CREDITS

Published by the Junior League of Little Rock Publications, a subsidiary of The Junior League of Little Rock, Incorporated.

The Junior League of Little Rock, Incorporated, is an organization of women committed to promoting voluntarism, developing the potential of women, and improving the community through the effective action and leadership of trained volunteers. Its purpose is exclusively educational and charitable.

Edited, designed and manufactured in the United States of America by
Favorite Recipes® Press
an imprint of

FRP™

2451 Atrium Way
Nashville, Tennessee 37214

Book Design: Brad Whitfield
Project Editor: Jane Hinshaw
Production Design: Susan Breining

Library of Congress Number: 97-72872
ISBN: 0-9606724-3-5
First printing: 1997   30,000 copies

Any inquiries or orders for additional copies of this book should be directed to:
Junior League of Little Rock Cookbook Committee
3600 Cantrell Road, Suite 102
Little Rock, Arkansas 72202
P.O. Box 7453
Little Rock, Arkansas 72217
Telephone (501) 666-0658 or Fax (501) 666-0589

Cover and Chapter Opener Photography – Shigeta & Associates, Chuck Sharrard, Chicago, Illinois

Photographers – Bruce Andrews and David Morey

Food Stylists – Terri Maki and Mary Helen Steinler

Props – Kathy Schroedter and Rene Miller

Art – Kevin Kresse and Chester Storthz Advertising

Entertaining Chapter Photography – Mark Matthews, Peerless Photography

Flowers – Tipton & Hurst

Logo – Cranford Johnson Robinson Woods

Legal Assistance – Friday, Eldredge & Clark

"American Thanksgiving" © Copyright 1997 James Morgan

"Just Desserts" and "Green Salads" © Copyright 1997 Crescent Dragonwagon, from her vegetarian cookbook

"A World Away Without Beans and Buttermilk" © Copyright 1997 Jack Butler, an excerpt from "A World Away Without Beans and Buttermilk", originally published in the "Arkansas Times."

Muffy VanderBear® © Copyright design North American Bear Company, Inc. on pages 176 and 177. All rights reserved.

© Fabric Traditions by Susan Winget Designs on pages 176 to 203.

Crab Meat Brunch Scramble – © Copyright 1995, Southern Living, Inc. Reprinted with permission.

APRON STRINGS

TIES TO THE SOUTHERN TRADITION OF COOKING

Growing up in a family that loves to celebrate any occasion with good times and good food, I am aware of lots of apron strings that have wrapped themselves around me, tying me closer and closer to those wonderful cooks that just seem to come naturally in a Southern family.

I have many recollections of special aprons that have ties to the past; a few are tucked away in my kitchen drawer. There's the one with the chocolate pie smeared all over it. That's the recipe my Mother whipped up any time my brother or sister and I had "special" friends over — it worked on my husband. Then there's the "fish fry" apron we insist my Dad wear every year when he mixes up his secret batter for family reunions on the Saline River. Other aprons are stained with memories from my childhood: the one that my Great Aunt Minnie wore when the two of us stirred together a batch of prize-winning pinwheel cookies for the Ashley County Fair when I was six; or the apron that still conjures up cinnamony smells from the dozens of hot apple pies that my Grandmother Deckelman always had waiting for my Dad when we came to visit. He never did tell her Karo Pecan was his favorite.

And there are several handmade aprons from another grandmother that make a special appearance at holiday time every year. When we put on these red gingham Christmas aprons, we're ready to make Mama Pierce's famous turkey and dressing. While she's no longer here to be our "sage" advisor, I can't imagine that cornbread concoction tasting any better up in heaven. There are many words of wisdom from the kitchens of our grandmothers and many others shared in this cookbook. Brent Bumpers shares his Grandmother Ola's secret for fried okra. Max Brantley recalls his grandmother Lily's "inky black" chicory coffee; Charles Allbright, his Granny Ramey's holiday dinners. And Crescent Dragonwagon remembers the joy of getting her "just desserts" from a mother who indulged her with "small white bakery boxes tied with string."

Then there are other Southerners, including best-selling author John Grisham, who delight us with even more "gritty" tales of food and memories full of flavor. It seems most of us are tied to traditions from our past that we savor in the present. In *Apron Strings: Ties to the Southern Tradition of Cooking*, The Junior League of Little Rock celebrates this culinary heritage with more than 300 recipes, as well as dozens of entertaining tips and stories. Whether it's a Sunday lunch at Grandmother's, a rousing Razorback tailgate party or just a relaxing picnic at the lake, all these apron strings lead to ties that bind family and friends. That's the best reason of all to entertain. Life is just more delicious that way.

SHARON DECKELMAN MOSLEY

We would like to honor our previous two cookbooks, Little Rock Cooks *and* Traditions: A Taste of the Good Life. *Since these cookbooks are no longer in print, and we continue to receive requests for them, some of the favorite recipes from each book have been included in* Apron Strings.
Also, League members cook JLLR recipes for our Gourmet-to-Go booth at our fund-raiser, Holiday House.
The apron symbol marks these tried and true favorites.

Fifty recipes have been analyzed for nutritional content. The information appears in chart form on page 250. The heart symbol marks these recipes.

Contents

Contents

A World Away Without Beans and Buttermilk

You've probable gotten one of those telephone calls. They come more frequently during the holidays. What it is, it's a grown child calling for that special recipe, the one he or she grew up eating, and now wants to try out on a loved one or friends.

These are very targeted phone calls. You don't do a lot of sidebar chatting, don't catch up on what's been happening lately. These phone calls are strictly about getting the necessary information, time's a-wasting.

I don't know that there are any human transactions that create a warmer glow for me. For the genuine pleasure, the sheer happiness of realizing that you've contributed something to the next wave of humans, I'll take one of those phone calls any day. It's pleasant to be the repository of the old wisdom. But the feeling is bigger than that. It's your children saying, "We remember, it mattered to us. Now we want to serve it to someone that we care about. When we serve it to them, we'll be saying, this is me. This is my past. This is who I am."

Recently, I set a new distance record for one of those recipe calls. My daughter, Lynnika, is living quite happily in Japan nowadays. When asked what they wanted for Christmas, she and Luke wanted plain, simple things, things that aren't expensive here but are almost not to be found in Japan. They wanted dried beans. We shipped them bags and bags—pintos, black beans, white beans, speckled peas, black-eyed peas. Imagine a Southerner *living in a country where you can't get black-eyed peas.*

So naturally, not long after the beans and peas arrived, we got the call. Daughter needed the recipe for cornbread. Luke claimed he had real cornbread, but clearly, since he admitted what he'd eaten had sugar in it...

And while we were at it, how about the recipe for biscuits as well?

I was even able to deal with the problem of a certain unavailable ingredient, buttermilk. Simple. Dilute plain yogurt with a little water or milk and beat to the right consistency. It has basically the same microorganisms creating basically the same acids, and as for flavor—you can't tell the difference.

I don't know yet how everything turned out for Lynnika and Luke, but I can tell you, their call made my New Year. I confess I'm a little worried about them, now, though. I haven't been worried about her living so far from home. I haven't been worried about the language barrier, or the high price of everything in Japan. But I'm worried now.

Imagine living in a country where you can't get buttermilk.

JACK BUTLER

ABOUT THE AUTHORS

CHARLES ALLBRIGHT has been a columnist for the *Arkansas Democrat-Gazette* since 1991. He began his journalism career as a reporter, editorial writer, and columnist for the *Arkansas Gazette* in 1955, and served as a speech writer and director of public relations for Winthrop Rockefeller from 1966 to 1973.

RICHARD ALLIN began as a political writer for the *Commercial Appeal* in Memphis. He joined the *Arkansas Gazette,* now the *Arkansas Democrat-Gazette,* as a reporter, later becoming a columnist, a post he has held for 30 years. He is the author of the *Southern Legislative Dictionaries* and *The Wad and Gudge Creek Chronicles.*

MAX BRANTLEY, the editor of the *Arkansas Times* since 1992, has been a journalist for twenty-four years. He is a political columnist who frequently appears on AETN's weekly public affairs program "Arkansas Week." An avid cook with particular interest in barbecue and bread baking, one of his favorite breads, the southern dinner roll, is truly an Arkansas tradition.

JACK BUTLER, author of six critically acclaimed books, is the Director of Creative Writing at the College of Santa Fe. He lived in Arkansas for twenty-five years and still writes a food column for the *Arkansas Times.* His third novel, *Living in Little Rock with Miss Little Rock,* was nominated for the 1993 Pulitzer Prize and the 1993 Pen/Faulkner award. A collection of his food columns, *Mosey Froghead's Barbecue Sauce (And other Recipes)* is forthcoming in 1997.

WAYNE CRANFORD is the chairman emeritus of Cranford Johnson Robinson Woods in Little Rock. He is the chairman of the President's Advisory Committee on the Arts at the John F. Kennedy Center for the Performing Arts in Washington, D.C. Mr. Cranford is the chairman of the Governor's Mansion Commission and also a member of the National Governmental Affairs Committee of the American Association of Advertising Agencies.

CRESCENT DRAGONWAGON ("It's a children's book name, like Dr. Seuss," she says.) was born in New York City, but has lived since 1972 in Eureka Springs, Arkansas. There, with her husband, Ned Shank, she owns and runs a country inn and restaurant. Her last cookbook, *Dairy Hollow House Soup & Bread: A Country Inn Cookbook,* was nominated for both the Julia Child and James Beard Cookbook Awards, and has sold over 200,000 copies. She is currently at work on a vegetarian cookbook.

HELAINE R. FREEMAN is a feature writer and columnist for the *Arkansas Democrat-Gazette.* She began working for the *Arkansas Democrat* at the age of 19 and her dream of writing a humor column for a major newspaper was fulfilled when she began writing her biweekly column, "Let's Talk" in 1989.

JOHN GRISHAM is one of America's most popular authors, with eight novels, beginning with *A Time to Kill.* Five of his novels have been made into motion pictures. Mr. Grisham spent his early years in tiny Black Oak, Arkansas, but moved to Mississippi where he graduated from Mississippi State University and Ole Miss Law School. He now lives in Virginia and Mississippi with his family.

JAMES MORGAN'S work has appeared in such publications as *The New Yorker, Atlantic Monthly, GQ, Men's Health,* and *The Washington Post Magazine.* He is the author of two books, *Leading with my Heart* (with Virginia Kelley) and *If These Walls had Ears: The Biography of a House.*

LIBBY SMITH is the travel editor of the *Arkansas Democrat-Gazette.* A former travel agent who enjoys cooking, Ms. Smith's favorite travel destination for food is Hawaii. She feels that Pacific Rim cuisine, a combination of influences from the Orient, the United States, and the South Pacific, is at its finest in the islands.

NANCY L. SNYDERMAN, M.D., a surgeon of otolaryngology, is a medical correspondent for ABC News and can be seen on "Good Morning America" and "Prime Time Live." She writes monthly columns for *Good Housekeeping* and *Parenting* and is the author of *Nancy Snyderman's Guide to Good Health for Women Over Forty.* Dr. Snyderman began her broadcasting career at KATV and KARK-TV in Little Rock in 1985.

PHYLLIS K. SPEER is the Regional Education Coordinator for the Arkansas Game and Fish Commission. An accomplished cook who specializes in the gourmet preparation of wild game, she appears monthly on AETN's "Arkansas Outdoors." Ms. Speer serves on the National Advisory Committee of the "Becoming an Outdoorswoman" program.

PATTI UPTON is president and chief executive officer of Aromatique, Inc., a decorative fragrance business which combines her talent for business with her love of fashion and art. She has been recognized by her colleagues with numerous awards and has been featured in the national media. Her fragrance line, "The Natural State," has contributed over $700,000 to benefit The Nature Conservancy.

Before the Arts

APPETIZERS AND BEVERAGES

Pesto Terrine with Italian Pita Wedges
Smoked Salmon Appetizer
Caviar Torte
Duck Paté
Baked Brie
Full Bar
Cranberry Spritzers

Great Beginnings – The Best Part of the Show

It's been said that since people have more leisure time today, development and appreciation of the arts is critical. And we all know that the arts are universally enjoyed, superseded only by the one thing that all humans love to do. And that's eating.

I've always thought that the best part of a lot of Broadway musicals was the overture. Maybe it's the excitement that you share with the rest of the audience and the anticipation of something new that's about to happen, but I always like those short and snappy previews of the show-stoppers to come.

The same is true for appetizers. Most times, when evening comes, you just can't beat tasty hors d'oeuvres.

There also seems to be a certain trendiness in the matter of appetizers. I remember in the 60s, you could hardly go to a dinner party where they didn't pass those asparagus roll-ups in buttered white bread that had been run into the oven just long enough to get crispy and brown. Then smoked salmon became a staple, and for a while it was those little balls made of sausage, cheese, and biscuit dough.

Recently, I've had the opportunity to help plan special events for the President's Advisory Committee on the Arts (P.A.C.A.) both at The Kennedy Center and other sites in Washington like Blair House and various embassies, and throughout the country. And some of the most memorable foods have been passed around on silver trays before everyone sits down to dinner.

For example, at Spago in Los Angeles we had roasted new potatoes with caviar, smoked salmon on brioche, and a selection of Spago's famous pizzas.

In Santa Fe, we passed red and yellow pepper polenta diamonds, Blue Mountain snapper canapés with black bean salsa, tiny risotto fritters, and grilled swordfish medallions. And back in Washington, during Kennedy Center Honors weekend, there were buckwheat blinis with caviar and crème fraîche, wild onion tarts, and jerk spiced chicken in coconut pastry with Jamaican mango sauce.

I'm sure that some of our P.A.C.A. members preferred the formal dinner offerings, but I'll always remember the appetizers as the best part of the show.

WAYNE CRANFORD

CHEESY PESTO CROSTINI

1 medium eggplant
1½ teaspoons salt
1 tablespoon minced garlic
¼ cup chopped fresh basil, or
   1½ tablespoons dried
¼ cup olive oil
pepper to taste

1 baguette
½ cup pesto (page 19)
1 (8-ounce) jar roasted red bell
   peppers, slivered
1 cup shredded provolone cheese
½ cup crumbled feta cheese

- Peel and chop the eggplant. Spread on paper towels and sprinkle with the salt; let stand for 30 to 45 minutes. Pat firmly with paper towels to dry.
- Sauté the eggplant with the garlic and basil in the olive oil in a 10-inch skillet for 10 minutes or until the eggplant is tender and beginning to brown. Season with pepper.
- Preheat the broiler.
- Slice the baguette ¼ inch thick. Spread with the pesto. Top with the eggplant mixture and 2 slivers of roasted bell pepper arranged in an X.
- Sprinkle with the provolone cheese and the feta cheese. Place on a baking sheet.
- Broil for 4 minutes or until the cheese melts. Serve immediately.

SERVES THIRTY

BURGUNDY MUSHROOMS

Combine 1 cup butter, 2 cups Burgundy, 1 cup boiling water, 2 teaspoons Worcestershire sauce, 2 beef bouillon cubes, 2 chicken bouillon cubes and ½ teaspoon each dillseeds, garlic powder and pepper in a large saucepan. Bring to a simmer over medium heat. Add 3 pounds fresh mushrooms and reduce the heat. Simmer, covered, for 6 hours; mushrooms will appear dark. Simmer, uncovered, for 3 hours longer. Serve as an appetizer or a side dish. Do not be concerned about the length of cooking time; they will be delicious.

SPICY CHICKEN WINGS

½ cup reduced-sodium soy sauce
2 cloves of garlic, minced
⅓ cup packed brown sugar
2 teaspoons freshly grated ginger, or
   1 teaspoon ground ginger
24 chicken wings
garlic powder to taste

To marinate the chicken
• Combine the soy sauce, garlic, brown sugar and
  ginger in a bowl and mix well.
• Cut each chicken wing into 3 portions,
  discarding the tip portions. Rinse the remaining
  portions and pat dry.
• Add the chicken to the marinade and marinate
  in the refrigerator for 2 hours or longer.

To bake the chicken
• Preheat the oven to 350 degrees.
• Arrange the chicken in a single layer in a
  shallow baking dish. Pour the marinade over
  the top.
• Bake for 1½ hours, turning and basting several
  times. Sprinkle with garlic powder. Broil for
  1 to 2 minutes or until crisp.

SERVES EIGHT TO TWELVE

CRAB MEAT CANAPÉS

3 (5-ounce) jars Old English cheese
1½ cups butter, softened
1 teaspoon Worcestershire sauce
½ teaspoon Tabasco sauce
5 green onions, chopped
2 teaspoons parsley flakes
1 tablespoon garlic powder
1 pound fresh crab meat
18 English muffins, split

• Preheat the oven to 400 degrees.
• Combine the cheese, butter, Worcestershire
  sauce, Tabasco sauce, green onions, parsley
  flakes and garlic powder in a bowl and mix
  well. Fold in the crab meat.
• Spread the mixture on the cut sides of the
  muffins; place on a baking sheet.
• Bake for 15 to 20 minutes or until golden
  brown. Cut each into 4 wedges. Serve warm.

*Note: Do not substitute margarine for the butter
in this recipe. These can be frozen.*

YIELDS TWELVE DOZEN

SMOKED SALMON APPETIZER

1 cup mayonnaise
2 tablespoons Dijon mustard
2 tablespoons drained capers
1 tablespoon fresh lemon juice
1 tablespoon chopped fresh dill
lettuce leaves
1 cup finely chopped green onions

1 cup finely chopped radishes
1 cup finely chopped cucumber
1 cup drained capers
1 pound smoked salmon, sliced
thinly sliced dark pumpernickel
bread, toasted

For the sauce
• Combine the mayonnaise, Dijon mustard, capers, lemon juice and dill in a bowl and mix well.
• Place in a serving bowl in the center of a serving platter.

To assemble the appetizer
• Arrange 5 lettuce cups around the sauce.
• Mound the green onions, radishes, cucumber, capers and salmon in the lettuce cups. Arrange the bread around the edge.

SERVES TWENTY

CREAM CHEESE SPREAD

16 ounces cream cheese, softened
½ cup unsalted butter, softened

2 tablespoons whipping cream
1 tablespoon Hungarian paprika

• Combine the cream cheese, butter and whipping cream in a mixer bowl and beat until smooth.
• Add the paprika and mix well.
• Chill for up to 12 hours.
• Serve with the Smoked Salmon Appetizer as an alternative to the dill sauce if preferred.

YIELDS TWO AND ONE-HALF CUPS

Cooking with your children can provide them with some treasured childhood memories. However, it can also provide you with some terrible stress and an incredible mess. I have discovered a neat trick. The perfect kitchen work surface for children is the opened dishwasher door. There they can happily stir, knead, and mix to their hearts' content. It is easier for the little ones to reach, and clean-up becomes a snap: just shut the door and run the next load of dishes!

Marynell Branch Kalkbrenner

HERBED GARDEN MUSHROOMS

3 ounces cream cheese, softened
1/2 cup freshly grated Parmesan cheese
1/4 teaspoon Worcestershire sauce
1 tablespoon chopped fresh parsley
1 1/2 teaspoons chopped fresh thyme
1 teaspoon chopped fresh oregano
ground nutmeg, salt and pepper to taste
18 large fresh mushroom caps

• Preheat the oven to 350 degrees.
• Combine the cream cheese, Parmesan cheese, Worcestershire sauce, parsley, thyme, oregano, nutmeg, salt and pepper in a small bowl and mix well.
• Spoon or pipe the mixture into the mushroom caps. Place in a 9x12-inch baking dish.
• Bake for 20 minutes or until tender.

Garnish with fresh herbs.

SERVES EIGHTEEN

SUMMER BRUSCHETTA

1 1/2 pounds Roma tomatoes
1/2 cup fresh basil leaves
1 tablespoon fresh oregano leaves
1 tablespoon minced garlic
1 tablespoon balsamic vinegar
1 tablespoon olive oil
1 teaspoon fresh lemon juice
salt and pepper to taste
1/2-inch crusty French bread slices
garlic-flavored olive oil

For the tomato spread
• Seed and chop the tomatoes; chop the basil and oregano. Combine with the garlic, vinegar, 1 tablespoon olive oil and lemon juice in a bowl. Season with salt and pepper. Spoon into a serving bowl.

For the bruschetta
• Brush the bread with garlic-flavored olive oil. Grill for 5 to 8 minutes or until toasted.
• Serve with the tomato mixture.

Note: The bread can be toasted ahead of time and the tomato mixture prepared and allowed to stand at room temperature for up to 2 hours. Do not spread ahead of time. This is best in the summer using fresh tomatoes and herbs from the garden.

SERVES SIX TO EIGHT

BAKED BRIE

1 sheet frozen puff pastry, thawed   *Cranberry-Ginger Chutney*
1 (8-ounce) round Brie cheese

- Preheat the oven to 350 degrees.
- Roll the pastry thin on a lightly floured surface. Place the cheese round in the center and wrap the pastry to enclose the cheese completely.
- Place seam side down on a baking sheet; imprint the top with a cookie cutter.
- Bake for 10 to 15 minutes or until golden brown.
- Serve with Cranberry-Ginger Chutney and sliced small rounds of sourdough bread or wafer crackers.

Variation: Substitute crescent roll dough for the puff pastry.

SERVES EIGHT TO TEN

CRANBERRY-GINGER CHUTNEY

1½ cups fresh cranberries   *2 tablespoons minced fresh ginger*
16 dried apricots, cut into   *2 tablespoons orange juice*
*   quarters*   *¾ teaspoon ground cinnamon*
⅓ cup dried currants   *¼ teaspoon cayenne pepper*
¾ cup packed light brown sugar

- Combine the cranberries, apricots, currants, brown sugar, ginger, orange juice, cinnamon and cayenne in a heavy medium saucepan and mix well.
- Cook over medium heat until the brown sugar dissolves, stirring constantly.
- Increase the heat to high and bring to a boil. Boil for 3 minutes, stirring constantly.
- Spoon into a bowl and let stand until cool. Store in an airtight container in the refrigerator for up to 1 week.

Note: This is delicious served with roast pork, turkey, venison or game birds.

YIELDS THREE CUPS

SPINACH BREAD APPETIZER

Cut 1 loaf of French bread into halves horizontally and spread the cut sides with ½ cup butter or margarine. Thaw and drain 2 packages of frozen chopped spinach. Combine with 2 cups shredded Monterey Jack cheese, ½ cup grated Parmesan cheese, ½ cup light mayonnaise, 1 teaspoon garlic seasoning and salt and pepper to taste; mix well. Spread on the French bread and place on a baking sheet. Broil until bubbly. Cut into bite-sized pieces or allow guests to cut as they serve themselves. Serves 8 to 10.

BRIE WITH TOMATOES

1 (15-ounce) Brie cheese round
4 large tomatoes
1 cup fresh basil
3 to 4 cloves of garlic, crushed
1/4 cup olive oil
1/4 teaspoon salt
1/2 teaspoon freshly ground pepper
toasted Italian bread slices

- Remove and discard the rind from the cheese; cut into 1/2- to 3/4-inch pieces.
- Seed the tomatoes and cut into 1/2-inch pieces. Cut the basil into 1/8-inch-wide strips.
- Combine the cheese, tomatoes, basil, garlic, olive oil, salt and pepper in a bowl and mix lightly.
- Let stand, covered, at room temperature for 1 hour.
- Serve with toasted bread slices.

Note: This is also delicious as a salad or served over pasta as a meatless main dish.

SERVES EIGHT

BARBECUED SHRIMP

1 pound butter
1 pound margarine
3/4 cup Worcestershire sauce
1/2 cup finely ground pepper
1 teaspoon Tabasco sauce
3 cloves of garlic, crushed
4 lemons, sliced
1 teaspoon ground rosemary
2 teaspoons salt
6 pounds unpeeled shrimp

- Preheat the oven to 400 degrees.
- Melt the butter and margarine in a saucepan. Add the Worcestershire sauce, pepper, Tabasco sauce, garlic, lemon slices, rosemary and salt and mix well. Cook until heated through.
- Divide the shrimp between 2 large shallow baking pans. Pour the heated sauce over the shrimp and mix well.
- Bake for 15 to 20 minutes or until the shrimp are firm and opaque, turning once.
- Serve with French bread to dip into the sauce.

Note: This makes a wonderful main course for twelve people. Serve with corn on the cob.

SERVES SIXTEEN TO TWENTY

CAVIAR TORTE

6 hard-cooked eggs, finely
   chopped
⅓ cup butter, softened
1 teaspoon red wine vinegar
2 teaspoons Dijon mustard
dill to taste
salt to taste

6 scallions, finely chopped
8 ounces cream cheese, softened
⅔ cup sour cream
3 tablespoons mayonnaise
6 ounces black lumpfish caviar,
   rinsed, drained

- Combine the eggs, butter, vinegar, Dijon mustard, dill and salt in a small bowl and mash with a fork until smooth.
- Spread evenly over the bottom of a 9-inch springform pan. Sprinkle with the scallions.
- Blend the cream cheese and sour cream in a small bowl. Spread over the scallions.
- Chill, covered, for 2 hours or until firm.
- Remove the torte from the refrigerator and place on a serving plate; remove the side of the pan. Spread top with the mayonnaise.
- Spoon the caviar over the top.
- Serve with toast points.

SERVES TWENTY

POOR MAN'S CAVIAR

Rinse and drain one 16-ounce can black-eyed peas. Combine with one 4-ounce can chopped green chiles, ⅓ cup oil-free Italian salad dressing, 1 tablespoon vinegar, ½ teaspoon Italian seasoning and crushed red pepper flakes to taste. Chill for 4 to 6 hours. Add 2 chopped tomatoes and ½ cup chopped green onions. Serve as a salad or as an appetizer with pita wedges or Melba toast rounds. Serves 10.

CRAB ROLL

10 ounces cream cheese, softened
2 (6-ounce) cans claw crab meat, drained
½ (12-ounce) bottle cocktail sauce
½ (5-ounce) jar prepared horseradish
1 teaspoon Tabasco sauce (optional)
red pepper to taste

- Combine the cream cheese and crab meat in a bowl and mix well with the fingers. Shape into a roll and wrap with plastic wrap. Chill for 2 hours or longer.
- Combine the cocktail sauce, horseradish, Tabasco sauce and red pepper in a bowl and mix well.
- Place the crab roll on a serving plate. Spoon the sauce over the top.
- Serve with crackers.

SERVES EIGHT

JALAPEÑO CHEESE SPREAD

16 ounces jalapeño cheese, softened
8 ounces cream cheese, softened
3 tablespoons minced green bell pepper
3 tablespoons chopped green onions
1 (2-ounce) can chopped pimento, drained
1 (16-ounce) can chopped sauerkraut

- Combine the jalapeño cheese, cream cheese, green pepper, green onions and pimento in a bowl and mix well.
- Drain the sauerkraut and press to remove moisture; do not rinse. Add to the cheese mixture and mix well.
- Shape into a ball or log on foil.
- Serve at room temperature with crackers.

Garnish with sliced olives and paprika.

SERVES TWELVE

PESTO TERRINE

24 ounces cream cheese, softened
8 ounces light sour cream

1 package sun-dried tomatoes
Fresh Pesto

- Blend the cream cheese and sour cream in a small bowl.
- Cut the sun-dried tomatoes into quarters. Soak in boiling water in a bowl for 10 minutes. Drain and discard any hard pieces.
- Line 2 miniature loaf pans with plastic wrap.
- Spread ⅓ of the cream cheese mixture in the prepared pans. Layer the Fresh Pesto, half the remaining cream cheese mixture, tomatoes and remaining cream cheese mixture in the prepared pans.
- Fold the plastic wrap over the top and press the layers lightly. Chill until serving time.
- Remove the terrine from the pans by lifting the plastic wrap and invert onto serving plates.
- Serve with Italian Pita Wedges (page 21) or crackers.

Garnish with finely chopped walnuts and fresh parsley or basil leaves.

Variation: This can also be made in a ring mold.

SERVES TEN

BAKED TORTILLA CHIPS

Cut two 8- or 10-inch flour tortillas into 8 to 10 wedges each and place on an ungreased baking sheet. Brush with 2 tablespoons melted butter; sprinkle with ½ teaspoon each garlic powder, Italian seasonings and lemon pepper. Bake at 325 degrees for 5 to 6 minutes or until light brown and crisp. Store cooled chips in an airtight container. These are especially good with Hot Spinach Dip (page 23) and Caponata (page 21).

FRESH PESTO

1 bunch fresh basil
¼ cup fresh parsley
½ cup grated Parmesan cheese
2 cloves of garlic

1 tablespoon olive oil
3 tablespoons water
¼ cup finely crushed walnuts or
 pine nuts

- Combine the basil, parsley, cheese, garlic, olive oil, water and nuts in a food processor container.
- Process until smooth.

YIELDS TWO CUPS

SMOKED CATFISH PATÉ

1 pound catfish fillets
½ cup water
½ cup vermouth
16 ounces cream cheese, softened
1 clove of garlic, minced
2 tablespoons fresh lemon juice
2 teaspoons Creole seasoning
½ to 1 teaspoon liquid smoke (optional)
salt and pepper to taste

- Poach the catfish fillets in the water and vermouth in a saucepan until the fish flakes easily with a fork; drain.
- Combine the fish with the cream cheese, garlic, lemon juice, Creole seasoning, liquid smoke, salt and pepper in a food processor container and process until smooth.
- Spoon into a covered container. Chill for 2 to 48 hours.
- Serve with crackers or garlic toast.

SERVES SIXTEEN

CHILE CON QUESO

6 tablespoons margarine
¼ cup flour
1 teaspoon paprika
1 teaspoon garlic powder
1 teaspoon dry mustard
1 teaspoon cumin
1 cup milk
8 ounces Velveeta cheese, cubed
½ (10-ounce) can tomatoes with green chiles

- Melt the margarine in a saucepan. Stir in the flour, paprika, garlic powder, dry mustard and cumin.
- Add the milk. Cook until thickened, stirring constantly.
- Add the cheese and tomatoes with green chiles. Cook until the cheese melts, stirring to mix well.
- Serve warm or at room temperature with tortilla chips.

SERVES EIGHT TO TWELVE

CAPONATA

1 (1-pound) eggplant
salt to taste
1 cup minced green onions
1 cup minced celery
1 medium red bell pepper, minced
2 cloves of garlic, minced
4 teaspoons olive oil
1 (8-ounce) can tomato sauce

3 tablespoons tomato paste
¼ cup salad olives
2 tablespoons garlic-flavored red
  wine vinegar
1 tablespoon sugar
¼ teaspoon dried oregano
¼ teaspoon pepper
Italian Pita Wedges

- Cut the eggplant into halves lengthwise. Scoop out and chop enough pulp to measure 4 cups, reserving the shells.
- Sprinkle the shells lightly with salt and invert onto paper-towel-lined plates; store in the refrigerator.
- Sauté the eggplant pulp, green onions, celery, bell pepper and garlic in the olive oil in a heavy nonaluminum saucepan over medium heat for 10 minutes, stirring frequently.
- Add the tomato sauce, tomato paste, olives, vinegar, sugar, oregano and pepper. Cook over low heat for 25 minutes or until the vegetables are tender, stirring frequently.
- Spoon into a medium bowl. Chill, covered, for 8 hours.
- Spoon into the reserved eggplant shells.
- Serve with Italian Pita Wedges (at right).

Garnish with fresh basil or parsley.

Note: Nutritional analysis does not include the Italian Pita Wedges.

SERVES TWELVE

ITALIAN PITA WEDGES

Separate each of four 6-inch pita rounds into halves by cutting around the outer edges. Cut each half into 6 wedges. Place brown side down on an ungreased baking sheet. Brush with a mixture of 6 tablespoons sesame oil, 1 teaspoon dried whole oregano and ½ teaspoon garlic powder. Bake at 325 degrees for 10 minutes or until the wedges are golden brown. Store in an airtight container. Yields 4 dozen wedges.

For a great low-fat snack, omit the oil mixture and simply bake the wedges until golden brown.

CORN DIP

2 cups shredded medium Cheddar cheese
1 (4-ounce) can chopped green chiles
2 tablespoons chopped jalapeños
2 tablespoons dried chopped cilantro
1/2 cup mayonnaise
1 cup sour cream
1/2 teaspoon Tabasco sauce
2 (11-ounce) cans whole kernel corn, drained
salt to taste

• Combine the cheese, green chiles, jalapeños, cilantro, mayonnaise, sour cream and Tabasco sauce in a large bowl and mix well. Stir in the corn and salt.
• Chill for 8 hours or longer.
• Serve with corn chips.

Variation: You may substitute light sour cream and light mayonnaise for the sour cream and mayonnaise in this recipe.

SERVES TWELVE

PEANUT FRUIT DIP

8 ounces cream cheese, softened
3/4 cup packed light brown sugar
1 cup sour cream
1/3 cup coffee liqueur
6 ounces unsalted peanuts, finely chopped
8 ounces whipped topping

• Combine the cream cheese, brown sugar, sour cream and liqueur in a bowl and mix just until combined; do not overmix.
• Stir in the peanuts. Fold in the whipped topping.
• Chill for 24 hours.
• Serve with apples, grapes, strawberries, bananas or gingersnaps.

Variation: To reduce the fat in this recipe, use light cream cheese and light sour cream. The peanuts can even be omitted if desired.

SERVES TWELVE

ROSY SHRIMP DIP

8 ounces cream cheese, softened
1 cup light mayonnaise
3 tablespoons chili sauce
2 tablespoons lemon juice

1 small onion, grated
1 teaspoon horseradish
1 pound tiny cooked peeled
   shrimp

- Combine the cream cheese, mayonnaise, chili sauce, lemon juice, onion and horseradish in a bowl and mix well.
- Fold in the shrimp. Chill, covered, for up to 3 days.
- Serve with crackers.

SERVES TWELVE

HOT SPINACH DIP

2 (10-ounce) packages frozen
   chopped spinach
1/2 cup chopped onion
1 pickled jalapeño, chopped
   (optional)
8 ounces cream cheese, softened
2 cups shredded Monterey Jack
   cheese

1/3 cup half-and-half
1 teaspoon hot sauce
1 (11-ounce) can chopped
   tomatoes with green chiles
1 cup chopped fresh tomatoes

- Preheat the oven to 350 degrees.
- Thaw the spinach and press to remove excess moisture.
- Combine the spinach with the onion, jalapeño, cream cheese, shredded cheese, half-and-half, hot sauce and canned tomatoes with green chiles in a bowl; mix well. Fold in the fresh tomatoes.
- Spoon into a greased 2-quart baking dish. Bake for 20 to 30 minutes or until bubbly.
- Serve with baked tortilla chips or crackers.

SERVES SIXTEEN

SPECIAL DIP

Combine 2 bunches chopped green onions, 2 bunches chopped fresh cilantro, 3 drained 2-ounce cans chopped green chiles, three 2-ounce cans chopped black olives, 3 chopped large tomatoes, 1 cup finely shredded Monterey Jack cheese, 1 cup finely shredded Cheddar cheese and 1/2 cup Italian salad dressing in a bowl and mix well. Serve with chips. Serves 12.

23

TEQUILA DIP

6 ounces cream cheese, softened
3 tablespoons tequila
½ teaspoon hot sauce
white pepper to taste
2 or 3 medium ripe avocados
2 tablespoons plus 1 teaspoon lime juice
½ teaspoon lemon juice
lime juice for rubbing the bowl rim
salt for the bowl rim

• Beat the cream cheese in a mixer bowl until smooth. Stir in the tequila, hot sauce and white pepper.
• Mash the avocados in a bowl and stir in lime juice and lemon juice.
• Add the avocado mixture to the cream cheese mixture and mix well.
• Rub the rim of a serving bowl with lime juice. Invert the bowl onto a saucer of salt to coat the rim.
• Spoon the dip carefully into the prepared bowl.

Garnish with a lime wedge.

YIELDS THREE CUPS

SUGARED PECANS

3 cups pecan halves
1 cup sugar
½ cup water
1 teaspoon cinnamon
1 teaspoon vanilla extract

• Preheat the oven to 300 degrees.
• Spread the pecans on a baking sheet. Toast for 15 minutes.
• Combine the sugar, water and cinnamon in a saucepan. Cook to 238 degrees on a candy thermometer, soft-ball stage.
• Remove the saucepan from the heat and stir in the vanilla. Beat until smooth and shiny; do not overbeat, as mixture will harden quickly.
• Add the pecans and stir to coat well. Spread on waxed paper, separating immediately with a fork; mixture will be very hot.
• Let stand until cool. Store in an airtight container.

Note: The pecans can be toasted by microwaving on High for 3 minutes if preferred.

YIELDS THREE CUPS

Fried Walnuts

6 cups water
4 cups walnut halves
½ cup sugar

vegetable oil
seasoned salt

- Bring the water to a boil in a 4-quart saucepan. Add the walnuts and return the water to a boil. Boil for 1 minute.
- Rinse the walnuts with hot water in a coarse sieve. Combine with the sugar in a large bowl and stir gently until the sugar dissolves.
- Heat 2 inches oil to 300 degrees in a skillet.
- Add the walnuts and fry until golden brown, stirring frequently; drain. Sprinkle with seasoned salt and spread on a paper towel to drain.
- Heat in a 250-degree oven for 1 minute if the walnuts are not as crisp as desired.

YIELDS FOUR CUPS

Pecan Praline Crunch

1 (16-ounce) package oat squares cereal
2 cups pecans
¼ cup margarine

½ cup packed brown sugar
½ cup light corn syrup
½ teaspoon baking soda
1 teaspoon vanilla extract

- Preheat the oven to 250 degrees.
- Mix the cereal and pecans in a bowl.
- Bring the margarine, brown sugar and corn syrup to a boil in a saucepan. Remove from the heat and stir in the baking soda and vanilla.
- Pour over the cereal mixture, stirring to coat well. Spread in a baking pan.
- Bake for 1 hour, stirring every 20 minutes.
- Store in an airtight container.

YIELDS EIGHT CUPS

Gunpowder Dip

To prepare the spice mix for the dip, combine ½ cup dried parsley, ⅓ cup each dried minced onion and chili powder, ¼ cup each dried chives and cumin and 2 tablespoons salt and store in an airtight container until needed. To make the dip, combine 3 tablespoons of the spice mix with 1 cup mayonnaise and 1 cup sour cream or low-fat yogurt and whisk until smooth. Chill for 2 to 4 hours. Serve with tortilla chips or fresh vegetables. Yields 2 cups.

ALMOND TEA

2 cups strong brewed tea
6 cups water
1 cup sugar
Juice of 2 large lemons
1 teaspoon vanilla extract
2½ teaspoons almond extract

• Combine the tea, water, sugar, lemon juice and flavorings in a noncorrosive saucepan. Heat just until heated through; do not boil.
• Store leftovers in the refrigerator and reheat in the microwave.

Note: 2 tablespoons instant tea and 2 additional cups water can be substituted for the brewed tea in this recipe.

SERVES SIX TO EIGHT

HOT SPICED TEA

6 cups water
4 family-size tea bags
4 cinnamon sticks
2 whole cloves
1 cup sugar
1 (12-ounce) can frozen lemonade concentrate
1 (12-ounce) can frozen orange juice concentrate
1 (46-ounce) can pineapple juice

• Bring the water to a boil in a saucepan. Add the tea bags, cinnamon sticks, cloves and sugar, stirring to mix well.
• Remove the saucepan from the heat and let stand, covered, for 1 hour to brew.
• Strain the tea into the saucepan and add lemonade concentrate, orange juice concentrate and pineapple juice.
• Heat just to serving temperature and serve warm.

SERVES SIXTEEN

ORANGE JULIUS

1 (6-ounce) can frozen orange
   juice concentrate
1/2 cup confectioners' sugar

1 1/3 cups milk
1 teaspoon vanilla extract
ice cubes

- Combine the orange juice concentrate, confectioners' sugar, milk and vanilla in a blender container and process at medium speed until smooth.
- Add enough ice cubes to raise the ingredients level to the fill line on the blender.
- Blend at high speed until the mixture is slushy.

Note: Leftover Orange Julius can be frozen.

SERVES FOUR

CRANBERRY SPRITZERS

3 cups cranberry juice cocktail
1/2 cup orange juice
1/2 cup pineapple juice

1 (16-ounce) bottle sparkling
   water

- Combine the cranberry juice cocktail, orange juice, pineapple juice and sparkling water in a pitcher and mix well.
- Chill in the refrigerator.
- Serve over crushed ice in glasses.

Garnish with orange slices.

SERVES SIX

The kitchen can be an exciting place to learn math. Children love to measure, pour, and stir, quite unaware that they are putting their math skills to work. Slices of pizza and pieces of fudge are a great way to fill the tummy as well as the mind, while learning fractions. The recipe for Orange Julius (at left) is one that I have used repeatedly in my math program.

Ann Fincher Evans

PINK LEMONADE

1¼ cups sugar
½ cup boiling water
juice of 7 or 8 medium lemons
4½ cups cold water
1 or 2 drops of red food coloring

- Add the sugar to the boiling water, stirring to dissolve completely.
- Add the lemon juice, cold water and food coloring and mix well.
- Chill until serving time.
- Serve over ice in glasses.

Garnish with lemon slices.

SERVES SIX

LONG ISLAND TEA

¼ cup sweet-and-sour drink mix
¼ cup tequila
½ cup light rum
½ cup vodka
½ cup gin
3 cups ginger ale
2 cups cola
1 cup water

- Combine the drink mix, tequila, rum, vodka, gin, ginger ale, cola and water in a large container and mix well.
- Chill until serving time.
- Serve over ice in glasses.

Garnish with lemon wedges.

Note: This is great to make ahead and keep chilled for parties, but beware of its punch!

SERVES TWELVE

BLUE MARGARITAS

*½ (10-ounce) can frozen
  margarita mix*
5 ounces tequila

*¼ cup blue curaçao
juice of ½ lime
salt to taste*

- Combine the margarita mix, tequila, blue curaçao and lime juice in a blender container.
- Add salt to taste and enough ice to fill the blender. Process until smooth.
- Serve in glasses with salt-crusted rims if desired.

SERVES FOUR TO SIX

MUDDY BLARYS

*1 (42-ounce) can vegetable juice
  cocktail*
*1 (5½-ounce) can zesty vegetable
  juice cocktail*
¼ cup lime juice

*2 tablespoons Worcestershire sauce
1 tablespoon Tabasco sauce
1 teaspoon celery seeds
2 cups vodka (optional)*

- Combine the vegetable juice cocktails, lime juice, Worcestershire sauce, Tabasco sauce, celery seeds and vodka in a pitcher and mix well.
- Chill until serving time. Stir before serving.
- Serve over ice in glasses.

Variation: For a spicier drink, add 2 cans of the zesty vegetable juice cocktail and reduce the lime juice to 2 tablespoons.

SERVES EIGHT TO NINE

*My cousin gave me a delicious
Italian Cream Liqueur as a
Christmas gift and I have been
making it for friends as a holiday
gift ever since. Poured into a gift
bottle and decorated with a bow, it's
a gift any loved one would enjoy!
Include the directions to serve it
chilled. To make this treat, combine
1½ cups whipping cream, one
14-ounce can sweetened condensed
milk, 1 cup Frangelico liqueur,
¾ cup vodka, 1 teaspoon vanilla
extract and ½ teaspoon almond
extract and blend well. Store in the
refrigerator for up to 1 month.*

Susie Fletcher Smith

MOOD-ENHANCING MILK PUNCH

½ gallon vanilla ice cream
½ gallon milk
2 cups brandy or bourbon
nutmeg

- Let the ice cream stand at room temperature for several minutes to soften.
- Combine the ice cream with the milk and brandy in a mixer bowl and mix until smooth.
- Pour into a 1-gallon container. Place in the freezer for 24 hours.
- Let stand at room temperature for 1 hour before serving. Spoon into a punch bowl or pitcher and sprinkle with nutmeg.

YIELDS ONE GALLON

───────────

HOLIDAY SANGRIA

½ cup green grapes
½ cup red grapes
4 cups sugar-free lemonade
4 cups sugar-free ginger ale
2 cups chilled white wine
¼ cup orange liqueur
1 lime, sliced into thin wedges

- Fill 2 ice trays with water and arrange the grapes in the sections. Freeze until firm.
- Combine the lemonade, ginger ale, wine and orange liqueur in a punch bowl or glass pitcher and mix well.
- Add the grape ice cubes and lime wedges.

SERVES TEN

───────────

White Wine Sangria

3 oranges
3 lemons
3 limes
4 or 5 ripe peaches or nectarines
1 cup fresh or canned pineapple
   chunks

1/2 cup (or more) sugar
3 bottles dry white wine,
   chilled
1/2 cup brandy (optional)

- Wash the whole oranges, lemons and limes and cut into very thin slices, discarding the seeds. Combine in a 4-quart pitcher.
- Peel the peaches and slice into thin wedges, discarding the seeds. Add to the pitcher. Add the pineapple. Fold in the sugar and let stand for 30 minutes. Add the wine and brandy. Cover and chill for 3 to 4 hours.
- Taste for sweetness and add additional sugar dissolved in a small amount of additional wine if needed.
- Serve over ice in large stemmed glasses or from a punch bowl.

Variation: Substitute frozen peaches for fresh peaches or nectarines when not in season.

SERVES FIFTEEN

Wine Slushes

For a delicious summer party drink, combine 1 can of frozen lemonade concentrate, 2 juice cans of water and 2 juice cans of red or white wine in a freezer container and place in the freezer for 8 hours or longer. Let stand at room temperature until slushy before serving. Serves 8.

Brandy Slush

12 cups brewed tea
1 (12-ounce) can frozen orange
   juice concentrate, thawed
1 (12-ounce) can frozen lemonade
   concentrate, thawed

2 to 3 cups brandy
lemon-lime soda

- Combine the tea, orange juice concentrate, lemonade concentrate and brandy in a pitcher and mix well. Pour into loaf pans. Freeze until slushy.
- Spoon into a punch bowl and add enough lemon-lime soda to thin to the desired consistency.

SERVES THIRTY-SIX

TROPICAL PUNCH

3 (46-ounce) cans pineapple juice
2 (12-ounce) cans frozen orange juice
*   concentrate*
3 (12-ounce) cans frozen lemonade concentrate
3½ quarts water
½ cup sugar
1 quart ginger ale, chilled

- Combine the pineapple juice, orange juice concentrate, lemonade concentrate, water and sugar in a large container and mix well.
- Chill until serving time.
- Combine the juice mixture with the ginger ale in a punch bowl at serving time and mix gently.

Garnish with orange slices, cherries and strawberries.

Variation: Vodka or rum may be added to this punch base if desired.

SERVES SEVENTY-FIVE

HOT BUTTERED RUM

2 cups butter, softened
1 (1-pound) package light brown sugar
1 (1-pound) package confectioners' sugar
2 teaspoons ground cinnamon
2 teaspoons ground nutmeg
1 quart vanilla ice cream, softened
light rum
whipped cream
cinnamon sticks

- Combine the butter, brown sugar, confectioners' sugar, cinnamon and nutmeg in a mixer bowl and beat until smooth. Add the ice cream and mix well.
- Spoon into a 2-quart freezer container. Freeze until firm.
- Place 3 tablespoons of the slightly thawed mixture in a large mug for each serving.
- Add 1½ ounces rum and fill with boiling water; stir to mix well.
- Top with whipped cream and serve with a cinnamon stick.

Note: Butter mixture may be refrozen for later use.

SERVES TWENTY-FOUR

CAFÉ BRÛLOT

2 oranges
2 lemons
1 quart bourbon
1 quart brandy
sugar cubes

5 cinnamon sticks
2 tablespoons whole cloves
1 tablespoon whole allspice
coffee (optional)

- Wash the whole oranges and lemons. Peel in a continuous spiral.
- Combine the bourbon, brandy, 10 sugar cubes, cinnamon sticks, cloves and allspice in a large container.
- Add the fruit peels. Let stand, covered, for 8 hours or longer.
- Strain the mixture into a brûlot bowl, discarding the spices and reserving the fruit peels. Add the fruit peels to the bowl.
- Fill a ladle with brandy and add 1 sugar cube. Hold over a flame to heat and then ignite the brandy in the ladle.
- Ease the flame onto the brûlot mixture in the bowl to ignite. Turn off the lights and lift the flaming fruit peels from the bowl.
- Place 2 sugar cubes in each serving cup. Ladle the brûlot into the cups and add coffee if desired.

Note: This recipe comes from Henry Sylvester Stevens who uses Old Charter, Old Grand-Dad or Old Taylor bourbon and Three-Star Hennessy brandy in it.

SERVES A CROWD

Every Christmas Eve, my grandfather, PaPa, would make Café Brûlot for the family. Making Café Brûlot has been a familiar ritual in many southern homes throughout the years. On a silver tray, PaPa would arrange a collection of little dishes and boxes holding cloves, allspice, sugar, cinnamon, orange and lemon rinds, along with a decanter of brandy and bourbon. All of which he would pour into a silver bowl. By candlelight, PaPa would light the brandy mixture, setting the orange and lemon rinds on fire. While our delightful concoction blazed, we would sing a Christmas carol, and all the while my grandfather would scoop up the flaming rinds with a ladle for show. As we finished singing, the flame would be extinguished by placing the silver top on the bowl. The warming drink was then ladled into demitasse cups, and we would settle back to listen to PaPa read The Night Before Christmas.

Heather Davenport McCastlain

Razorback Tailgate Party

Soups and Sandwiches

Brie with Tomatoes
Assorted Crackers and Baguettes
Black Bean Chili
Veggie Sandwiches
Saucepan Brownies
Chilled Soft Drinks

For You Non-Cooking Sports Fans Out There

I don't cook. Actually, I did cook—before I got married. Then I stopped cooking. Nothing. Nada. Zilch. Why did I stop cooking, you ask? Because, after being told for years by my mom to forget about women's liberation and to have my husband's dinner ready even if both of us work, I hauled off and married a man who likes only junk food.

Why does Curtis like only junk food? Because, he says, he had no choice but to eat home-grown, home-cooked meals during his days as a Wabbaseka, Arkansas, farm boy—and he vowed that when he grew up, he'd eat what he darn well pleased. I tried cooking just for myself, but no matter how little I cooked I'd always end up with about a week's worth of leftovers, and I just can't do leftovers after the second or third night. So food would be wasted. It's been easier to just eat what he eats.

Anyway, Curtis's vow also included watching what he darn well pleased on the telly, since he and his siblings had to work the farm and didn't get to watch much television. And, like many other hubbies out there, most of what he watches is sports.

Mom warned me before we got married that sports was something I wasn't going to be able to drag Curtis away from, so she said I shouldn't even go into the marriage with thoughts of changing him. "Fine," I said. "I can stand being a football widow."

Football widow, my foot. I'm also a basketball widow, a baseball widow, and a horse-racing widow. Maybe it's a good thing. If it weren't for all these sports, he'd probably notice how many times I go to the mall.

Football and fast food run hand in hand, and most evening mealtimes, Curtis can be found sitting cross-legged on the floor, scarfing pizza from Mazzio's™, Shotgun Dan's™, or Tony's™; chili from Backyard Burgers™; burgers from McDonald's™ or Burger King™, or—and this is about the closest he gets to a regular meal—a "to-go" plate from Western Sizzlin™. But sometimes he gets a hankering for homemade fast food, and that's when he pulls out the grill—or I clean the cobwebs out of the pots and pans; find out whether the cook top burners are still working; and try not to burn the homemade fries.

One main dish Curtis likes is Manwich™ sloppy joes. Theoretically, the beef gets all its flavor from the Manwich™ sauce, but I like to jazz my beef up a bit for even more flavor. On the next page is a recipe I came up with the last time we had this dish.

HELAINE R. FREEMAN

CREAM OF ARTICHOKE SOUP

6 artichoke hearts
4 tomatoes
1 cup chicken stock
2 cups milk
1 cup half-and-half
1 medium yellow onion, chopped
1 clove of garlic, minced

2 tablespoons chopped basil
1 teaspoon oregano
red or white pepper to taste
3/4 cup butter
1/2 cup flour
salt and black pepper to taste

- Cut the artichoke hearts into quarters. Peel, seed and purée the tomatoes.
- Combine the artichokes, tomatoes, chicken stock, milk and half-and-half in a saucepan. Bring just to a simmer over medium heat, stirring frequently.
- Sauté the onion, garlic, basil, oregano and red pepper in the butter in a skillet.
- Stir in the flour gradually. Cook until bubbly and golden brown, stirring constantly.
- Stir the flour mixture into the soup. Cook over medium heat until thickened, stirring constantly. Season with salt and black pepper.

Garnish with fresh basil.

SERVES SIX TO EIGHT

CURTIS FREEMAN'S
QUICK MANWICH™
SLOPPY JOES

Mix 1 to 2 pounds ground beef in a big ole saucepan, skillet, pot, anything except maybe a wok. Add diced onion strong enough to make you boo-hoo, garlic powder, Mrs. Dash™, black pepper, soy sauce and, if feeling really wicked, green peppers. At some point, turn the burner up to about medium (but not too high) heat. (It's near impossible to tell how high our burners are; a while back I got a wild hair, sprayed oven cleaner on our dials, and obliterated the settings—a mistake Curtis never misses an opportunity to scold me about.) Stir the beef frequently and get it all brown, then drain the grease off (or heck, leave it in if you want to) before adding 1 to 2 cans of Manwich™. Turn heat down low and let simmer for 5 to 10 minutes so the flavor of the Manwich™ permeates the beef; stir a few more times. Spoon out on toasted buns and en-joy! You may also use the recipe without the Manwich™ and just make plain burgers.

Helaine R. Freeman

ALMOND SOUP

³/₄ cup sliced natural almonds
6 tablespoons margarine
6 tablespoons flour
1¹/₂ (12-ounce) cans chicken broth
3 cups half-and-half
1 tablespoon instant minced onion
1¹/₂ tablespoons dry sherry or cooking wine

- Crush the almonds. Sauté in the margarine in a saucepan over medium heat until light brown.
- Stir in the flour. Cook until bubbly.
- Add the chicken broth, half-and-half and instant onion. Bring to a boil and cook until thickened, stirring constantly. Stir in the wine.

Garnish with parsley and additional almonds.

Note: This mild and light soup is a great first course for a heavy meal such as Thanksgiving dinner.

SERVES EIGHT

BRIE AND PORTOBELLO SOUP

8 ounces Brie cheese
4 portobello mushrooms
3 medium shallots, finely chopped
1 clove of garlic, minced
3 tablespoons butter
2 tablespoons flour
4 cups whipping cream
2 (16-ounce) cans chicken broth
¹/₂ cup dry sherry
¹/₂ cup toasted chopped pecans

- Remove the rind from the cheese and chop the cheese. Clean and chop the mushrooms, discarding the gills.
- Sauté the shallots and garlic in the melted butter in a saucepan over medium heat for 5 minutes.
- Stir in the flour and cook for 2 minutes.
- Whisk in 1 cup of the cream or enough to make a thick white sauce. Cook until thickened, whisking constantly.
- Add the cheese. Cook until melted, stirring constantly. Add the remaining cream, chicken broth, wine and mushrooms and mix well.
- Reduce the heat and simmer, uncovered, for 20 minutes or until the mushrooms are tender.
- Top the servings with the toasted pecans.

SERVES SIX

BRIE AND ROASTED GARLIC SOUP

2 heads of garlic
2 tablespoons olive oil
1 medium onion, finely chopped
¼ cup olive oil
2 ribs celery, finely chopped
1 carrot, finely chopped
¼ cup flour
6 cups chicken stock

7 ounces Brie cheese
1 teaspoon chopped fresh oregano,
or ½ teaspoon dried
½ teaspoon chopped fresh thyme,
or ¼ teaspoon dried
1 teaspoon chopped fresh parsley
salt and white pepper to taste

- Preheat the oven to 325 degrees.
- Separate the garlic heads into cloves and place the unpeeled cloves in a glass baking dish. Drizzle with 2 tablespoons olive oil.
- Bake, covered with foil, for 30 minutes or until the garlic is very tender and golden brown. Cool in the dish on a wire rack.
- Sauté the onion in ¼ cup olive oil in a large heavy saucepan over medium heat for 10 minutes or until translucent.
- Add the celery and carrot and sauté for 10 minutes or until the vegetables are tender.
- Stir in the flour. Cook for 3 minutes, stirring constantly. Stir in the chicken stock gradually. Bring to a boil and cook until thickened, stirring constantly.
- Reduce the heat and simmer for 15 minutes, stirring occasionally.
- Peel the garlic and remove the rind from the cheese; chop the cheese.
- Combine the garlic with 1 cup of the soup in the food processor container. Process until smooth.
- Stir the purée into the soup with the oregano, thyme and parsley. Bring to a simmer over medium-low heat.
- Add the cheese gradually, cooking until melted after each addition and stirring constantly. Season with salt and white pepper.

SERVES SIX

SOUP GARNISHES

Add interest to soups with different garnishes. Try shredded cheese, grated hard-cooked egg, lemon slices, sunflower or sesame seeds, a dollop of sour cream or yogurt, alfalfa sprouts, or roasted nuts.

CREAMY BROCCOLI SOUP

4 cubes chicken bouillon
4 cups water
1 cup chopped celery
1 cup chopped onion
1 cup chopped carrot
2 (10-ounce) packages frozen chopped broccoli
2½ cups chopped peeled potatoes
2 (10-ounce) cans cream of chicken soup
1 pound Velveeta cheese, cubed
2 tablespoons Worcestershire sauce

- Combine the chicken bouillon, water, celery, onion and carrot in a large heavy saucepan.
- Cook for 20 minutes. Add the broccoli and potatoes. Cook until the vegetables are tender.
- Stir in the cream of chicken soup and cubed Velveeta cheese. Cook until the cheese melts, stirring to mix well.
- Add the Worcestershire sauce and serve immediately.

SERVES TWELVE

BLACK BEAN CHILI

2 (28-ounce) cans tomatoes
1 pound ground pork
1 pound ground beef chuck or sirloin
2 onions, chopped
3 cloves of garlic, minced
1 green bell pepper, chopped
1 red bell pepper, chopped
1 jalapeño, chopped
4 beef bouillon cubes
2 cups water
½ cup chili powder
2 tablespoons masa
2 tablespoons cumin
2 teaspoons oregano
2 teaspoons salt
1 tablespoon black pepper
1 teaspoon white pepper
2 (16-ounce) cans black beans

- Purée 1 can of the tomatoes until smooth. Cut the remaining can of tomatoes into small pieces.
- Sauté the pork and beef in a nonstick skillet until brown. Transfer to a large stockpot.
- Add the onions, garlic, bell peppers and jalapeño to the skillet and sauté until the onions are slightly translucent.
- Add to the stockpot. Add the tomatoes, bouillon cubes and 2 cups water.
- Combine the next 7 ingredients in a small bowl. Add enough water to make a thin paste. Add to the stockpot.
- Simmer for 1½ hours. Drain and rinse the beans. Add to the chili. Simmer for 20 to 30 minutes longer.
- Serve with corn chips and sour cream.

SERVES TEN

WHITE CHICKEN CHILI

6 boneless skinless chicken breasts
3 cups water
1 teaspoon lemon pepper
1 teaspoon ground cumin
2 cloves of garlic, minced
1 cup (or more) chopped onion
2 (9-ounce) packages frozen Shoe
   Peg corn
2 (4-ounce) cans chopped green
   chiles

1 teaspoon ground cumin
3 tablespoons lime juice
red pepper to taste
2 (15-ounce) cans Great Northern
   beans
crushed tortilla chips
shredded Monterey Jack cheese
Salsa Verde (page 158)

- Rinse the chicken well. Bring the water, lemon pepper and 1 teaspoon cumin to a boil in a large saucepan. Add the chicken.
- Simmer, covered, over low heat for 25 to 30 minutes. Remove the chicken and cut into 1-inch pieces. Return to the broth.
- Sauté the garlic in a small skillet sprayed with nonstick cooking spray for 1 minute. Add to the chicken mixture.
- Add the onion to the skillet. Cook until tender; add to the chili.
- Add the corn, green chiles, 1 teaspoon cumin, lime juice and red pepper. Bring to a boil. Add the undrained beans. Cook until heated through.
- To serve, crumble tortilla chips into each serving bowl and sprinkle with the cheese. Ladle in the chili and top with Salsa Verde.

Garnish with fresh cilantro.

Variation: Prepared red or green salsa can be substituted for the Salsa Verde to top this chili.

SERVES TWELVE

STRAWBERRY SOUP

Combine 15 ounces thawed frozen strawberries with their juice and 16 ounces sour cream and beat until smooth. Add 1/2 ounce grenadine syrup, 1/2 cup confectioners' sugar and 1 tablespoon vanilla, beating constantly until smooth. Add 1/4 cup half-and-half and mix gently. Chill for 4 hours. Shake or stir before serving. Serves 6.

CHICKEN-WILD RICE SOUP

1/2 medium onion, minced
6 tablespoons margarine
1/4 cup flour
3 cups chicken broth
2 cups chopped cooked chicken
2 cups cooked long grain and wild rice
1/2 cup finely shredded carrot
1 (4-ounce) can sliced mushrooms
3 tablespoons chopped slivered almonds, lightly
* toasted*
1/2 teaspoon salt
1 cup half-and-half, or 1 (12-ounce) can
* evaporated skim milk*
2 tablespoons dry sherry (optional)

- Sauté the onion in the melted margarine in a large saucepan until tender.
- Stir in the flour. Cook until bubbly.
- Add the chicken broth gradually. Bring to a boil over medium heat and cook for 1 minute, stirring constantly.
- Add the chicken, rice, carrot, mushrooms, almonds and salt. Simmer for 5 minutes.
- Stir in the half-and-half and wine. Heat just to serving temperature.

Garnish with chopped parsley or chives.

Note: Use the long grain and wild rice mix for this recipe and cook it according to the package directions, adding the seasoning packet.

SERVES SIX TO EIGHT

CHILLED CUCUMBER SOUP

1 (10-ounce) can chicken broth
2 cups plain yogurt
1 cup grated peeled and seeded cucumber
1 teaspoon minced green onions
1/4 cup half-and-half
1 teaspoon fresh lemon juice
1 teaspoon chopped fresh dill, or
* 1/2 teaspoon dried*
salt and pepper to taste

- Combine the chicken broth and yogurt in a bowl and mix well. Add the cucumber, green onions, half-and-half, lemon juice, dill, salt and pepper and mix well. Adjust the seasonings.
- Chill, covered, for 4 hours or longer.

Garnish with dill.

SERVES FOUR TO SIX

CRAB AND CORN BISQUE

1 medium onion, chopped
1 clove of garlic, minced
½ cup unsalted butter or
   margarine
¼ cup flour
2 cups clam juice
2 cups chicken broth
1½ cups smoked corn
1 teaspoon Creole seasoning

¾ teaspoon chopped fresh thyme
½ teaspoon cayenne pepper
½ teaspoon freshly ground black
   pepper
2 cups half-and-half
1 pound lump crab meat
4 green onions, chopped
   (optional)

- Sauté the onion and garlic in the melted butter in a heavy saucepan over medium heat for 5 minutes or until translucent.
- Stir in the flour all at once. Cook for 3 to 4 minutes, stirring constantly.
- Add the clam juice and chicken broth. Bring to a boil.
- Stir in the corn, Creole seasoning, thyme, cayenne and black pepper.
- Cook, uncovered, over medium heat for 25 minutes. Add the half-and-half. Cook for 10 minutes. Adjust the seasonings.
- Pick over the crab meat, discarding any bits of shell but leaving the meat in lumps.
- Add the crab meat to the soup with the green onions. Cook for 5 to 6 minutes or until heated through. Serve hot.

Variation: Substitute drained whole kernel corn for the smoked corn.

SERVES EIGHT TO TEN

My son's recent holiday telephone call shows how history does tend to repeat itself. It seems he and his wife were unable to get home for Thanksgiving, but that didn't mean that he didn't feel "at home." Since the meal was to be her first Thanksgiving dinner with all the trimmings, she wanted to make sure it was just right. As my son described it, the kitchen walls looked like mine during holiday meal preparation time—always filled with post-it notes and lists everywhere. Of course, his words made us miss them even more.

Carol Scholtens

GAZPACHO

1 (10-ounce) can tomato soup
1 (13-ounce) can tomato juice
1¼ cups water
1 tablespoon olive oil
2 tablespoons red wine vinegar
1 tablespoon Italian salad dressing
1 tablespoon lemon or lime juice
½ teaspoon Tabasco sauce
1 teaspoon Worcestershire sauce
½ teaspoon salt
¼ teaspoon pepper
¾ cup chopped peeled cucumber
¾ cup chopped tomato
½ cup chopped green bell pepper
½ cup chopped onion
2 cloves of garlic, minced

• Combine the soup, tomato juice, water, olive oil, vinegar, salad dressing, lemon juice, Tabasco sauce, Worcestershire sauce, salt and pepper in a large bowl.
• Add the cucumber, tomato, green pepper, onion and garlic and mix well. Chill for 6 hours or longer.
• Serve with tortilla chips.

Garnish with cucumber slices.

ONION SOUP

4 cups thinly sliced yellow onions
1½ cups butter
1¾ cups flour
3 quarts beef stock
1 tablespoon Worcestershire sauce
1½ teaspoons salt
1 teaspoon white pepper
2 tablespoons whipping cream

• Cook the onions in the melted butter in a heavy saucepan over low heat until tender but not brown.
• Stir in the flour. Cook for 10 minutes, stirring frequently.
• Add the beef stock, Worcestershire sauce, salt and white pepper. Increase the heat and bring the mixture to a low boil.
• Reduce the heat and simmer, covered, for 15 minutes. Remove from the heat and stir in the cream.

Garnish with croutons and grated Parmesan cheese.

Note: Add ½ to ¾ cup of the beef stock with the flour if needed to prevent the mixture from scorching.

FRIENDSHIP SOUP

1 pound chopped chicken
vegetable oil
12 cups water

1 (28-ounce) can chopped
tomatoes
Friendship Soup Mix

- Rinse the chicken well and pat dry. Sauté in a small amount of oil in a large saucepan; drain. Add the water and undrained tomatoes.
- Remove the heart-shaped pasta carefully from the top of the Friendship Soup Mix and reserve.
- Add the remaining soup mix ingredients to the soup. Simmer for 45 minutes or until the peas are nearly tender.
- Add the heart-shaped pasta. Simmer for 15 minutes or until the peas and pasta are tender.

Note: To reheat this soup, add an additional small can of tomatoes.

FRIENDSHIP SOUP MIX

1/3 cup instant chicken bouillon
1 1/2 tablespoons Italian seasoning
1/4 cup onion flakes
1/2 cup dried split peas
1/2 cup alphabet macaroni

1/4 cup barley
1/2 cup dried lentils
1/2 cup uncooked rice
1 1/4 cups (about) heart-shaped or
other pasta

- Layer the chicken bouillon, Italian seasoning, onion flakes, dried peas, alphabet macaroni, barley, lentils and rice in the order listed in a 1-quart jar.
- Fill the jar with about 1 1/4 cups heart-shaped or other pasta.
- To give as a gift, decorate the jar and include a clever card with directions for cooking the soup.

SERVES TEN TO TWELVE

When preparing edible "care packages" to be mailed, prevent breakage by filling the spaces between items with miniature marshmallows. For example, place fragile food, such as cookies, in a metal tin and surround the cookies with the miniature marshmallows. Place the tin in a sturdy cardboard box, and fill the space around the tin with peanuts in the shell. Family members who are away from home will surely appreciate this triple treat.

RED BELL PEPPER SOUP

4 medium red bell peppers, chopped
6 green onion bulbs, chopped
1/2 cup chopped onion
1 medium carrot, finely shredded
3 tablespoons margarine
2 cups chicken broth
2 cups whipping cream
salt and pepper to taste

- Sauté the bell peppers, green onions, onion and carrot in the margarine in a saucepan until tender.
- Add the chicken broth and cream. Reduce the heat and simmer for 30 minutes.
- Process in a blender or food processor until smooth. Return to the saucepan.
- Simmer for 15 minutes longer. Season with salt and pepper.

Garnish servings with a red, green or yellow bell pepper ring or fresh parsley.

SERVES FOUR TO SIX

——

BAKED POTATO SOUP

4 large baking potatoes
2/3 cup butter or margarine
2/3 cup flour
6 cups milk
3/4 teaspoon salt (optional)
freshly ground pepper to taste
4 green onions, chopped
12 slices bacon, crisp-fried, crumbled
1 1/4 cups shredded Cheddar cheese
1 cup sour cream

- Preheat the oven to 400 degrees.
- Wash the potatoes and pierce several times with a fork. Bake for 1 hour or until tender; cool.
- Cut the potatoes into halves and scoop the pulp into a small bowl, discarding the skins.
- Melt the butter in a heavy saucepan over low heat. Stir in the flour. Cook for 1 minute, stirring constantly.
- Add the milk gradually, stirring well after each addition. Cook over medium heat until thickened and bubbly, stirring constantly. Season with salt and pepper.
- Add the potato pulp, 2 tablespoons of the green onions, 1/2 cup of the bacon and 1 cup of the cheese. Cook until heated through.
- Stir in the sour cream. Add additional milk if needed for the desired consistency.
- Sprinkle the servings with the remaining green onions, bacon and cheese.

Note: Skim milk and low-fat sour cream and cheese may be used to reduce the fat in this soup. The recipe can be increased and freezes well.

SERVES SIX TO EIGHT

——

SMOKED TOMATO SOUP

2 pounds tomatoes
1 clove of garlic, minced
½ onion, chopped
2 tablespoons olive oil
3 quarts (about) rich chicken
   stock

juice of 1 lemon
Worcestershire sauce to taste
salt and pepper to taste

- Peel and seed the tomatoes (see method at right). Smoke the tomatoes in a column smoker with apple wood, mesquite wood, hickory wood or pecan shells for 30 to 45 minutes or until the flavor permeates the tomatoes.
- Sauté the garlic and onion in the olive oil in a saucepan until the onion is translucent.
- Add the tomatoes and enough chicken stock to make of the desired consistency. Simmer over low heat for 45 minutes.
- Process in small batches in a food processor or emersion blender.
- Return the mixture to the saucepan and season with lemon juice, Worcestershire sauce, salt and pepper. Cook just until heated through.

Garnish with sour cream and chives.

SERVES SIXTEEN

PEELING TOMATOES

This recipe for Smoked Tomato Soup was shared by Peter Brave, the owner of Brave New Restaurant in Little Rock. He tells us that to peel and seed tomatoes, you should first score them with an X on the bottom. Place them in boiling water and blanch for 30 seconds, drain in a colander and plunge the colander into ice water to stop the cooking. The skins will slip easily from the tomatoes. Cut the tomatoes into halves and squeeze gently to remove the seeds.

POTLUCK, INC.

Peter Brave is also the Chairman of the Board of Potluck, Inc., a project of the Junior League. Potluck, Inc. is a nonprofit organization that "rescues" unserved perishable food from local restaurants and delivers it to local hunger agencies.

MINESTRONE

1 cup finely chopped onion
1 cup finely chopped celery
2 tablespoons olive oil
1 tablespoon butter
4 large cloves of garlic, minced
3 extra-large cubes chicken bouillon
2 cups sliced quartered carrots
1 teaspoon salt
1 teaspoon pepper
2 cups frozen corn
2 cups frozen green peas
2 cups frozen green beans
1 (16-ounce) can kidney beans
9 cups water
1 (10-ounce) package frozen chopped spinach
1 cup uncooked small tubular pasta

- Sauté the onion and celery in the olive oil and melted butter in an 8-quart saucepan until the onion is tender but not brown.
- Add the garlic and bouillon cubes; crush the cubes with a spoon and stir to mix well. Add the carrots, salt and pepper.
- Cook, covered, over low heat for 5 minutes or until the carrots are tender-crisp.
- Add the corn, peas and green beans and mix well. Cook, covered, over medium heat for 5 minutes or until the vegetables thaw.
- Purée the kidney beans with 1 cup of the water in a food processor. Add to the soup with the remaining 8 cups water. Bring to a boil.
- Add the spinach. Bring to a simmer over high heat. Reduce the heat and simmer for 30 minutes.
- Add the pasta. Cook until the pasta is tender.

SERVES TEN

CREAM OF SPINACH SOUP

1 (10-ounce) package frozen chopped spinach
1 (10-ounce) can cream of mushroom soup
2 tablespoons chopped onion
2 cups milk
1 tablespoon Worcestershire sauce
5 drops of Tabasco sauce
¼ teaspoon dried chervil
¼ teaspoon dried marjoram
salt and pepper to taste

- Thaw the spinach and press to remove excess moisture.
- Combine with the mushroom soup, onion, milk, Worcestershire sauce, Tabasco sauce, chervil, marjoram, salt and pepper in a blender container and process until smooth.
- Chill until serving time.

Garnish with chopped pimento or crumbled crisp-fried bacon.

Variation: Heat in a saucepan and serve warm.

SERVES FOUR

TORTILLA SOUP

1 (4-ounce) can whole green chiles
1 (14-ounce) can stewed tomatoes
1 large onion, chopped
2 cloves of garlic, minced
1½ cups chopped cooked chicken
   or turkey
4 cups chicken stock
1 (10-ounce) can tomato soup
1 teaspoon ground cumin

½ teaspoon lemon pepper
2 teaspoons chili powder
2 teaspoons Worcestershire sauce
salt and pepper to taste
5 corn tortillas
vegetable oil
1 or 2 avocados, chopped
shredded Cheddar cheese

- Rinse and chop the green chiles, discarding the seeds. Combine with the tomatoes, onion and garlic in a large saucepan. Cook over medium heat for 5 to 10 minutes.
- Add the chicken, chicken stock, tomato soup, cumin, lemon pepper, chili powder, Worcestershire sauce, salt and pepper. Simmer, covered, for 1 hour.
- Sauté the tortillas in a small amount of oil in a skillet. Tear into bite-size pieces.
- Drop the tortillas into the soup. Heat for 10 to 20 minutes but do not boil.
- Place the avocados and shredded cheese in soup bowls and ladle the soup into the bowls.

Garnish with sour cream.

Note: This soup can be prepared in advance and chilled or frozen prior to adding the tortillas. It is a wonderful soup to take to new mothers, with the instructions for reheating and adding the tortillas, avocados, cheese and sour cream.

SERVES FOUR TO SIX

ARKANSAS TOMATOES

Warren, Arkansas, is the home of the famous Bradley County Pink Tomato. In 1987, the Arkansas General Assembly recognized the South Arkansas Vine-Ripe Pink Tomato as both the state fruit and vegetable. The tomato is botanically a fruit, but is used as a vegetable. It is a delicious choice for a summertime lunch sandwich.

TOMATO SANDWICH

Brush sliced sourdough bread with olive oil. Layer ¼-inch slices of tomato and ¼- to ½-inch slices of buffalo mozzarella cheese on the bread and sprinkle with basil and freshly ground pepper.

ROASTED RED PEPPER SPREAD

2 cups chopped roasted red bell peppers
6 cups shredded Cheddar cheese
1 cup mayonnaise
1 (16-ounce) jar medium picante sauce
4 teaspoons sugar

- Combine the peppers, cheese, mayonnaise, picante sauce and sugar in a bowl and mix well. Chill until serving time.
- Serve spread on toasted wheat bread with lettuce leaves.

Note: You may use commercial roasted peppers or roast them in the oven. To roast, cut red bell peppers into halves lengthwise and discard the seeds. Place them cut side down on a baking sheet and bake at 400 degrees until the skin is puffed and brown. Remove from the oven. Let stand under a cloth towel for 20 minutes, peel the skin away and use as needed.

YIELDS TEN CUPS

VEGGIE SANDWICHES

2 (10-ounce) packages frozen chopped spinach
½ onion, finely chopped
1 tablespoon minced green bell pepper
6 tablespoons mayonnaise
1 tablespoon lemon juice
½ teaspoon salt
⅔ to 1 cup sliced mushrooms
3 tablespoons margarine, softened
12 slices rye or pumpernickel bread
6 slices Swiss cheese
6 slices provolone cheese
6 slices Cheddar cheese
2 tablespoons sunflower kernels
1 cup alfalfa sprouts

- Cook the spinach using the package directions; drain well. Combine with the onion, green pepper, mayonnaise, lemon juice and salt in a large bowl and mix well.
- Sauté the mushrooms in a small amount of the margarine in a skillet and set aside.
- Spread 1 side of the bread slices with margarine. Grill 6 of the slices on a griddle and set aside.
- Place the remaining slices on the griddle. Layer 1 slice Swiss cheese, 1 slice provolone cheese and 1 slice Cheddar cheese on each slice of bread.
- Grill until the cheeses melt. Remove from the heat.
- Sprinkle with the sunflower kernels, mushrooms and alfalfa sprouts. Top with the spinach spread and the reserved grilled bread.

SERVES SIX

PORTOBELLO MUSHROOM SANDWICHES

1 large zucchini
1 yellow bell pepper
1 red bell pepper
2 medium or 1 large portobello
   mushroom caps
2 thin slices large red onion

⅓ cup olive oil
8 slices bread, lightly toasted
1 tablespoon roasted garlic
   mayonnaise
spinach leaves
4 ounces goat cheese

- Cut the zucchini lengthwise into ¼-inch slices. Cut the bell peppers into quarters lengthwise, discarding the seeds. Brush all sides of the zucchini, bell peppers, mushroom caps and onion slices with the olive oil.
- Grill over medium-high heat or broil 5 inches from the heat source for 10 to 12 minutes or until roasted, turning once. Remove to a plate and cool to room temperature.
- Separate the onion slices into rings. Slice the mushrooms crosswise. Spread 1 side of each bread slice lightly with mayonnaise.
- Layer the spinach leaves and vegetables on 4 slices of bread. Cut the cheese crosswise into 8 slices. Arrange on the layers. Top with the remaining bread.
- Cut the sandwiches into halves and secure with wooden picks. Wrap in plastic wrap and chill for up to 8 hours.
- Let stand until room temperature before serving.

Note: Roasted garlic mayonnaise is available commercially in most specialty stores.

SERVES FOUR

CUCUMBER SANDWICHES

Combine 16 ounces softened cream cheese with 2 peeled, seeded and shredded cucumbers, ¼ cup sour cream or mayonnaise, 1 tablespoon dillweed, 1 teaspoon Greek seasoning and 1 teaspoon celery seeds in a mixer bowl or food processor bowl and mix well. Spread on trimmed bread rounds or slices and garnish with a thin cucumber slice.

Just the Girls

SALADS

Salsa Verde with Chips
Strawberry Romaine Salad
Confetti Corn Salad
Chicken Fiesta
Island Fruit Trifle
Blue Margaritas

A Gathering of the Women Folk: Girls' Night Out

As I reflect on the makings of a great "Girls' Night Out," I quickly realize the list is short and succinct: Joy's Fruit Salad (see below), some Chardonnay, sourdough baguettes, and friends who are women folk. When I say women folk, I mean the kind who are trustworthy and conversational, such as our family's nanny and mothers whose children are friends of my daughter. They just have to be good conversationalists. We always gather at somebody's house, but not on a regularly scheduled basis.

When it's my house for Girls' Night Out, I serve the fruit salad I grew up with: the one my mother, Joy, made all year round. She used to make it for us as dessert using seasonal fruits. She and my dad would have cheese in theirs, but Mom never made us eat ours with cheese. Since becoming an adult, I also add gorgonzola and walnuts.

None of the girls want to eat much in the evening when we get together. So I put the salad in a big bowl in the middle of the table, and we eat it as an entree. A sourdough baguette or two accompany, and we just rip off pieces of bread. Everybody has her own plate, and we sit around and talk about everyday things.

While many of our conversations deal with topics like the children's basketball games and horses, we occasionally veer off in the direction of more "worldly" matters. I will never forget the night I predicted that "Live with Regis and Kathie Lee" would never be a success. "Who would want to hear about where they ate dinner the night before?" I had wondered aloud. I soon found out that I am not the one to consult about TV programming!

For Joy's Fruit Salad, mix any fruit with low-fat or nonfat vanilla yogurt. Never use fruits that are not in season - this makes them more exciting when they are available. For example, use lots of honeydew melons, cantaloupes, strawberries, and grapes in the summer. The amount of fruit can vary according to personal preference. Children love it, too, but they may pass on the cheese as I used to do.

NANCY L. SNYDERMAN, M.D.

AMBROSIA SALAD

1 (15-ounce) can mandarin
  oranges, drained
1 (20-ounce) can pineapple
  chunks, drained
1 cup flaked coconut
1 cup sour cream
1 cup miniature marshmallows

2 (3-ounce) packages orange
  gelatin
2 cups boiling water
1 pint orange sherbet
1 (11-ounce) can mandarin
  oranges, drained

For the fruit mixture
• Combine the large can of oranges, pineapple, coconut, sour cream and marshmallows in a bowl and mix well.
• Chill, covered, for 8 to 10 hours.

For the ring mold
• Dissolve the gelatin in the boiling water in a bowl. Add the sherbet, stirring until melted.
• Chill until partially set. Stir in the small can of mandarin oranges. Pour into a 1½-quart ring mold. Chill until set.

To assemble the salad
• Unmold the ring mold onto a serving plate. Fill the center with the fruit mixture.

Variation: Substitute ½ cup whipping cream for the sour cream and 2 cups orange juice for the water.

SERVES TEN TO TWELVE

One of my favorite girls' night out activities in college centered around cooking. Several girls would go to the grocery store and purchase all of the ingredients for a stir-fry, including loads of fresh vegetables, rice, chicken, and seasonings. We would then borrow an apartment from an older friend, get out the stir-fry pan, and spend the evening creating a delicious meal. The conversation and camaraderie flowed over chopping vegetables and cooking rice. We felt like true adults, out of the sorority house, preparing our own food, and living independently. I still make stir-fry today for a hungry family on a busy night.

Cecile Stuckey Rose

FRESH FRUIT SALAD

½ cup dry white wine
½ cup honey
½ teaspoon cinnamon
¼ teaspoon allspice
1 tablespoon amaretto
4 cups fresh fruit
3 tablespoons chopped fresh mint

For the dressing
• Combine the wine, honey, cinnamon, allspice and amaretto in a bowl and stir until the honey is well mixed.

For the salad
• Select fresh fruit such as raspberries, strawberries, orange sections, melon balls, kiwifruit, peach slices or pear slices.
• Combine the fruit in a large bowl and toss lightly to mix.
• Pour the dressing over the fruit. Chill, covered, for several hours.
• Sprinkle with the mint immediately before serving.

SERVES FOUR

MEDITERRANEAN BREAD SALAD

1 clove of garlic, minced
1 tablespoon red wine vinegar
salt and pepper to taste
¼ cup olive oil
1 pound tomatoes
¼ cup fresh basil leaves
2 cups (1-inch) cubes crusty French or Italian bread
¼ cup sliced black olives
½ cup feta cheese

For the dressing
• Mash the minced garlic into a paste in a large bowl. Add the vinegar, salt and pepper and whisk together.
• Whisk in the oil gradually.

For the salad
• Cut the tomatoes into 1-inch chunks. Chop the basil leaves.
• Combine the tomatoes, basil, bread cubes, olives and cheese in a bowl and toss to mix.
• Add the dressing and toss gently to mix. Let stand at room temperature for 15 minutes before serving.
• Serve with lamb or pork.

SERVES FOUR

CURRIED CHICKEN SALAD

1 (16-ounce) package white rice
1 cup cauliflowerets (optional)
1 (8-ounce) bottle French
　dressing
1 cup mayonnaise
1 teaspoon curry powder
1 tablespoon salt
1/2 teaspoon pepper

1/2 cup milk
6 to 7 cups chopped cooked
　chicken
1 cup thin green bell pepper rings
2 cups chopped celery
1 cup thinly sliced red onion
1 cup coarsely chopped red bell
　pepper

- Cook the rice using package directions. Cool completely.
- Combine the rice with the cauliflower and French dressing in a bowl and toss to mix. Chill, covered, for 2 hours or longer.
- Combine the mayonnaise, curry powder, 1 tablespoon salt and pepper in a bowl. Add the milk gradually, stirring to mix. Add the chicken and toss lightly.
- Chill, covered, for 2 hours or longer.
- Combine the rice mixture, chicken mixture, green pepper rings, celery, onion and red bell pepper in a bowl and mix well just before serving.
- Serve accompanied with bowls of chutney, hard-cooked eggs, pineapple chunks, canned onion rings, peanuts and shredded coconut.

SERVES TWENTY

Birthday clubs are a perfect ruse to get a group of girlfriends together. We have a group of ten friends who have met for monthly lunch for more than five years. The problems of the world and our lives are solved in one hour by us, all talking at once. It is a wonder that there is time to eat! To lessen the complication of gifts, we give a group gift with the preceding month's birthday girl responsible for fulfilling the request; everyone else brings a funny card. Mile-marker birthdays warrant special treatment. For fortieth birthdays, we try to have an overnight getaway, and the honoree receives a whimsical old-lady sculpture by Jane Hankins, a local artist. Each is unique and treasured. We have been known to don black tulle and bejeweled sunglasses—in public!

Becky Butler Scott

CHICKEN SALAD

¾ cup mayonnaise
¾ cup sour cream
2 tablespoons lemon or lime juice
2 tablespoons chopped fresh dill
salt and pepper to taste
5 cups chopped cooked chicken
¾ cup diced celery
¾ cup seedless green or red grapes
¾ cup chopped walnuts
1 (11-ounce) can mandarin oranges, drained
* (optional)*

For the dressing
- Combine the mayonnaise, sour cream, lemon juice, dill, salt and pepper in a bowl and mix well.

For the salad
- Combine the chicken, celery, grapes, walnuts and mandarin oranges in a bowl and toss to mix.
- Pour the dressing over the chicken mixture and mix well.

Variation: For a Mexican flavor, use grilled or smoked chicken, substitute cilantro for the dill and add ⅓ cup chopped red onion.

SERVES EIGHT

ASPARAGUS VINAIGRETTE

½ cup vegetable oil
2 small cloves of garlic, minced
1 small shallot, minced
1 teaspoon sugar
juice of ½ lemon
1 tablespoon Dijon mustard
¼ cup chopped fresh parsley
1 tablespoon tarragon vinegar
2 pounds very thin fresh asparagus
1 (2-ounce) jar pimento strips

For the vinaigrette
- Combine the oil, garlic, shallot, sugar, lemon juice, mustard, parsley and vinegar in a bowl and whisk until well mixed.

For the asparagus
- Trim any tough ends from the asparagus spears and discard. Rinse in cold water.
- Bring a large saucepan of water to a boil over medium heat. Add the asparagus. Cook for 3 to 5 minutes or just until tender-crisp; do not overcook.
- Drain immediately and plunge into cold water; drain well. Arrange on a serving platter.
- Drizzle the vinaigrette over the asparagus. Top with the pimento strips. Chill, covered, until serving time.

SERVES EIGHT

BLACK BEAN SALSA SALAD

¼ cup red wine vinegar
juice of 1 lemon
cumin to taste
1 clove of garlic, minced
chili powder and cayenne to taste
1 jalapeño, chopped
3 (15-ounce) cans black beans
1 (15-ounce) can white or yellow
   corn

2 (10-ounce) cans tomatoes with
   green chiles
1 bunch green onions, chopped
1 yellow bell pepper, chopped
1 green bell pepper, chopped
1 red bell pepper, chopped
2 cups chopped tomatoes
1 cup chopped cilantro

For the dressing

• Combine the vinegar, lemon juice, cumin, garlic, chili powder, cayenne pepper and jalapeño in a bowl and mix well.

For the salad

• Drain the beans and corn. Combine with the tomatoes with green chiles, onions, bell peppers, chopped tomatoes and cilantro in a bowl and mix well.
• Add the dressing to the salad. Chill, covered, for up to 24 hours. Drain the excess liquid before serving.

Variation: For **Black Bean Salsa**, *serve this salad undrained. It is good as an appetizer with chips or as an accompaniment.*

SERVES TWENTY

There are few meals not improved by a really good green salad. Nothing makes me quite so happy—or tells me quite as much about a restaurant's attention to detail—as a salad. Because there are only so many accurate words to describe salads—fresh, crisp, green, refreshing—these descriptions become tired, but a perfect salad never is. Learn to do a green salad right, have the ingredients for the salad on hand, take the time (not much) needed to do it, and you will have a reliable source of pleasure throughout your days.

Crescent Dragonwagon, *from her vegetarian cookbook*

BEAN AND TOMATO SALAD

2 tablespoons balsamic vinegar
1 tablespoon red wine vinegar
2 teaspoons sugar
2 teaspoons Dijon mustard
1 teaspoon salt
¼ cup olive oil
freshly ground pepper to taste
¼ cup finely chopped red onion
1½ pounds fresh green beans
salt to taste
1 pint cherry tomatoes, cut into halves

For the dressing
• Combine the vinegar, sugar, mustard, 1 teaspoon salt, oil and pepper in a bowl and whisk until well mixed. Stir in the onion.

For the salad
• Cook the beans with salt to taste in boiling water in a saucepan for 3 minutes or until tender-crisp. Drain and place in a serving bowl.
• Drizzle the dressing over the warm green beans. Top with the cherry tomatoes.
• Serve at room temperature.

SERVES EIGHT

BROCCOLI SALAD

1 cup mayonnaise
¼ cup sugar
2 tablespoons cider vinegar
5 to 6 cups broccoli florets
1 cup raisins
¼ cup chopped red onion
6 slices crisp-fried bacon, crumbled
½ cup sunflower kernels

For the dressing
• Combine the mayonnaise, sugar and vinegar in a bowl and mix well.

For the salad
• Cut the broccoli into bite-size pieces. Combine the broccoli, raisins and onion in a bowl and mix well.
• Pour the dressing over the salad and toss gently to mix. Chill, covered, until serving time.
• Sprinkle with the bacon and sunflower kernels just before serving.

Variation: Add 1 cup shredded Cheddar cheese.

SERVES TEN

CAESAR SALAD

1 clove of garlic
1 egg
2 tablespoons lemon juice
1/2 cup grated Parmesan cheese
1 teaspoon Worcestershire sauce

1/2 teaspoon salt
1/2 teaspoon pepper
1/2 cup vegetable oil
1 head romaine lettuce, chopped
1 cup croutons

For the dressing
- Combine the garlic, egg, lemon juice, cheese, Worcestershire sauce, salt and pepper in a blender container.
- Process until well mixed. Add the oil gradually, processing constantly at high speed until smooth.
- To avoid the danger of salmonella in uncooked eggs, use an equivalent amount of pasteurized egg substitute. You may also bring 2 inches of water to a boil in a small saucepan, remove from the heat, and lower the egg carefully into the water; let stand for 1 minute. Cool slightly before removing the shell.

For the salad
- Combine the romaine lettuce and croutons in a large bowl and toss to mix.
- Add the dressing just before serving and toss to mix.

Variation: Add cooked chicken or shrimp for a main-dish salad.

SERVES SIX

TOMATO AND FETA SALAD

Mix 1/2 cup olive oil, 1/2 cup red wine vinegar, 1 teaspoon each dried oregano and thyme and salt to taste in a bowl. Combine 2 pints of cherry tomato halves, 1/2 cup pitted black olives and 2 teaspoons crushed garlic in a bowl. Add the dressing and 1 1/2 cups crumbled feta cheese and toss lightly. Chill until serving time. For variety, add 1 sliced cucumber and/or 1/2 cup chopped green onions. Serves 10.

COLESLAW

1 teaspoon celery seeds
2 tablespoons sugar
3 tablespoons vinegar
1 teaspoon salt
1 teaspoon monosodium glutamate
pepper to taste
⅓ cup vegetable oil
4 to 5 cups shredded cabbage
1 bunch green onions, chopped
1 to 2 carrots, grated
2 tablespoons sesame seeds

For the dressing
- Combine the celery seeds, sugar, vinegar, salt, MSG and pepper in a bowl and beat well.
- Add the oil gradually, beating well until mixed.

For the salad
- Combine the cabbage, green onions and carrots in a bowl and mix well.
- Add the dressing to the coleslaw and toss to mix. Chill, covered, for up to 24 hours.
- Sprinkle with the sesame seeds just before serving.

SERVES EIGHT TO TEN

CONFETTI CORN SALAD

½ cup apple cider vinegar
¼ cup sugar
salt and pepper to taste
1 (16-ounce) can white whole kernel corn
1 (16-ounce) can yellow whole kernel corn
1 (14-ounce) can black beans (optional)
1 (2-ounce) jar chopped pimento
1 large green bell pepper, chopped
1 large sweet yellow or purple onion, chopped
1 large tomato, chopped
1 cucumber, chopped

For the dressing
- Combine the vinegar, sugar, salt and pepper in a bowl and mix until the sugar dissolves.

For the salad
- Combine the corn, black beans, pimento, bell pepper, onion, tomato and cucumber in a large bowl and toss lightly to mix.
- Add the dressing to the salad and toss to mix.
- Chill, covered, for several hours before serving.

SERVES TWELVE

HEARTS OF PALM SALAD

¼ small onion, chopped
3 tablespoons cider vinegar
2 teaspoons spicy brown mustard
½ teaspoon sugar
½ teaspoon salt
¼ teaspoon pepper

1 cup vegetable oil
12 ounces bacon
1 (7-ounce) can hearts of palm
1 (8-ounce) can artichoke hearts
2 bunches romaine lettuce
4 ounces bleu cheese, crumbled

For the dressing
- Combine the onion and vinegar in a blender container. Process until the onion is puréed.
- Add the mustard, sugar, salt and pepper. Process until well mixed. Add the oil gradually, processing constantly at high speed until thickened.

For the salad
- Fry the bacon in a large skillet over medium heat until crisp. Drain on paper towels; cool and crumble.
- Drain the hearts of palm and chop. Drain the artichoke hearts and cut into quarters. Tear the romaine lettuce into bite-size pieces.
- Combine the hearts of palm, artichoke hearts, romaine lettuce, bleu cheese and bacon in a large bowl and toss to mix.
- Add the dressing and toss to mix just before serving.

SERVES TWELVE

On the Christmas before our wedding, my fiancé's mother gave me a very special Christmas present: a recipe box that was filled not only with her son's favorite recipes, but also with all the old family recipes that had been lovingly passed down for generations. It was such a thoughtful way to welcome me into the family, and, of course, it gave me a tremendous jump-start on cooking for my new husband.

Mallory Lemon Rottman

MARINATED POTATO SALAD

1 pound small new potatoes
salt to taste
3/4 cup vinaigrette salad dressing
1 (13-ounce) can artichoke hearts
10 to 12 cherry tomatoes
1 small green bell pepper, sliced
1 small red bell pepper, sliced
1/2 small red onion, sliced
1 (4-ounce) can sliced olives
1/4 cup chopped parsley
pepper to taste

- Boil the potatoes with salt in water to cover in a saucepan over medium heat for 15 to 20 minutes or until tender; drain.
- Cut the potatoes into bite-size pieces. Place in a large bowl.
- Pour the salad dressing over the potatoes.
- Drain the artichoke hearts and cut into halves. Cut the cherry tomatoes into halves.
- Add the artichoke hearts, tomatoes, green and red bell peppers, onion, olives, parsley, salt and pepper to the potatoes and mix well.
- Chill, covered, for 4 to 24 hours, stirring occasionally. Spoon into a serving bowl.
- Serve with anything from hamburgers to fried chicken and fish.

SERVES SIX

ROASTED POTATO SALAD

4 cups quartered unpeeled new potatoes
6 slices bacon
1/2 cup sour cream
1/2 cup mayonnaise
1/4 cup chopped green onions
1/4 teaspoon salt
1/4 teaspoon pepper

- Preheat the oven to 425 degrees.
- Place the potatoes on a baking pan sprayed with nonstick cooking spray.
- Bake the potatoes for 40 minutes or until tender and golden brown. Remove from the oven and cool slightly.
- Fry the bacon in a large heavy skillet until crisp. Drain on paper towels and crumble.
- Combine the sour cream, mayonnaise, green onions, salt and pepper in a large bowl and mix well. Add the potatoes and bacon and toss gently to mix.
- Serve warm or at room temperature.

SERVES SIX

STRAWBERRY ROMAINE SALAD

1 cup vegetable oil
3/4 cup sugar
1/2 cup red wine vinegar
2 cloves of garlic, minced
1/2 teaspoon salt
1/2 teaspoon paprika
1/4 teaspoon ground white pepper

1 large head romaine lettuce
1 head Boston lettuce
1 pint strawberries, sliced
1 cup shredded Monterey Jack
  cheese
1 cup sugar-toasted walnuts

For the dressing
- Combine the oil, sugar, vinegar, garlic, salt, paprika and pepper in a large jar. Cover and shake vigorously.
- Store for up to 1 week in the refrigerator.

For the salad
- Cut or tear the romaine and Boston lettuce into bite-size pieces. Combine with the strawberries, cheese and walnuts in a bowl and toss to mix.
- Shake the dressing and add just before serving. Toss to mix.

Garnish with 1/2 jicama, cut into strips.

SERVES SIX

SIMPLE VINAIGRETTE

Mash 2 cloves of garlic with 1/2 teaspoon salt. Mix in 3 tablespoons vinegar. Combine with 3 tablespoons fresh lemon juice, 1/2 cup olive oil, 1/2 cup vegetable oil and 1/4 teaspoon dry mustard in a covered jar and shake to mix well. Yields 1 1/2 cups.

SUMMER SALAD COMPOSÉE

⅛ pound peppered bacon
6 ripe tomatoes
2 avocados
2 tablespoons lemon juice
½ cup Italian salad dressing or vinaigrette
⅓ cup minced red onion

- Fry the bacon in a large skillet until crisp. Drain on paper towels; cool and crumble.
- Peel the tomatoes and remove the cores. Cut into thin slices.
- Peel the avocados and slice lengthwise. Toss with the lemon juice in a shallow dish.
- Drain the avocado slices and arrange in the center of a serving platter. Arrange the tomato slices on each side.
- Drizzle the dressing over the avocado and tomato. Sprinkle the onion on the tomato and the bacon on the avocado.

SERVES EIGHT

INDIAN SPINACH SALAD

¼ cup white wine vinegar
¼ cup vegetable oil
2 to 3 tablespoons chutney
2 teaspoons sugar
½ teaspoon salt
curry powder to taste
1 teaspoon dry mustard
1 (2-ounce) package slivered almonds
1 bunch fresh spinach, torn
1 (11-ounce) can mandarin oranges, drained
3 tablespoons sliced green onions

For the dressing
- Combine the vinegar, oil, chutney, sugar, salt, curry powder and dry mustard in a bowl and mix well. Chill, covered in the refrigerator.

To toast the almonds
- Preheat the oven to 350 degrees.
- Place the almonds on a nonstick baking pan. Toast at 350 degrees for 5 to 10 minutes, stirring occasionally. Cool.

For the salad
- Combine the almonds, spinach, mandarin oranges and green onions in a bowl and toss to mix.
- Add the desired amount of dressing and toss to mix.

Variation: Substitute romaine lettuce or other assorted greens for the spinach.

SERVES EIGHT

STRAWBERRY SPINACH SALAD

½ cup sugar
2 teaspoons salt
2 teaspoons dry mustard
⅔ cup vinegar
4 scallions, chopped
3 tablespoons poppy seeds
2 cups vegetable oil

1 cup sugar
1 cup pecans, broken
1 (10-ounce) package fresh
  spinach, torn
1 cup diagonally-sliced celery
1 pint strawberries, cut into
  halves

For the dressing
- Combine ½ cup sugar, salt, dry mustard, vinegar, scallions and poppy seeds in a bowl and mix well.
- Add the oil gradually, mixing constantly.
- Store, covered, in the refrigerator.

To caramelize the pecans
- Combine 1 cup sugar and pecans in a heavy skillet. Cook over low heat until the sugar has melted and the pecans are brown and coated, stirring constantly. Remove to waxed paper to cool.

For the salad
- Combine the spinach, caramelized pecans, celery and strawberries in a bowl and toss to mix.
- Add the dressing and toss to mix.

SERVES FOUR TO SIX

Many cooks agree that the one item in the kitchen that they could not do without is a food processor. It will chop, slice, shred, or combine vegetables, meats, and nuts. It is a perfect tool for making sauces and dressing, especially those, like mayonnaise, which are so dependent upon proper emulsification. This recipe for celery seed dressing is a good example of food processor magic.

CELERY SEED DRESSING

Combine 1¼ cups sugar, 2 teaspoons dry mustard, 1 tablespoon grated onion and ⅓ cup white vinegar in a food processor or blender container and process until smooth. Add ⅓ cup additional vinegar alternately with 2 cups vegetable oil, processing constantly. Stir in 1 tablespoon celery seeds. Store in the refrigerator. This is good served over fresh fruit. Yields 3 cups.

TOMATO BASIL SALAD

1/4 cup olive oil
1/4 cup vegetable oil
1 tablespoon wine vinegar
1 tablespoon fresh lemon juice
1 clove of garlic, crushed
1 tablespoon chopped fresh basil
1 teaspoon salt
1/4 to 1/2 teaspoon freshly ground pepper
5 ripe medium tomatoes
1 bunch green onions, chopped
1 tablespoon chopped parsley

For the dressing
- Combine the olive oil, vegetable oil, vinegar, lemon juice, garlic, basil, salt and pepper in a bowl and mix well.

For the salad
- Cut the tomatoes into 1/4-inch slices. Arrange on a serving platter, overlapping the edges.
- Drizzle with the dressing.
- Combine the green onions and parsley. Sprinkle over the top.
- Chill, covered, for 2 to 6 hours before serving.

Variation: Substitute sliced Vidalia onion for the green onions and add 2 teaspoons oregano.

RASPBERRY VINAIGRETTE

1/3 cup raspberry preserves
1 teaspoon salt
1/4 teaspoon freshly ground pepper
1 1/2 teaspoons coarse-grained or Creole mustard
1/4 cup olive oil
4 teaspoons rice vinegar
4 teaspoons cider vinegar
1 tablespoon dry white wine

- Combine the preserves, salt, pepper, mustard, olive oil, vinegars and wine in a jar. Cover and shake until well mixed.
- Store in the refrigerator.
- Serve over mixed greens sprinkled with toasted walnuts.

Note: Warm the preserves briefly in the microwave for easier mixing.

SERVES FOUR

HONEY MUSTARD VINAIGRETTE

¾ cup olive oil
¼ cup red wine vinegar
1 tablespoon prepared mustard
2 tablespoons honey

1 tablespoon dried minced parsley
1 teaspoon salt
¼ teaspoon freshly ground pepper

- Combine the olive oil, vinegar, mustard and honey in a jar.
- Add the parsley, salt and pepper and shake to mix well.

YIELDS ONE AND ONE-FOURTH CUPS

RÉMOULADE SAUCE

½ cup tarragon vinegar
¼ cup horseradish mustard
1 teaspoon salt
½ teaspoon cayenne
1 tablespoon paprika
2 tablespoons catsup

1 clove of garlic, mashed
1 cup vegetable oil
½ cup finely minced green onions
*   and tops*
½ cup finely minced celery

- Combine the vinegar, mustard, salt, cayenne pepper, paprika, catsup and garlic in a blender container. Process at low to medium speed until well mixed.
- Add the oil gradually, processing constantly until well mixed.
- Add the green onions and celery. Process until mixed.
- Store, covered, in the refrigerator for 24 hours.
- Serve over chilled lettuce and cooked shrimp.

SERVES TEN

INSTANT SALADS

There are several things that you can keep on hand to perk up your salads. Marinated artichoke hearts, stuffed green olives, fresh Parmesan or feta cheese, fines herbes, and your favorite Italian salad dressing only need the addition of fresh greens, purple onion, and tomatoes for a variety of instant salads.

Hot Off the Grill

Meats

Black Bean Salsa
Marinated Potato Salad
Beef Tenderloin with
Grand Marnier Sauce
Shrimp Kabobs
Pineapple Salsa
Tootie Bread
Fruit Cobbler with Ice Cream

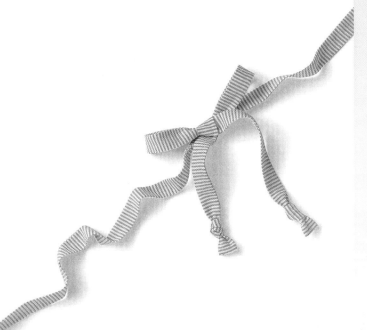

In Defense of Grits

After years of indifference, my wife, Renee, and I finally befriended some New Yorkers. They came to stay with us for a long weekend. We weren't really nervous about what to feed them, and since I'll eat almost anything, we decided to go with things like bagels, salmon, and decorative magazine dishes favored by those who live in the Upper East.

Over a quiet breakfast, as I chewed on a bagel and thought about scrambled eggs and Tabasco™, one of our guests made a profane comment about grits. Though I tried not to show it, I was deeply wounded by what was said. I vowed revenge.

I called my friend, John Currence, the chef of my favorite restaurant in the world, the City Grocery in Oxford, Mississippi, and he faxed me his recipe for Shrimp and Grits. John has prepared this dish for us a thousand times, and we've even begun cooking it ourselves. When our guests inquired about the main course for dinner, I simply said we were having grits. They went for a long walk.

Renee added extra bacon to the recipe, and I loaded up on the cayenne pepper and the Tabasco™. Our guests said nothing when we served them in the candlelight. Since they are our friends, they began by picking at the dish, their noses still pointed to the North.

They ate like refugees. I've never seen two Yankees so gorge themselves on grits. But, I've never known one recipe do so much for such a humble food.

JOHN GRISHAM

JOHN CURRENCE'S SHRIMP AND GRITS

2 cups chopped smoked bacon
3 tablespoons olive oil
1½ pounds (26- to 30-count)
  shrimp
salt and pepper to taste
1 tablespoon minced garlic

3 cups sliced white mushrooms
2 tablespoons lemon juice
3 tablespoons white wine
2 cups sliced scallions
Cheese Grits

- Cook the bacon in a skillet until it begins to brown; remove the bacon with a slotted spoon to drain and reserve 2 tablespoons drippings.
- Heat a large skillet until very hot. Add the olive oil and reserved bacon drippings and heat until the oil begins to smoke.
- Add the shrimp and sprinkle immediately with salt and pepper.
- Sauté until the shrimp turn pink and the skillet has returned to the original temperature.
- Add the garlic and bacon. Cook for several minutes, stirring to prevent overbrowning.
- Add the mushrooms and sauté briefly. Add the lemon juice and wine. Cook for 30 seconds, stirring constantly. Add the scallions and sauté for 20 seconds; do not brown.
- Serve over Cheese Grits. Enjoy, burp, and reminisce about those fine meals at City Grocery.

SERVES THREE OR FOUR, DEPENDING ON HOW HUNGRY EVERYONE IS

CHEESE GRITS

1 cup quick-cooking grits
¼ cup unsalted butter
¾ cup shredded extra-sharp white
  Cheddar cheese
½ cup grated Parmesan cheese

1 teaspoon cayenne
1½ tablespoons paprika
1 teaspoon Tabasco sauce
salt and pepper to taste

- Cook the grits using the package directions. Whisk in the butter, cheeses, cayenne, paprika and Tabasco sauce.
- Season with salt and pepper. Keep warm until serving time.

SERVES THREE OR FOUR

RAMBLING ON ABOUT BARBECUE SAUCE

No old family secrets here. Just years of experimenting with lots of spices and liquids to make the best barbecue sauce in these parts, if I do say so myself. From my old barbecue cook-off days, I have concocted my tasty, hot, peppery, blow-your-head-off barbecue sauce for my bibulous friends. I make it in a big stockpot on my home stove on Sunday afternoons, fourteen bottles at a time. You should enjoy my barbecue sauce on the side after the meat is cooked. Reddish-brown is better, not that yellow, mustardy or see-through peppery sauce. Arkansas has some of the best barbecue sauces in the world, contrary to the erstwhile opinion of other southerners, Yankees, and Texans. You'll know you've had good barbecue sauce if it stays with you a few days, like mine does. Don't buy that thick, clumpy barbecue sauce. Mine's the best and it's free—but I don't deliver. You have to drop by the house and visit a while to get a bottle. Bring some red wine, too!

Pat Miller

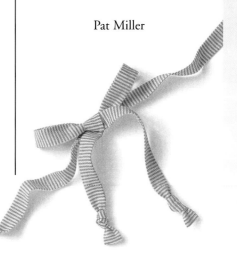

BEEF TENDERLOIN

1 (2½- to 3-pound) beef fillet, trimmed, tied
salt and pepper to taste
Grand Marnier Sauce (at right)

- Preheat the broiler and place the fillet in a broiler pan; season with salt and pepper.
- Broil until brown. Reduce the oven temperature to 450 degrees. Roast for 10 to 12 minutes for rare.
- Slice the beef and serve with Grand Marnier Sauce (at right).

SERVES SIX

GRAND MARNIER SAUCE

1 teaspoon dried thyme
1 bay leaf
8 peppercorns
3 whole cloves
2 strips orange peel
4 teaspoons arrowroot
⅓ cup Grand Marnier
12 shallots
2 tablespoons butter
1 pound mushrooms, sliced
2 cloves of garlic, minced
½ cup dry white wine
2½ cups beef broth
1 tablespoon tomato paste
3 tablespoons each sugar and red wine vinegar
½ cup orange juice
½ teaspoon lemon juice
salt and pepper to taste

- Tie the first 5 ingredients in a cheesecloth bag. Dissolve the arrowroot in a small amount of the Grand Marnier.
- Sauté the shallots in the butter in a saucepan over medium heat until golden brown.
- Add the mushrooms. Sauté until tender. Add the garlic. Sauté for 1 minute. Stir in the wine and remaining Grand Marnier. Cook for 1 minute. Add the beef broth, tomato paste and cheesecloth bag. Simmer for 30 minutes.
- Combine the sugar and vinegar in a saucepan. Cook until syrupy, stirring constantly.
- Stir in the orange juice. Cook until smooth, stirring constantly. Add to the sauce and bring to a boil. Stir in the arrowroot mixture. Simmer until thickened, stirring constantly.
- Remove the cheesecloth bag. Stir in the lemon juice; season to taste.

SERVES SIX

BARBECUED BRISKET

1/4 cup Worcestershire sauce
1 1/2 cups catsup
1/2 teaspoon Tabasco sauce
1/2 cup sugar
1/2 teaspoon sage

1 teaspoon celery salt
1 (4-pound) beef brisket
1 teaspoon salt
1 teaspoon pepper

For the barbecue sauce
- Combine the Worcestershire sauce, catsup, Tabasco sauce, sugar, sage and celery salt in a saucepan. Heat until the sugar melts, stirring constantly.

For the brisket
- Preheat the oven to 275 degrees.
- Spoon 1/3 of the sauce into a roasting pan. Sprinkle the beef with the salt and pepper. Place in the prepared pan.
- Pour 1/3 of the sauce over the top. Cover tightly with foil.
- Roast for 4 to 5 hours or until very tender. Cut into thin slices.
- Serve on buns, topped with the remaining sauce.

Variation: Grill over medium-low heat until done to taste.

SERVES TWELVE

CHANUKAH BRISKET

1 envelope onion soup mix
1/2 cup packed brown sugar
2 cups catsup

1 beef brisket
garlic powder and pepper to taste

- Preheat the oven to 325 degrees.
- Combine the soup mix, brown sugar and catsup in a bowl and mix well.
- Rub the brisket with garlic powder and pepper. Coat well with the catsup mixture. Place in a roasting pan and cover with heavy foil. Roast the brisket for 3 1/2 hours.
- Serve in the gravy formed by the roasting process.

SERVES TWELVE

Of all the aromas coming from a Jewish kitchen, none is more familiar than that of a brisket. Baking for hours, the smell of brisket permeates the household and signals the ritual of tradition. For many Jews of eastern European descent, brisket is the mainstay of holiday meals. It can be prepared in advance, it miraculously improves with every reheating, and it provides ample quantity for relatives who gather for celebrations. Each Jewish cook has a preferred recipe, often handed down from grandmother to mother to daughter, embellished along the way with this or that ingredient. Accompanying the brisket at the holiday table can be all sorts of vegetables and noodle puddings. Perhaps the ultimate favorite is the Chanukah specialty of potato pancakes or latkes. Made of grated potatoes, the latkes are fried to a crisp brown in oil, which is a symbolic ingredient in Chanukah dishes, and are often graced with homemade applesauce. Eaten together, brisket and latkes are a warming reminder of home and heritage.

Janet Lampell Aronson

MARINATED FLANK STEAK

1½ cups vegetable oil
½ cup soy sauce
½ cup honey
¼ cup wine vinegar
1 medium onion, chopped
4 to 6 cloves of garlic, minced
1 tablespoon ground ginger
1 (3-pound) flank steak, trimmed
1 pound fresh mushrooms, sliced

To marinate the steak
- Combine the oil, soy sauce, honey, vinegar, onion, garlic and ginger in a large shallow dish. Add the steak and turn to coat well.
- Marinate, covered, in the refrigerator for up to 3 days, turning the steak several times each day.

To cook the steak
- Remove the steak from the marinade, reserving the marinade.
- Grill over very hot coals for 5 minutes on each side for medium-rare, basting with a portion of the reserved marinade near the end of the grilling time.
- Slice the steak diagonally across the grain into ¼-inch slices.

For the mushroom sauce
- Remove the lower layer of the reserved marinade with a basting tube, discarding the oil.
- Combine the marinade with the mushrooms in a saucepan. Cook until the mushrooms are tender. Serve with the steak.

Note: This makes great fajitas.

SERVES SIX

PEPPERED RIBEYE

2 tablespoons tomato paste
1 teaspoon paprika
½ teaspoon garlic powder
1 cup soy sauce
¾ cup red wine vinegar
½ cup black peppercorns, ground
1 teaspoon ground cardamom
1 (5-pound) ribeye roast, trimmed
1 cup water

For the marinade
- Combine the tomato paste, paprika and garlic powder in a small bowl. Stir in the soy sauce and vinegar.

For the steak
- Combine the ground peppercorns and cardamom. Press firmly over the surface of the beef.
- Place in a 9x13-inch baking pan. Pour the marinade over the top. Chill, covered, for 6 hours or longer, basting occasionally.
- Let the roast stand at room temperature for 1 hour or longer.
- Preheat the oven to 300 degrees.
- Drain the roast, discarding the marinade. Wrap with heavy foil and place in a shallow roasting pan. Roast for 2 hours for medium-rare.

For the gravy
- Combine 1 cup of the drippings with the water in a saucepan. Bring to a boil over medium-high heat.
- Serve with the roast.

SERVES EIGHT

BEEF FILLETS IN PASTRY

6 (6-ounce) beef fillets, trimmed
3 tablespoons butter
6 tablespoons sherry
12 ounces mushrooms, minced

6 frozen puff pastry shells,
    thawed, or puff pastry sheets
salt and pepper to taste
Béarnaise Sauce

- Sear the steaks on both sides in the melted butter in a heavy skillet until brown, or longer for well-done steaks.
- Add 1 tablespoon of the wine and cook until the wine evaporates. Transfer the steaks to a platter and let stand until cool.
- Add the remaining 5 tablespoons wine and mushrooms to the skillet. Cook over medium heat until the liquid evaporates, stirring constantly.
- Chill the mushrooms in the refrigerator.
- Roll each pastry shell to an 8-inch circle on a lightly floured surface.
- Spoon the mushrooms onto the circles and place 1 steak on each. Sprinkle with salt and pepper.
- Fold the pastry to enclose the steaks and press to seal. Place seam side down on a baking sheet. Chill, covered, for 15 minutes to 8 hours.
- Preheat the oven to 425 degrees.
- Bake the steaks in pastry on the lowest oven rack for 10 minutes. Bake on the top oven rack for an additional 8 to 10 minutes or until golden brown.
- Serve with Béarnaise Sauce and fresh seasonal vegetables.

BÉARNAISE SAUCE

¼ cup dry white wine
¼ cup white wine vinegar
2 tablespoons minced green onions
1 teaspoon dried tarragon
1 teaspoon dried chervil

pepper to taste
3 egg yolks
1 cup unsalted butter, softened
1 tablespoon fresh tarragon
1 tablespoon chopped parsley

- Combine the wine, vinegar, green onions, dried tarragon, chervil and pepper in a saucepan. Cook over low heat until the liquid is reduced by ½. Strain the mixture and cool.
- Beat the egg yolks until thick in a double boiler bowl. Beat in the vinegar mixture gradually. Place over hot water. Cook until thickened, whisking in the butter gradually. Stir in the fresh tarragon and parsley.

SERVES SIX

Never let it be said that the kitchen or cooking is in any way, shape, or form, back-pedaling for a woman. Preparing a wholesome meal for her family, graciously welcoming guests to her home and table, making the potluck potato salad special by carefully positioning a radish rose in the center, all radiate from the central core of womanhood. Yes, we are architects and bank presidents, but we are also, first and foremost, nurturers—and nothing is more nurturing and loving than food. Simple food or extravagant food—it matters not, as long as it is prepared and shared lovingly. The coziness of the family kitchen, the smell of grandmother's yeast rolls, learning from your mother how to properly measure flour, letting your own children lick the beaters just as you did, always having enough for that unexpected guest, these are Southern traditions of cooking. No matter how far we as women have come regarding career options, this is a heritage that we can ill afford to lose.

Nancy Allenbaugh Puddephatt

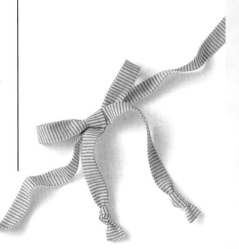

BEEFY BAKED BEANS

1 pound ground beef
½ cup chopped onion
½ cup chopped green bell pepper
2 (16-ounce) cans baked beans
2 (16-ounce) cans pork and beans
2 (16-ounce) cans ranch-style beans
½ cup molasses
1 cup packed brown sugar
½ cup barbecue sauce

• Preheat the oven to 350 degrees.
• Brown the ground beef with the onion and green pepper in a saucepan, stirring until the ground beef is crumbly; drain.
• Add the beans, molasses, brown sugar and barbecue sauce and mix well. Spoon into a 9x13-inch baking dish.
• Bake for 30 minutes or until bubbly.

Variation: For **Vegetarian Baked Beans,** *omit the ground beef.*

SERVES EIGHT TO TEN

MEXICAN CASSEROLE

1 cup uncooked rice
1 teaspoon salt
1 pound ground beef
4 cups thinly sliced zucchini
½ cup chopped onion
1 green bell pepper, chopped
½ cup water
1 envelope taco seasoning mix
1 (10- to 12-ounce) jar picante sauce
1 cup shredded Cheddar cheese
¾ cup crushed tortilla chips

• Preheat the oven to 350 degrees.
• Cook the rice with the salt using the package directions. Brown the ground beef in a saucepan, stirring until crumbly. Add the zucchini, onion, green pepper, water and taco seasoning and mix well.
• Layer the rice, beef mixture, picante sauce and cheese in the order listed in a 9x13-inch baking dish.
• Bake for 20 minutes. Sprinkle with the tortilla chips and bake for 10 minutes longer.
• Serve with black beans and Mexican cheese melted in a flour tortilla as a side dish or with black beans topped with melted Monterey Jack cheese and warm buttered tortillas.

SERVES EIGHT

♥

ENCHILADA CASSEROLE CON ESPINACAS

1 (10-ounce) package frozen
    chopped spinach
2 pounds ground chuck
1 large onion, chopped
1 (16-ounce) can tomatoes
1 teaspoon ground cumin
salt and pepper to taste
12 to 16 flour tortillas
1/2 cup melted butter
2 (4-ounce) cans chopped green
    chiles

1 1/2 cups shredded Cheddar cheese
1 (10-ounce) can golden
    mushroom soup
1 (10-ounce) can cream of
    mushroom soup
1 cup sour cream
1/4 cup milk
1/4 teaspoon garlic powder
1/2 cup shredded Cheddar cheese

- Cook the spinach using the package directions; drain and press to remove excess moisture.
- Brown the ground beef in a large skillet, stirring until crumbly; drain. Add the spinach, onion, tomatoes, cumin, salt and pepper and mix well.
- Dip half the tortillas in the melted butter and arrange over the bottom and sides of a large shallow baking dish.
- Layer the ground beef mixture, green chiles and 1 1/2 cups cheese in the prepared dish.
- Dip the remaining tortillas in the butter and arrange over the top.
- Combine the soups, sour cream, milk and garlic powder in a bowl and mix well. Spread over the layers.
- Chill, covered with plastic wrap, for 8 hours or longer.
- Preheat the oven to 325 degrees.
- Sprinkle the casserole with 1/2 cup cheese. Bake, uncovered, for 45 to 60 minutes or until bubbly.
- Serve with black beans and a green salad.

SERVES TWELVE

BEEF TENDERLOIN

Combine 1/2 cup melted butter, one 5-ounce bottle of Worcestershire sauce, the juice of 1 or 2 lemons, 1 tablespoon prepared mustard and 2 minced cloves of garlic. Combine half the mixture with a 2- to 4-pound beef tenderloin in a sealable plastic bag. Marinate in the refrigerator for 8 hours or longer; refrigerate the remaining marinade. Remove the tenderloin from the marinade and discard the marinade. Grill over hot coals for 15 minutes on each side. Let stand at room temperature until cool and slice. Heat the reserved marinade until heated through and serve with the tenderloin.

For **Oven-Baked Tenderloin,** place the tenderloin in a preheated 450-degree oven and reduce the temperature immediately to 350 degrees. Roast for 30 minutes or to 140 to 150 degrees on a meat thermometer. Serves 6 to 8.

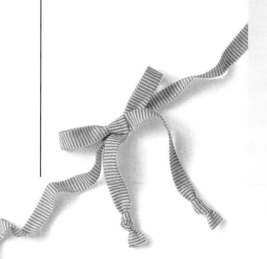

SPAGHETTI SAUCE

2 pounds ground beef
1½ onions, chopped
½ green bell pepper, chopped
2 tablespoons butter
2 (14- to 16-ounce) cans tomatoes, chopped
2 (15-ounce) cans tomato sauce
1 (12-ounce) can tomato paste
¼ teaspoon Worcestershire sauce
½ teaspoon vinegar
1 tablespoon sugar
1 tablespoon basil
1 teaspoon oregano
1½ teaspoons garlic powder
¼ teaspoon pepper

- Brown the ground beef in a saucepan, stirring until crumbly; drain.
- Sauté the onions and green pepper in the butter in a skillet.
- Add the sautéed vegetables to the ground beef. Add the remaining ingredients and mix well.
- Simmer, covered, over medium heat for 3 hours, stirring frequently.
- Serve over cooked spaghetti.

SERVES EIGHT

SANTA FE STEW

2 pounds ground beef or turkey
2 yellow onions, chopped
1 envelope ranch salad dressing mix
1 envelope taco seasoning mix
1 (15-ounce) can kidney beans
2 (15-ounce) cans pinto beans
2 (15-ounce) cans whole kernel corn
2 (15-ounce) cans diced tomatoes
2 (16-ounce) cans jalapeño black-eyed peas
Worcestershire sauce and Tabasco sauce to taste
salt and pepper to taste
12 ounces Cheddar cheese, shredded

- Brown the ground beef with the onions in a large saucepan, stirring until the ground beef is crumbly; do not drain.
- Add the salad dressing mix, taco seasoning mix and the undrained beans, corn, tomatoes and peas.
- Simmer, covered, for 20 minutes. Remove from the heat and let stand for 10 minutes.
- Season to taste with Worcestershire sauce, Tabasco sauce, salt and pepper.
- Top servings with the shredded cheese.

SERVES TEN

ORIENTAL PORK CHOPS

¼ cup soy sauce
2 tablespoons dry sherry
¼ cup pineapple juice
1 tablespoon vegetable oil
1 tablespoon brown sugar

1 clove of garlic, minced
1 teaspoon 5-spice powder
¼ teaspoon hot pepper sauce
4 (1-inch-thick) center-cut
  pork chops

To marinate the pork chops
- Combine the soy sauce, wine, pineapple juice, oil, brown sugar, garlic, 5-spice powder and pepper sauce in a sealable plastic bag.
- Add the pork chops and turn to coat well.
- Marinate in the refrigerator for 2 to 12 hours, turning several times. Drain, reserving the marinade.

To grill the pork chops
- Preheat the grill or broiler to low-medium.
- Grill or broil the pork chops 4 to 5 inches from the heat source for 10 minutes on each side.
- Brush with the reserved marinade and cook for 5 to 10 minutes longer or until cooked through, turning occasionally; do not overcook or baste during the last 3 minutes of cooking time.
- Serve with garlic mashed potatoes and steamed sugar snap peas or steamed broccoli.

Variation: This marinade can also be used with sirloin steaks 1 inch or more thick. Adjust the cooking time to achieve the desired degree of doneness.

SERVES FOUR

RUBS, PASTES, MARINADES

Most barbecue purists agree sauces should be used only after the meat is cooked. However, rubs, pastes, and marinades may all be used on foods before cooking. Rubs are a mixture of dried herbs and spices which are rubbed on meat before it is cooked. Rubs are best used on meats with a higher fat content, on bulky pieces of meat that are difficult to marinate, or when you do not have time to marinate. Pastes are rubs which are suspended in a liquid. Because they add moisture as well as flavor, pastes work well with lean meat. Marinades are liquids used to add flavor and/or tenderize meat. They are usually composed of an oil, spices, and an acid such as lemon juice, vinegar, wine, or soy sauce. Plan on ⅓ to ½ cup of marinade per pound of meat. Food should always be marinated in nonmetallic containers or sealable plastic bags in the refrigerator. Any marinade which has come in contact with uncooked meat should be boiled for at least one minute to kill all bacteria before being used as a sauce for cooked meat.

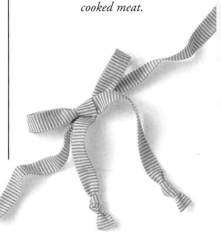

CRANBERRY PORK ROAST

1 (2- to 3-pound) boneless pork loin roast
salt and pepper to taste
1 cup sweetened dried cranberries
¼ cup honey
1 teaspoon grated orange peel
¼ teaspoon cloves
¼ teaspoon nutmeg

- Sprinkle the roast with salt and pepper. Place in a slow cooker.
- Combine the cranberries, honey, orange peel, cloves and nutmeg in a bowl and mix well. Pour over the roast.
- Cook on Low for 8 to 10 hours.

SERVES SIX TO EIGHT

PORK LOIN ROAST- BLUEBERRY SAUCE

½ cup soy sauce
½ cup dry sherry
1 teaspoon minced garlic
1 tablespoon dry mustard
1 teaspoon ground ginger
1 teaspoon dried thyme
1 (3- to 4-pound) boned pork loin roast
1 (10-ounce) jar blueberry or black currant jelly
2 tablespoons sherry
1 tablespoon soy sauce

To marinate the pork
- Combine ½ cup soy sauce, ½ cup sherry, garlic, dry mustard, ginger and thyme in a bowl and mix well.
- Combine with the pork roast in a sealable plastic bag and mix well.
- Let stand at room temperature for 2 to 3 hours, turning occasionally. Drain, reserving the marinade.

To cook the roast
- Preheat the oven to 325 degrees.
- Place the roast in a shallow baking pan. Roast, uncovered, for 1½ to 2 hours.
- Roast for 1 hour longer or until the roast reaches 160 to 165 degrees on a meat thermometer, basting with the reserved marinade.

For the sauce
- Combine the jelly, 2 tablespoons sherry and 1 tablespoon soy sauce in a small saucepan. Bring to a simmer over low heat.
- Serve with or over the pork roast.

SERVES EIGHT

ROAST PORK WITH MUSHROOM SAUCE

1 (3-pound) boneless rolled pork
   loin roast
1 teaspoon dried thyme
1/2 teaspoon salt
1/2 teaspoon pepper
1/3 cup apple cider or apple juice

2 tablespoons vermouth
1 cup chicken broth
1 cup whipping cream
12 ounces fresh mushrooms, sliced
2 tablespoons butter or margarine

For the roast pork
- Preheat the oven to 450 degrees.
- Sprinkle the roast with the thyme, salt and pepper.
- Place in a 9x13-inch baking pan. Roast for 20 minutes. Reduce the oven temperature to 325 degrees and roast for 1 1/4 hours longer.
- Remove from the baking pan to a serving platter, reserving the pan drippings. Let stand for 10 minutes before slicing.

For the sauce
- Combine the reserved pan drippings with the apple cider, vermouth, chicken broth and whipping cream in a medium saucepan.
- Bring to a boil over medium-high heat. Cook for 20 minutes or until the mixture thickens, stirring frequently.
- Sauté the mushrooms in the butter in a small skillet until tender. Add to the sauce. Cook until heated through.
- Serve over the sliced roast.

SERVES EIGHT

DRY RIBS

Remove the membrane from the backs of 4 racks of pork baby back ribs, or slice the membranes between the ribs. Starting with the back side of the ribs, apply a medium sprinkling of seasoned salt, a light sprinkling of garlic powder and a medium to heavy sprinkling of lemon pepper to both sides. Coat with paprika. Soak 2 handfuls of hickory chunks in water. Mound 8 to 10 pounds of charcoal in the fire pan of a smoker and add a light application of lighter fluid. Start the fire, allow to burn for 20 minutes, and add the hickory chunks. Add the ribs and smoke for 5 hours if the outside temperature is 70 degrees or above. Add about 30 minutes of cooking time for each 5- to 10-degree drop in outside temperature. Wrap in heavy-duty foil and leave on the smoker until ready to serve for moist and tender ribs.

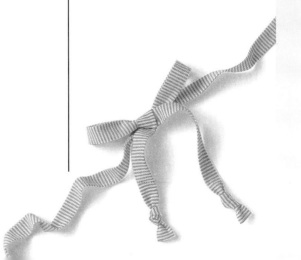

PORK TENDERLOIN-MUSTARD SAUCE

¼ cup soy sauce
¼ cup bourbon
2 tablespoons brown sugar
1 (3-pound) pork tenderloin
1 tablespoon dry mustard
1½ teaspoons vinegar
½ cup sour cream
⅓ cup mayonnaise
1 tablespoon chopped green onions
salt to taste

To marinate the pork
- Combine the soy sauce, bourbon and brown sugar in a bowl and mix well. Add the pork.
- Marinate in the refrigerator for several hours, turning occasionally. Drain, reserving the marinade.

To cook the pork
- Preheat the oven to 325 degrees.
- Place the pork in a baking pan. Roast for 45 to 60 minutes or until cooked through, basting frequently with the reserved marinade.

For the sauce
- Dissolve the dry mustard in the vinegar in a bowl. Mix in the sour cream and mayonnaise. Stir in the green onions and salt.
- Serve with the sliced tenderloin.

SERVES SIX

PORK TENDERLOIN TERIYAKI

¼ cup soy sauce
2 tablespoons vegetable oil
2 teaspoons light brown sugar
1 clove of garlic, minced
1 teaspoon ground ginger
½ teaspoon pepper
2 (12-ounce) pork tenderloins

To marinate the pork
- Combine the soy sauce, oil, brown sugar, garlic, ginger and pepper in a jar. Cover and shake to mix well.
- Combine with the pork tenderloins in a shallow dish.
- Marinate, covered, in the refrigerator for several hours. Drain, reserving the marinade.

To cook the pork
- Preheat the oven to 325 degrees.
- Place the tenderloins on a rack in a roasting pan. Roast for 45 to 55 minutes or until cooked through, basting occasionally with the reserved marinade.

SERVES SIX

♥

PORK TENDERLOIN WITH SPINACH

¼ *cup pine nuts*
2 cloves of garlic, minced
1 tablespoon butter
12 ounces fresh spinach leaves
salt and freshly ground pepper to
  taste

1 tablespoon vegetable oil
1 (1- to 1½-pound) pork
  tenderloin in 2 pieces
1 cup red wine
2 cups beef broth

- Preheat the oven to 350 degrees.
- Sauté the pine nuts and garlic in the melted butter in a large saucepan for 1 minute.
- Add the spinach. Cook until the spinach is wilted. Season with salt and pepper. Remove to a bowl.
- Heat the oil in the same skillet over medium heat.
- Add the tenderloin and brown on 1 side. Remove from the skillet.
- Spread the spinach mixture between the pieces over the unbrowned side and secure with butcher's cord. Place in a roasting pan and add the wine.
- Roast, uncovered, for 35 minutes for each pound or to 160 to 165 degrees on a meat thermometer. Remove to a warm platter.
- Place the roasting pan on the stove top. Add the beef broth.
- Cook until thickened, stirring to deglaze the pan.
- Serve over the sliced pork.

SERVES FOUR TO SIX

HARDWOODS FOR GRILLING

The variety and size of hardwood used are important considerations when grilling or smoking foods. Chips or larger chunks should be used for grills, while chunks or logs are considered more appropriate for smokers. Chips and chunks should be soaked in water, wine, beer, or juice for at least thirty minutes before being added to the fire. **Hickory** *and* **mesquite** *are the most popular woods, but a wide variety of hardwoods may be used. While hickory is definitely the king of southern barbecue, mesquite is often associated with the flavors of the Southwest. Other wood choices include, but are not limited to, the following:*

Pecan, *a mellow flavor good with almost any meat or cheese*
Oak, *a heavy smoke flavor good with pork, lamb, or beef*
Cherry, *a fruity flavor good with ham, game, or poultry*
Apple, *a mild, sweet flavor good with chicken or turkey*
Alder, *a delicious choice for fish*

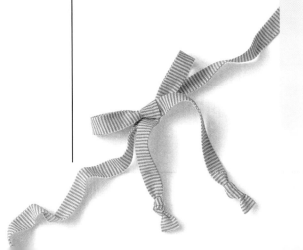

STROMBOLI

1 pound ground sausage
8 ounces ground beef
1 (15-ounce) can tomato sauce
¼ cup grated Parmesan cheese
½ teaspoon rosemary
¼ teaspoon garlic salt
1 loaf Italian or French bread
2 cups shredded mozzarella cheese

- Brown the sausage and the ground beef in a saucepan, stirring until crumbly; drain.
- Stir in the tomato sauce, Parmesan cheese, rosemary and garlic salt.
- Slice off and reserve the top ½ inch of the bread; hollow out the loaf, leaving a ½-inch shell.
- Layer half the mozzarella cheese, the meat mixture and the remaining cheese in the bread shell; replace the top. Cover with foil.
- Preheat the oven to 350 degrees.
- Place the stromboli on a baking sheet. Bake for 10 to 15 minutes or until heated through.
- Slice to serve.

SERVES EIGHT

LAMB WITH FETA CRUST

3 tablespoons feta cheese, crumbled
2 cloves of garlic, minced
½ cup seasoned bread crumbs
½ teaspoon kosher salt
freshly ground pepper to taste
1 rack of lamb, at room temperature
2 teaspoons Dijon mustard

- Preheat the oven to 400 degrees.
- Mix the cheese, garlic, bread crumbs, salt and pepper in a bowl until crumbly.
- Coat the lamb with the Dijon mustard. Pat the cheese mixture over the lamb.
- Place on a baking sheet sprayed with nonstick cooking spray.
- Bake for 30 minutes for medium-rare.
- Let stand for 10 minutes before slicing.

SERVES FOUR

VEAL PICCATA

2 lemons
1 pound (¼-inch-thick) veal
1 cup flour
½ teaspoon salt

pepper to taste
2 tablespoons vegetable oil
½ cup butter
2 tablespoons chopped parsley

- Cut 1 of the lemons into 10 to 12 thin slices. Squeeze enough juice from the remaining lemon to measure 2 tablespoons.
- Place the veal between waxed paper and pound thin with the dull side of a knife or a meat mallet.
- Mix the flour, salt and pepper together. Coat the veal with the flour mixture.
- Heat the oil and half the butter in a heavy skillet until very hot. Add the veal and sauté until brown. Remove to a warm platter.
- Remove the skillet from the heat. Add the lemon juice, stirring to deglaze the skillet. Add the remaining butter.
- Cook over medium-low heat until the butter melts, stirring constantly. Stir in the parsley.
- Serve over the veal.

Garnish with the lemon slices.

SERVES FOUR

BARBECUE SAUCE

Combine 2 cups cola, 2 cups catsup, 2 cups vinegar, 3 tablespoons sugar, ½ minced large onion, 3 tablespoons chili powder, 3 tablespoons salt and 1½ tablespoons pepper in a saucepan. Bring to a boil and reduce the heat. Simmer until the volume is reduced by 1 inch in the saucepan or until the sauce is of the desired consistency. Yields 1 quart.

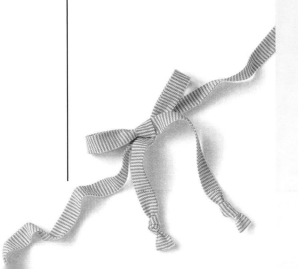

Servin' Up Arkansas

POULTRY

Smoked Catfish Paté
Oven-Crispy Chicken
Tomatoes with Bacon
Lemon Rice
Angel Biscuits with Strawberry Jam
Pecan Pie
Almond Tea

The Bounty of Arkansas

Deer, fish, morels, chanterelles, pawpaws, hickory nuts, persimmons,
muscadines, poke, mustard, blackberries, gooseberries, mussels, eels, turtles,
raccoons, possums, bear, boar, turkeys, dove, corn, passenger pigeons, quail, ducks, geese,
dandelion, wild plum, horseradish, truffles, wild asparagus.

Native Americans selected from that vast natural menu for centuries before the arrival of
European explorers in the area that would become Arkansas.

This bounty, and more, was available to De Soto when he crossed the
Mississippi River into our future land in 1541. The first French explorers,
Marquette and Jolliet, nourished themselves from this enormous variety during their expeditions
from Quebec southward in 1693, and it was all there at the time of the American expansion
westward after the Louisiana Purchase in 1803.

With the exception of the passenger pigeon, extinct from over-hunting since 1914,
all the items of this great banquet can still be enjoyed by the
present inhabitants of the state called Arkansas.

What a magnificent natural larder has the divine plan of Nature
provided for us throughout our history! What a substantial foundation on which
to base and build a native cookery!

Now our time has come to cultivate and preserve these gifts of the ages, turning them to
our usage, working them as we will, enlarging the banquet as we are able.

We are, after all, part of a great movement.

RICHARD ALLIN

CHICKEN IN
APPLE BRANDY SAUCE

6 boneless skinless chicken breast
  halves
1/2 cup flour
salt and pepper to taste
2 tablespoons butter
2 tablespoons vegetable oil
3 tart apples, peeled, sliced
1/2 cup dry white wine
1 cup sparkling apple cider

3/4 cup apple brandy
1 1/2 cups low-salt chicken broth
1 cup whipping cream
1/4 cup chilled unsalted butter,
  sliced
1/2 teaspoon freshly ground white
  pepper
fresh lemon juice (optional)

• Preheat the oven to 400 degrees.

For the chicken
• Rinse the chicken and pat dry. Coat with flour, shaking off the excess.
  Season with salt and pepper.
• Melt 2 tablespoons butter in a large heavy skillet over high heat. Add
  the oil. Add the chicken to the skillet and brown the chicken on both
  sides. Remove the chicken to a baking dish, reserving the pan drippings.
• Roast until cooked through; keep warm.

For the sauce
• Sauté the apples briefly in the drippings in the skillet over medium-high
  heat; drain the skillet.
• Add the wine to the skillet and bring to a boil, stirring to deglaze
  the skillet.
• Add the apple cider. Cook for 7 minutes or until reduced by 1/2.
• Add the brandy and ignite. Cook until the flame subsides, shaking the
  skillet gently.
• Stir in the chicken broth. Cook for 8 to 10 minutes or until reduced
  by 1/2. Stir in the cream. Cook for 15 minutes or until the sauce is thick
  enough to coat a spoon. Whisk in 1/4 cup butter. Season with salt to taste
  and white pepper.
• Add the lemon juice only if the sauce is too sweet to suit your taste.

To serve
• Arrange the apple slices over the chicken. Spoon the sauce over the top
  and serve immediately.

SERVES SIX

*The first time I ever made
dinner for my boyfriend, I made
fried chicken with mashed potatoes
and gravy, his favorite meal. The
chicken and mashed potatoes turned
out great, but the gravy—well,
that's another story. Let's just say that
when he took me home that night,
he couldn't resist asking my
Dad if he had any holes in the
roof that needed patching. I will
always question the old saying "The
best way to a man's heart is
through his stomach," because he
married me anyway.*

Dana Winter Bauer

91

CHICKEN WITH GOAT CHEESE

1 (3½-pound) roasting chicken
4 ounces goat cheese
2 cloves of garlic, sliced
1 bunch fresh herbs such as parsley, basil
*   and chervil*
8 small white onions
8 shallots
4 cloves of garlic
3 tablespoons melted unsalted butter

- Preheat the oven to 400 degrees.
- Rinse the chicken inside and out and pat dry. Loosen the skin gently from the breast and legs with the fingers.
- Cut the goat cheese into ¼-inch rounds. Place the cheese rounds and sliced garlic carefully under the skin of the chicken.
- Place the fresh herbs in the chicken cavity. Truss the chicken and secure with butcher string.
- Place on a rack in a roasting pan. Arrange the onions, shallots and whole cloves of garlic around the chicken.
- Roast, uncovered, for 1 hour or until the chicken is cooked through, basting occasionally with the melted butter.

SERVES FOUR

CHICKEN DIABLO

4 chicken breasts
¼ cup butter
½ cup honey
¼ cup Dijon mustard
1 teaspoon curry powder
1 teaspoon salt

- Preheat the oven to 350 degrees.
- Rinse the chicken and pat dry. Arrange in a shallow baking pan.
- Melt the butter in a small saucepan. Stir in the honey, mustard, curry powder and salt.
- Pour over the chicken, turning to coat evenly. Bake, covered, for 45 minutes.
- Bake, uncovered, for 15 minutes longer or until the chicken is tender and brown, basting frequently with the pan juices.

SERVES FOUR

CHICKEN AND DUMPLINGS

1 large frying chicken
1 onion
1 rib celery
1 tablespoon butter
salt to taste

1/2 teaspoon pepper
2 cups flour
1/2 teaspoon salt
1/2 cup butter
1 can chicken broth (optional)

For the chicken
- Rinse the chicken inside and out. Combine with the onion, celery, 1 tablespoon butter, salt to taste, pepper and water to cover in a large stockpot.
- Cook until very tender; drain, reserving the broth. Remove the chicken from the bones and cut into large pieces. Strain the broth into a saucepan.

For the dumplings
- Combine the flour and 1/2 teaspoon salt in a bowl. Cut in 1/2 cup butter until crumbly. Add enough cold water to form a soft dough and mix lightly.
- Roll the dough on a floured surface. Cut into strips.
- Bring the reserved broth to a boil, adding the canned broth if needed.
- Add the chicken pieces.
- Stretch each dough strip and drop each dough strip into the broth. Cook, uncovered, for 10 minutes or until the dumplings are cooked through.

Variation: For thicker dumplings, sift 2 cups flour and 1/2 teaspoon each baking soda, baking powder and salt together. Add 1 cup buttermilk and 1 tablespoon vegetable oil or melted shortening and mix well. Add additional flour if needed for a more easily worked dough. Knead on a floured surface and roll until thin. Cut into strips. Drop into boiling broth and cook for 20 minutes or until cooked through.

SERVES SIX

Her name was Tu-Choo, at least to her grandchildren, since saying Gertrude was too difficult. She was the kind of grandmother every child loved because she always kept things in perspective. A good example is the wonderful mouth-watering chicken and dumplings she used to make, which I used to shower with catsup to make them taste even better. Tu-Choo merely watched as if I truly were enhancing her recipe. My mother, however, kept a more watchful eye on Tu-Choo when she began making her delicious homemade eggnog—the kind that's so fluffy you have to eat it with a spoon. Tu-Choo loved to serve it to us in petite cobalt blue cups, but all the while, Mom was making sure that she didn't add too much rum to it.

Michelle Carter

93

CHICKEN FIESTA

¼ cup red wine vinegar
¼ cup olive oil
1 clove of garlic, minced
¼ cup Spanish green olives
1 cup sliced mushrooms
¼ cup capers
1 tablespoon caper juice
2 tablespoons chopped fresh oregano
3 bay leaves
1 teaspoon salt
1 teaspoon pepper
2 chickens, cut up, or chicken breasts
¼ cup packed light brown sugar
¼ cup vermouth or other dry white wine

To marinate the chicken,
- Combine the vinegar, olive oil, garlic, olives, mushrooms, capers, caper juice, oregano, bay leaves, salt and pepper in a large bowl.
- Rinse the chicken and pat dry. Add to the marinade.
- Marinate, covered, in the refrigerator for 8 hours or longer, turning frequently.

To cook the chicken
- Preheat the oven to 350 degrees.
- Remove the chicken to a baking dish and pour the marinade over the top. Sprinkle with the brown sugar. Add the wine to the baking dish.
- Bake for 50 minutes, basting with the pan juices.
- Remove the chicken, olives, capers and mushrooms to a serving dish; pour the pan juices over the top, discarding the bay leaves.
- Serve hot or at room temperature for a picnic.

SERVES SIX

CHICKEN DIJON

4 to 6 chicken breasts
salt and pepper to taste
¼ cup butter
2 tablespoons Dijon mustard
1 clove of garlic, minced
1 small onion, minced
1 tablespoon flour
2 tablespoons finely chopped parsley
¼ cup white wine
1 (10-ounce) can chicken broth

- Rinse the chicken and pat dry. Sprinkle with salt and pepper.
- Brown in the butter in a large skillet over low heat.
- Combine the Dijon mustard, garlic, onion, flour, parsley, wine and chicken broth in a bowl and mix well. Pour over the chicken.
- Simmer, covered, for 40 minutes or until the chicken is tender, turning occasionally.
- Remove the chicken to a serving bowl. Simmer the sauce until slightly thickened.
- Serve the sauce over the chicken.

SERVES FOUR TO SIX

CHICKEN AND PEPPER CASSEROLE

5 large poblano peppers
1 onion, chopped
1½ cups sour cream
½ cup whipping cream
2 tablespoons Tabasco sauce
1½ teaspoons ground cumin
½ teaspoon salt

1 teaspoon pepper
4 chicken breasts
1 large bunch fresh cilantro,
   finely chopped
3 large flour tortillas
2 cups shredded Monterey
   Jack cheese

To roast the peppers
- Preheat the broiler.
- Place the peppers in a broiler pan. Broil until blackened on all sides.
- Place in a sealable plastic bag and let stand for 10 minutes. Remove the skins and slice the peppers into 2-inch strips, discarding the seeds.

For the casserole
- Sauté the onion in a large nonstick saucepan. Add the sour cream, whipping cream, Tabasco sauce, cumin, salt and pepper.
- Simmer over low heat for 10 minutes.
- Rinse the chicken and pat dry. Cut into bite-size pieces.
- Add to the sauce. Cook for 10 minutes or until the chicken is partially cooked. Stir in the cilantro.
- Preheat the oven to 350 degrees.
- Layer the tortillas, chicken mixture, peppers and cheese ⅓ at a time in a greased baking dish.
- Bake for 30 to 40 minutes or until the chicken is cooked through.
- Serve with salad and rice.

Garnish with red chile peppers.

SERVES SIX TO EIGHT

SKINNY CHICKEN

The National Broiler Council tells us that it isn't necessary to remove the skin from chicken before cooking it. Although most chicken fat is in the skin, studies indicate that the chicken does not absorb fat from the skin during cooking. Leaving the skin on during cooking helps to maintain the natural moisture of chicken, while eliminating the need for adding fat in the form of marinades made with oil to keep skinned chicken from being dry. Chicken cooked in the skin will be more moist and palatable, but with no more fat than chicken cooked without the skin. To eliminate almost half the fat contained in chicken, the key is to remove the skin before serving.

MONTEREY CHICKEN

8 ounces Monterey Jack cheese
8 large boneless skinless chicken breast halves
1 (7-ounce) can chopped mild green chiles
1/2 cup fine dry bread crumbs
1/4 cup grated Parmesan cheese
1 tablespoon chili powder
1/4 teaspoon ground cumin
1/2 teaspoon salt
1/4 teaspoon pepper
6 tablespoons melted low-fat margarine
1 (15-ounce) can tomato sauce
1/3 cup chopped green onions
1/2 teaspoon ground cumin
pepper sauce, salt and pepper to taste

For the chicken
- Cut the cheese into 8 strips. Rinse the chicken and pat dry. Pound 1/4 inch thick.
- Top each piece of chicken with green chiles and 1 strip of the cheese. Roll the chicken to enclose the filling, tucking under the ends.
- Combine the bread crumbs, Parmesan cheese, chili powder, 1/4 teaspoon cumin, 1/2 teaspoon salt and 1/4 teaspoon pepper in a bowl.
- Dip the chicken into the melted margarine and coat with the bread crumb mixture. Place in a baking dish and drizzle with any remaining margarine. Chill, covered, for 4 hours or longer.
- Preheat the oven to 400 degrees.
- Bake for 30 minutes or until cooked through.

For the sauce
- Combine the remaining ingredients in a saucepan. Bring to a boil and cook until slightly thickened. Serve over the chicken.

Garnish with sour cream and fresh lime wedges.

SERVES EIGHT

CHICKEN STROGANOFF

1 pound boneless skinless chicken breasts
2 tablespoons margarine
8 ounces fresh mushrooms, sliced
1 medium onion, chopped
2 cloves of garlic, minced
1 (10-ounce) can reduced-fat cream of chicken soup
2/3 cup nonfat sour cream
salt and pepper to taste

- Cut the chicken into strips; rinse and pat dry.
- Brown the chicken on all sides in 1 tablespoon of the margarine in a 12-inch skillet. Remove to a platter.
- Add the remaining 1 tablespoon margarine, mushrooms, onion and garlic to the skillet.
- Sauté for 10 minutes or until the vegetables are tender and the liquid has evaporated. Stir in the soup and sour cream. Bring just to a simmer.
- Add the chicken and cook just until heated through. Season with salt and pepper.
- Serve over hot yolk-free noodles.

SERVES FOUR

OVEN-CRISPY CHICKEN

4 small oranges
1 lemon
1/2 cup soy sauce
1 teaspoon orange peel
3/4 teaspoon ground ginger
1/8 teaspoon garlic powder

8 boneless skinless chicken breasts
4 cups cornflakes, very finely
  crushed
2 teaspoons ground ginger
1/2 teaspoon garlic powder
1 teaspoon salt

To marinate the chicken

- Grate the zest and strain the juice of the oranges and lemon; reserve the zest for the coating.
- Combine the orange juice, lemon juice, soy sauce, orange peel, 3/4 teaspoon ginger and 1/8 teaspoon garlic powder in a bowl and mix well.
- Rinse the chicken and pat dry. Pierce 4 or 5 times with a fork. Add to the marinade.
- Marinate in the refrigerator for 2 hours or longer.

For the coating

- Combine the reserved orange and lemon zest, cornflake crumbs, 2 teaspoons ginger, 1/2 teaspoon garlic powder and salt on a plate.

To bake the chicken

- Preheat the oven to 375 degrees.
- Remove the chicken from the marinade and dip into the crumb mixture, coating well. Arrange on a lightly greased baking sheet.
- Bake for 20 to 25 minutes or until cooked through, turning once to brown evenly.

Variation: Substitute Worcestershire sauce for the soy sauce for a different flavor.

SERVES EIGHT

Cutting up a chicken rather than buying the parts saves money. To cut the chicken, place it breast side up on a cutting board. Cut the skin between the thighs and the body.

Grasp each leg in turn, lift the chicken and bend the legs back until the bones separate at the hip joints; cut it from the body. Locate the joint in the leg by bending the leg together.

With the skin side down, cut between the thighs and drumsticks. With the chicken breast side up, cut the wings from the body by cutting inside of the wings just over the joint. Pull the wing away from the body and cut through the joint from the top down. Separate the breast and back by placing the chicken on its neck end and cutting through the joints along each side of the rib cage. Place the breast skin side down and cut into halves, cutting the wishbone in two at the V.

PRESIDENT CLINTON'S ENCHILADAS

2 (4-ounce) cans chopped green chiles
1 large clove of garlic, minced
vegetable oil
1 (28-ounce) can tomatoes
2 cups chopped onions
½ teaspoon oregano
1 teaspoon salt
3 cups shredded cooked chicken
2 cups sour cream
2 cups shredded Cheddar cheese
1 teaspoon salt
15 corn or flour tortillas
⅓ cup vegetable oil

For the sauce
- Sauté the chiles and garlic in a small amount of heated oil in a skillet.
- Drain and chop the tomatoes, reserving ½ cup liquid. Add the tomatoes, reserved liquid, onions, oregano and 1 teaspoon salt to the skillet.
- Simmer for 30 minutes or until thickened; set aside.

For the filling
- Combine the chicken, sour cream, cheese and 1 teaspoon salt in a bowl and mix well.

For the enchiladas
- Soften the tortillas in ⅓ cup heated oil in a skillet; drain.
- Preheat the oven to 250 degrees.
- Spoon the chicken filling onto the tortillas and roll to enclose. Arrange seam side down in a 9x13-inch baking dish. Spoon the sauce over the top.
- Bake for 20 minutes or until heated through.

SERVES SIX TO EIGHT

CHICKEN ENCHILADAS

2 large onions, thinly sliced
2 tablespoons butter
2 cups shredded cooked chicken
½ cup chopped pimentos
1 (4-ounce) can chopped green chiles
6 ounces cream cheese, chopped
2 tablespoons chopped fresh cilantro or
*   1 teaspoon dried*
½ teaspoon salt
½ teaspoon pepper
1 cup shredded Monterey Jack cheese
12 corn or flour tortillas
1 cup whipping cream
1 cup shredded Monterey Jack cheese

For the filling
- Separate the onion slices into rings. Sauté in the butter in a skillet over medium heat for 20 to 30 minutes or until translucent.
- Add the chicken, pimentos, green chiles, cream cheese, cilantro, salt, pepper and 1 cup Monterey Jack cheese. Cook over low heat until the cheeses melt, stirring to mix well.

For the enchiladas
- Soften the tortillas in an oiled skillet.
- Spoon the chicken mixture onto the tortillas and roll to enclose the filling.
- Arrange seam side down in a buttered 9x13-inch baking dish. Pour the cream over the enchiladas.
- Preheat the oven to 375 degrees. Bake for 20 minutes. Sprinkle with 1 cup Monterey Jack cheese. Bake until the cheese melts.

Garnish with sliced black olives, salsa and guacamole.

SERVES SIX

CHICKEN-BLACK BEAN ENCHILADAS

12 ounces boneless skinless chicken
   breasts
3 slices bacon
2 cloves of garlic, minced
1/2 cup picante sauce
1 (16-ounce) can black beans,
   drained
1 large red bell pepper, chopped

2 teaspoons ground cumin
1/4 teaspoon salt
1/2 cup chopped green onions
12 (6-inch) flour tortillas
1 1/2 cups shredded Monterey Jack
   cheese
1 cup picante sauce

For the filling
- Rinse the chicken and pat dry. Cut into strips.
- Fry the bacon in a saucepan. Remove the bacon with a slotted spoon and drain the skillet, reserving 2 tablespoons drippings. Crumble the bacon.
- Add the chicken and garlic to the reserved drippings in the skillet. Sauté until light brown.
- Add 1/2 cup picante sauce, black beans, bell pepper, cumin and salt. Simmer for 7 or 8 minutes. Add the green onions and bacon.

For the enchiladas
- Preheat the oven to 350 degrees.
- Spoon the chicken mixture onto the tortillas and sprinkle each with 1 tablespoon cheese. Roll the tortillas to enclose the filling.
- Place seam side down in a lightly greased 9x13-inch baking dish. Spoon 1 cup picante sauce over the top.
- Bake for 15 minutes. Sprinkle with the remaining cheese. Bake until the cheese melts.

Garnish with shredded lettuce, chopped tomato, chopped avocado and sour cream.

SERVES SIX

When I was younger and quite a novice in the kitchen, I set out to impress my boyfriend by preparing a chicken and broccoli casserole with rice. My mother, eager to help by giving advice, told me to be sure to wash the chicken before cooking it. Wash the chicken? Oh well, I figured a little Ivory soap never hurt me. So I "washed" the chicken. No one became ill, thank goodness, but to this day, I still get teased about my specialty—Soapy Chicken.

Rebecca Pfauser

CHICKEN WITH ARTICHOKES

1½ cups chopped scallions
½ cup butter
6 cups chopped cooked chicken
2 cups whipping cream
½ cup medium-dry sherry
¾ teaspoon thyme
1½ teaspoons salt
lemon juice to taste
salt to taste
pepper to taste
8 artichoke bottoms
½ cup slivered almonds
¼ cup grated Parmesan cheese

• Sauté the scallions in the butter in a large saucepan over medium-low heat for 5 minutes or until tender.
• Add the chicken, cream, wine, thyme and 1½ teaspoons salt. Cook for 30 minutes, stirring occasionally. Add the lemon juice and salt and pepper to taste.
• Preheat the broiler.
• Arrange the artichoke bottoms in a buttered shallow 2-quart baking dish. Spread with the chicken mixture and sprinkle with the almonds and cheese.
• Broil 5 inches from the heat source for 3 minutes or until the top is bubbly and golden brown.

SERVES EIGHT

WHITE PIZZA

2 tablespoons sun-dried tomatoes
1 cup prepared Alfredo sauce
1 cup ricotta cheese
1 (4-ounce) can mushrooms, drained
1 cup shredded cooked chicken
1 large Boboli bread round
¼ cup chopped fresh basil
1 teaspoon garlic powder
red pepper flakes to taste
2 teaspoons freshly ground black pepper
2 cups shredded Monterey Jack cheese

• Preheat the oven to 400 degrees.
• Soak the sun-dried tomatoes in water in a bowl until softened; drain.
• Layer the Alfredo sauce, ricotta cheese, mushrooms, chicken and tomatoes on the Boboli round.
• Sprinkle with the basil, garlic powder, red pepper flakes and black pepper. Top with the cheese.
• Bake for 8 to 10 minutes or until bubbly.

Variation: For **Low-Fat White Pizza,** *make an Alfredo sauce of 1 can evaporated skim milk, 1 tablespoon cornstarch, ⅔ cup Parmesan cheese, garlic powder and ¼ teaspoon salt. Prepare as for a white sauce. Substitute nonfat cottage cheese for the ricotta and process until smooth. Reduce the amount of Monterey Jack cheese to 1 cup.*

SERVES FOUR

GRILLED GAME HENS MERLOT

2 (1½-pound) Cornish game
  hens
¼ cup merlot
¼ cup lemon juice
2 tablespoons grated gingerroot

1 clove of garlic, minced
2 tablespoons butter
½ cup raspberry jelly
2 tablespoons lemon juice
¼ cup merlot

To marinate the game hens
- Ask the butcher to split the game hens lengthwise into halves. Rinse the hens and pat dry.
- Combine ¼ cup wine, ¼ cup lemon juice, gingerroot and garlic in a shallow dish. Add the game hens, coating well.
- Marinate in the refrigerator for 30 minutes to 12 hours, turning occasionally.

For the glaze
- Combine the butter, jelly, 2 tablespoons lemon juice and ¼ cup wine in a saucepan. Bring to a boil and cook until reduced to a glaze consistency.

To cook the game hens
- Remove the game hens from the marinade. Place on a grill rack coated with cooking spray over medium coals.
- Grill for 15 minutes on each side or until the juices run clear, basting frequently with the glaze.

SERVES FOUR

CHICKEN IN
PATTY SHELLS

Sauté 1 cup finely chopped onion and 1 minced clove of garlic in ¼ cup butter. Add ¼ cup flour and cook for 3 minutes, stirring constantly. Whisk in 1½ cups chicken stock. Add ¼ cup dry white wine, a dash of Tabasco sauce, 1 teaspoon salt and pepper to taste. Simmer for 5 minutes. Sauté 8 ounces sliced mushrooms in 1 tablespoon butter in a skillet. Add the mushrooms to the sauce with 3 cups chopped cooked chicken, ½ cup sour cream, 1 small jar chopped pimento and 6 slices crisp-fried and crumbled bacon. Simmer for 20 minutes, stirring occasionally. Serve in 6 patty shells, garnished with paprika. Serves 6.

101

STUFFED GAME HENS OLÉ

¾ cup chopped onion
¼ cup chopped celery
½ cup melted butter
2 corn bread muffins, crumbled
4 to 6 hot tamales, crumbled
Chili powder, salt and pepper to taste
1 (14-ounce) can chicken broth
2 Cornish game hens

For the stuffing
• Sauté the onion and celery in a small amount of the butter in a saucepan until tender.
• Add the corn bread crumbs, hot tamales, chili powder, salt, pepper and half the remaining butter. Moisten with enough chicken broth to make of the desired consistency.

To cook the game hens
• Preheat the oven to 350 degrees.
• Rinse the game hens inside and out. Stuff loosely with the stuffing mixture. Place in a baking dish and mound the remaining stuffing around the hens.
• Roast for 1 hour or until the hens are tender and golden brown, basting occasionally with the remaining butter and pan juices.

Note: This stuffing recipe can also be used with quail.

SERVES TWO

FRIED TURKEY

¾ cup melted butter
1 tablespoon Worcestershire sauce
Tabasco sauce to taste
1 tablespoon Creole seasoning
1 (12-pound) turkey
Creole seasoning to taste
vegetable oil

• Combine the butter, Worcestershire sauce, Tabasco sauce and 1 tablespoon Creole seasoning in a bowl and mix well.
• Rinse the turkey inside and out and pat dry.
• Inject the butter mixture into the turkey, using a cooking syringe and placing small amounts of the mixture throughout the turkey.
• Coat the entire turkey with additional Creole seasoning. Let stand in the refrigerator for 2 hours.
• Place enough oil in a deep fish-fryer to cover the entire turkey. Heat the oil to 350 degrees.
• Add the turkey cavity side up to the oil. Deep-fry for 4 minutes per pound or until cooked through.
• Remove the turkey, draining the oil from the cavity. Let stand for 30 minutes before carving.

SERVES TWELVE

ROAST TURKEY AND CORN BREAD DRESSING

1 (12-pound) turkey
1/2 cup butter or margarine
1 cup wine

Greek seasoning
Corn Bread Dressing

- Preheat the oven to 400 degrees.
- Rinse the turkey inside and out and place in a roasting pan.
- Melt the butter in a saucepan. Add the wine. Pour over the turkey and sprinkle the entire surface with Greek seasoning. Cover with foil.
- Reduce the oven temperature to 350 degrees. Roast using the directions on the turkey packaging, removing the foil during the last 30 minutes for even browning. Serve with Corn Bread Dressing.

CORN BREAD DRESSING

1 cup cornmeal
1 cup flour
1 tablespoon sugar
4 teaspoons baking powder
1/2 teaspoon salt
1 cup chopped celery
1 cup chopped onion
1 cup milk
1 egg

1/4 cup vegetable oil
16 saltine crackers
3 or 4 biscuits or 4 slices toasted bread
8 to 10 eggs
1/2 teaspoon sage
salt to taste
turkey broth

For the corn bread
- Preheat the oven to 425 degrees and place a greased 8-inch baking pan in the oven to heat. Mix the cornmeal, flour, sugar, baking powder, 1/2 teaspoon salt, celery and onion in a bowl. Add the milk, 1 egg and oil and mix well. Spoon into the heated baking pan.
- Bake for 20 to 25 minutes or until golden brown.

For the dressing
- Crumble the corn bread, crackers and biscuits into a large bowl. Add 8 to 10 eggs, sage, salt to taste and enough turkey broth to make a dressing thin enough to pour. Pour into a 3-quart baking dish.
- Bake at 375 to 400 degrees for 45 to 60 minutes or until brown.

SERVES TEN TO TWELVE

TURKEY AND DRESSING TIPS

When cooking a turkey, cover it with four layers of cheesecloth and saturate the cheesecloth with a mixture of three parts melted butter to one part wine. Baste the turkey over the cheesecloth as it roasts, keeping it moist. Remove the cheesecloth during the last thirty minutes of cooking time to allow even browning.
When making the dressing, celery and onion can be sautéed in 1/4 cup butter and added to the dressing rather than to the corn bread for a crunchier effect.

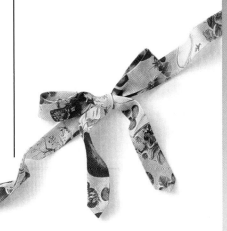

After the Hunt

GAME AND FISH

Gunpowder Dip
Champeau Duck Gumbo
Caesar Salad
Stuffed Game Hens Olé
Asparagus Spears
Special Potato Casserole
Breadsticks
Turtle-Pecan Swirl Cheesecake
Banana Pudding
Hot Buttered Rum

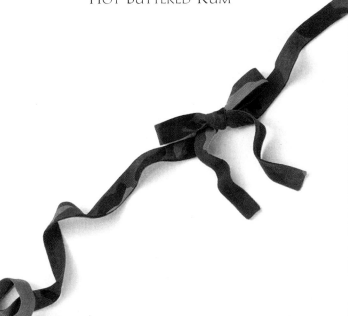

After the Hunt

For generations, the larder was filled with food from the wild.
Living off the land was a matter of necessity. Hunting was a practical and economical
way to provide sustenance for families. Our ancestors utilized a much larger variety of game.
Often, as we discuss types of game they enjoyed, peculiar, even grotesque expressions appear
on our faces as we try to imagine someone actually enjoying eating opossum, crow, armadillo, bear,
squirrel, turtle, skunk, or even rattlesnake. Admittedly, some are actually delectable.
However, I do find a few less than palatable.

Celebrating the bounty of the land by enjoying a dinner of wild game is a memorable experience.
The taste of game is distinctive, and when properly prepared it seldom disappoints.
Let your taste change to enjoy the natural flavors of this food. Well cared for
and well prepared game is an unparalleled delicacy.

Mealtime memories of time spent in our fields and forests are always better
when shared with friends and family. Whether the presentation is along the trail by a campfire,
in a cabin on the lake, or an elegant dinner at home using your best china,
it brings the outdoors indoors for all to enjoy.

Spending a morning in the forest, seeing nature awaken to a new day, brings alive senses
that on a day to day basis we often overlook. We are one with nature.
Being able to share some of the experience by providing delicious table fare and a story
or two of our adventure are the rewards no hunter could do without.

PHYLLIS K. SPEER

CHAMPEAU DUCK GUMBO

5 to 8 wild ducks
garlic powder and onion powder
   to taste
salt, red pepper and black pepper
   to taste
flour
1/2 cup vegetable oil
1/2 cup flour
3 quarts (or more) hot water
2 medium onions, chopped

1 cup chopped celery
1 green bell pepper, chopped
3 cloves of garlic, chopped
1/4 teaspoon ground cloves
8 bay leaves
1 teaspoon filé
1 pound sausage
6 ounces fresh or frozen sliced
   okra

- Cut the ducks into quarters, discarding the skin; rinse and pat dry.
- Coat completely with garlic powder, onion powder, salt, red pepper and black pepper. Sprinkle lightly with flour.
- Heat the oil in a heavy 6-quart saucepan.
- Stir in 1/2 cup flour. Make a roux by cooking over medium-high heat until the mixture is dark brown, stirring constantly; do not burn.
- Brown the duck quarters in the roux, beginning with the meatier pieces.
- Add enough hot water to cover the ducks by 1 inch or more. Add the onions, celery, green pepper, garlic, cloves, bay leaves and filé.
- Simmer, covered, for 30 minutes, stirring frequently. Reduce the heat and adjust the seasoning. Simmer for 3 1/2 hours longer.
- Brown the sausage in a skillet, stirring until crumbly; drain. Add to the gumbo. Add the okra. Cook for 30 minutes longer.
- Chill in the refrigerator overnight. Skim any congealed grease from the surface. Remove and bone the duck. Return the duck meat to the gumbo.
- Heat to serving temperature. Serve over rice.

SERVES SIX TO EIGHT

MEXICAN DOVES

Rinse the doves inside and out. Slice the breast meat away from the bone, but do not detach. Season inside and out with garlic salt, red pepper and black pepper. Place 1/2 jalapeño and 1 piece of onion between the breast and the bone of each dove. Slice bacon lengthwise into halves; wrap 1 slice around each dove and secure with wooden picks. Grill for 20 minutes or until cooked through, turning occasionally.

DUCK PATÉ

Breasts of 2 ducks
¼ cup finely chopped onion
¼ cup butter
¼ cup Italian salad dressing
3 tablespoons mayonnaise-type salad dressing
2 tablespoons lemon juice
1 tablespoon Worcestershire sauce
12 drops of Tabasco sauce
1 teaspoon liquid smoke
½ teaspoon dry mustard
¼ teaspoon red pepper (optional)
1½ teaspoons salt
½ teaspoon black pepper

- Rinse the duck breasts and pat dry. Sauté with the onion in the butter in a skillet. Drain, reserving 3 tablespoons drippings.
- Combine the duck with the Italian salad dressing, mayonnaise-type salad dressing, lemon juice, Worcestershire sauce, Tabasco sauce, liquid smoke, dry mustard, red pepper, salt, black pepper and 2 tablespoons of the reserved drippings in a food processor container. Process until smooth.
- Add the remaining 1 tablespoon drippings if needed for the desired consistency.
- Spoon into a serving dish or shape as desired.
- Serve with crackers.

SERVES FIFTEEN

DUCK CASSEROLE

2 ducks
1 onion
2 ribs celery
1 (5-ounce) package wild rice and long grain rice mix
½ cup chopped onion
½ cup melted butter
¼ cup flour
1 (6-ounce) can mushrooms
1½ cups half-and-half
1 tablespoon chopped parsley
1½ teaspoons salt
¼ teaspoon pepper
¼ cup slivered almonds

- Rinse the ducks inside and out. Combine with the whole onion and celery in a large saucepan and add water to cover.
- Cook for 2 hours. Remove the meat from the bones.
- Cook the rice using the package directions.
- Preheat the oven to 350 degrees.
- Sauté the chopped onion in the butter in a deep skillet. Stir in the flour. Cook for several minutes.
- Add the duck meat, rice, undrained mushrooms, half-and-half, parsley, salt and pepper and mix well.
- Spoon into a 2-quart baking dish and sprinkle with the almonds. Bake for 25 minutes.

SERVES SIX TO EIGHT

KINGDOM COME DUCK

4 ducks
2 apples, sliced
coarsely chopped celery
2 (10-ounce) cans consommé
1 (10-ounce) consommé can water

1½ cups butter
⅔ cup sherry
½ cup bourbon
1 (5-ounce) jar currant jelly
¼ cup Worcestershire sauce

To cook the ducks
- Preheat the oven to 350 degrees.
- Rinse the ducks inside and out and stuff with the apples and celery. Place breast down in a roasting pan and add the consommé and water.
- Roast, covered, for 3 hours or until very tender.
- Remove the breast meat from the ducks, reserving the remaining meat for another use. Place the duck breasts in a shallow greased baking dish.

For the sauce
- Combine the butter, wine, bourbon, jelly and Worcestershire sauce in a saucepan. Bring to a simmer over low heat.
- Thicken with a small amount of flour if necessary for the desired consistency.
- Pour over the duck. Bake just until heated through. Remove the duck to a serving platter.
- Pour the sauce into a bowl to serve at the table. Serve over rice.

Garnish with crumbled crisp-fried bacon.

SERVES SIX TO EIGHT

DUCK HUNTING

Stuttgart is world famous as a duck-hunting destination. Ducks migrating down the Mississippi flyway find the rice, soybeans, and flooded timber of the area very attractive. Blue-winged teal are the earliest migrant waterfowl to reach Arkansas each year, arriving in mid-July. Arkansas, historically, overwinters the largest population of Mallard ducks in the continental United States. The World Championship Duck Calling contest is held each year during Stuttgart's Wings over the Prairie Festival.

HURRICANE DUCK

Breasts of 3 ducks
1 (12-ounce) can lemon-lime soda
1 (7-ounce) can evaporated milk
12 slices bacon, cut into halves
1 (7-ounce) jar Chaka's® MMM Sauce

- Rinse the duck and pat dry; remove the membrane. Cut each duck breast into 4 pieces. Combine with the lemon-lime soda and evaporated milk in a bowl and coat well.
- Marinate in the refrigerator for several hours.
- Remove the duck from the marinade and wrap with the bacon; secure with wooden picks.
- Combine with the Chaka's® MMM Sauce in a bowl. Marinate in the refrigerator for 1 hour.
- Grill the duck over hot coals for 8 minutes or until cooked through and the bacon is crisp, turning once. Serve immediately.

Note: You can find Chaka's® MMM Sauce at specialty food markets.

SERVES SIX

STUFFED DUCK BREASTS

Breasts of 2 ducks, boneless
salt to taste
1 (8-ounce) bottle zesty salad dressing
2 tablespoons Worcestershire sauce
2 tablespoons lemon juice
1 onion, chopped
4 ounces mushrooms, chopped
1 or 2 jalapeños, chopped
pepper to taste
4 slices bacon

To marinate the duck
- Rinse the duck breasts well. Combine with salted water to cover in a bowl. Let stand in the refrigerator for 1 hour; drain.
- Combine the duck with the salad dressing, Worcestershire sauce and lemon juice in a bowl.
- Marinate in the refrigerator for 1 hour.

To stuff and cook the duck
- Combine the onion, mushrooms, jalapeños, salt and pepper in a small bowl.
- Remove the duck from the marinade and slice pockets in each. Spoon the stuffing into the pockets and wrap with the bacon; secure with wooden picks.
- Grill for 8 minutes on each side or smoke for 1 hour.

Note: For an extra-spicy flavor, use peppered bacon.

SERVES FOUR

TEAL IN WINE

10 teal or other ducks
salt to taste
2½ onions, cut into quarters
10 bay leaves
1 bottle red wine
½ cup vegetable oil

2 cups water
½ cup butter
2 tablespoons chopped parsley
4 (2-ounce) bottles onion juice
1 teaspoon cayenne
1 teaspoon white pepper

- Rinse the ducks well. Thaw frozen or soak fresh ducks in salted water to cover in a large container.
- Remove from the water and sprinkle with salt inside and out. Place ¼ onion and 1 bay leaf in the cavity of each. Place breast side down in a large heavy roasting pan.
- Preheat the oven to 350 degrees.
- Combine the wine, oil, 2 cups water, butter, parsley, onion juice, cayenne and white pepper in a saucepan. Bring to a boil. Pour half the mixture over the ducks.
- Roast the ducks, covered, for 2 hours. Turn the ducks over and baste with the remaining wine sauce.
- Roast, covered, for 2 hours longer; the meat will be tender enough to fall from the bones.
- Serve the cooking juices as gravy with wild rice.

SERVES TEN

MARINATED GRILLED DUCK

Combine one 10-ounce bottle of soy sauce, one 10-ounce bottle of olive oil, 3 tablespoons honey, 1 to 3 teaspoons ground ginger and garlic powder to taste. Marinate 10 to 12 duck breasts in the mixture in the refrigerator for 6 to 8 hours. Remove the duck from the marinade and wrap with bacon, securing with wooden picks. Grill for 1 hour or until cooked through.

SMOKED HERB-SEASONED QUAIL

1/3 cup vinegar
1 tablespoon Worcestershire sauce
2 cloves of garlic, minced
1 teaspoon sugar
1 tablespoon dried sage
1 tablespoon chopped fresh oregano, or
  1 teaspoon dried
1/4 teaspoon grated fresh nutmeg, or
  1/8 teaspoon ground
1/4 teaspoon dried thyme
1 1/2 cups vegetable oil
24 quail
24 thin slices bacon

To marinate the quail
- Combine the vinegar, Worcestershire sauce, garlic, sugar, sage, oregano, nutmeg and thyme in a bowl. Whisk in the oil gradually.
- Rinse the quail and pat dry. Combine with the marinade in a shallow nonaluminum dish.
- Marinate, covered, in the refrigerator for 8 hours or longer.

To cook the quail
- Drain the quail and wrap each with bacon; secure with wooden picks.
- Grill for 10 to 15 minutes or until cooked through, closing the grill during the last 5 minutes to smoke the quail.

SERVES TWELVE

OVEN-FRIED PHEASANT PARMESAN

1 (2 1/2-pound) pheasant
1 cup crushed herb-seasoned stuffing
2/3 cup grated Parmesan cheese
1/4 cup minced parsley (optional)
1/2 to 3/4 cup melted butter

- Preheat the oven to 375 degrees.
- Cut the pheasant into serving pieces and discard the skin. Rinse the pieces well and pat dry.
- Combine the stuffing, cheese and parsley in a bowl. Dip the pheasant in the melted butter and coat with the stuffing mixture.
- Arrange skin side up in a large shallow roasting pan. Drizzle with the remaining butter and sprinkle with the remaining stuffing mixture.
- Roast for 35 to 45 minutes or until cooked through; do not turn.

Note: Do not use low-fat butter in this recipe.

SERVES TWO

112

HERBED PHEASANT BREAST

2 cups flour
paprika, salt and pepper to taste
6 pheasant breasts
½ cup butter
2 teaspoons crushed garlic
½ teaspoon thyme
½ teaspoon marjoram

½ teaspoon sage
½ teaspoon chili powder
3 (10-ounce) cans cream of
  mushroom soup
2 (10-ounce) soup cans dry
  white wine

- Combine the flour, paprika, salt and pepper in a bowl.
- Rinse the pheasant and pat dry. Coat well with the flour mixture.
- Melt the butter with the half the garlic, thyme, marjoram, sage and chili powder in a skillet.
- Fry the pheasant in the butter mixture until golden brown. Arrange in a baking dish.
- Preheat the oven to 325 degrees.
- Combine the remaining garlic, thyme, marjoram, sage and chili powder with the soup and wine in a saucepan.
- Bring to a boil. Pour over the pheasant. Refrigerate for 2 hours or longer.
- Bake for 1½ hours.
- Serve on cooked wild rice.

SERVES SIX

TALKIN' SOUTHERN

Southerners, by birth, take their food and entertainment seriously. Hence, southern hospitality is a character trait, just as is Yankee ingenuity. When southerners talk about food, a subject so dear to the heart and stomach, suitable terms are used, and these recipes—old, new, southern, and eclectic—may inspire your taste buds to need some southern phrases to describe them. When a dish is more than good, it is described as awful good or 'specially good. Dishes that are delicious are also known as luscious, larruping, or lip-smacking. When one serving is not quite enough, you might use the expression "a heepa," meaning a great deal of, as in "I need a heepa those greens to come out even with my ham"; "a mess of," meaning a large quantity of, as in "A mess of catfish is what my plate needs"; or "prolly," meaning likely to, as in "I'm prolly going to need some more of Aunt Ellen's cream pie."
Our Junior League is "muchabliged" (southern for grateful) that you are using Apron Strings and hopes it inspires many good meals, memories, and conversations!

113

VENISON CHILI

4 pounds ground venison
2 large white onions, chopped
2½ quarts water
5 (8-ounce) cans tomato sauce
3 ounces chili blend seasoning mix
¼ cup chili powder
3 (16-ounce) cans chili beans
2 (1-ounce) squares unsweetened chocolate
salt and pepper to taste

• Combine the ground venison and onions with the water in a large saucepan. Cook until the venison is cooked through.
• Add the tomato sauce, chili seasoning and chili powder. Simmer over low to medium heat for 1½ hours.
• Add the beans and chocolate and cook for 30 minutes longer. Season to taste with salt and pepper.
• Serve over corn chips or tortilla chips in soup bowls.

Garnish with chopped onions and shredded cheese.

SERVES TEN

VENISON MANICOTTI

8 ounces ground venison or beef
1 clove of garlic, crushed
½ cup mayonnaise
1 cup cottage cheese
2 cups shredded mozzarella cheese
1 (8-ounce) package manicotti noodles
1 (28-ounce) jar spaghetti sauce
2 ounces Parmesan cheese, grated
1 teaspoon oregano
1 teaspoon basil

• Brown the ground venison with the garlic in a skillet, stirring until the venison is crumbly.
• Add the mayonnaise, cottage cheese and half the mozzarella cheese; mix well.
• Cook the noodles using the package directions; drain.
• Stuff the venison mixture carefully into the noodles. Arrange the noodles in a greased 9x13-inch baking dish.
• Preheat the oven to 350 degrees.
• Pour the spaghetti sauce over the manicotti. Sprinkle with the Parmesan cheese, remaining mozzarella cheese, oregano and basil.
• Bake, covered with foil, for 20 minutes. Bake, uncovered, for 10 to 15 minutes longer.

SERVES EIGHT

BLACKENED CATFISH

1 tablespoon paprika
1 teaspoon onion powder
1 teaspoon garlic powder
1/2 teaspoon dried thyme
1/2 teaspoon dried oregano
2 1/2 teaspoons salt

1 teaspoon ground red pepper
3/4 teaspoon white pepper
3/4 teaspoon black pepper
6 (1/2-inch-thick) catfish fillets
3/4 cup melted butter

For the seasoning mix

- Combine the paprika, onion powder, garlic powder, thyme, oregano, salt, red pepper, white pepper and black pepper in a shallow dish.

To cook the fish

- Heat a large cast-iron skillet over high heat for 15 minutes or until it is heated beyond the smoking point and a white ash forms in the bottom.
- Dip each catfish fillet into the melted butter and coat generously with the seasoning mix, patting it on by hand.
- Place the fillets in the hot skillet and pour 1 teaspoon butter over each, taking care that the butter does not flame up.
- Cook, uncovered, over high heat for 2 minutes or until blackened. Turn the fillets and top each with 1 teaspoon butter. Cook for 2 minutes longer.
- Serve immediately with additional melted butter.

Note: Fillets to be prepared in this manner must not be more than 3/4 inch thick, and thinner is better. This is a good dish to prepare outside because of the smoke.

SERVES SIX

DEALING WITH VENISON

The most tender cuts of venison come from the back and saddle. One of the best ways to remove the gamey taste of venison is to soak it overnight in a mixture of vinegar, water, and salt. Use 1/2 cup of vinegar to 1 gallon of water, and add 1/4 cup kosher salt. Venison can also be soaked in milk. In either case, always use plastic or glass bowls for this step rather than metal.

Age wild game to make it more tender. Venison should be hung for about two weeks at temperatures just above freezing before it is butchered. It can then be cut, packaged, and frozen for future use, although, like most game, it should not be frozen longer that six months to ensure the best texture and flavor.

BAKED DELTA CATFISH

2 cups dry bread crumbs
1/3 cup finely chopped pecans
1/2 cup grated Parmesan cheese
1/4 cup chopped parsley
1 teaspoon paprika
1/2 teaspoon oregano
1/4 teaspoon basil
2 teaspoons salt
1/2 teaspoon pepper
8 farm-raised catfish fillets
1 cup melted margarine

For the coating
- Combine the bread crumbs, pecans, cheese, parsley, paprika, oregano, basil, salt and pepper in a bowl.

To cook the fish
- Preheat the oven to 375 degrees.
- Dip the catfish into the melted butter and coat with the crumb mixture.
- Sear the coated fillets lightly on both sides in the remaining butter in a skillet.
- Remove to a greased 9x13-inch baking dish. Bake for 25 minutes or until the fish flakes easily.

Garnish with lemon wedges.

SERVES EIGHT

GRILLED FISH WITH SHRIMP

2 (6-ounce) swordfish steaks, cut 1 inch thick
salt and pepper to taste
2 tablespoons olive oil
1 clove of garlic, crushed
8 ounces fresh large shrimp
1/8 teaspoon salt
1/4 cup butter
1 tablespoon lemon juice
1 tablespoon Worcestershire sauce
1 tablespoon water
1 teaspoon freshly ground pepper

To prepare the fish
- Sprinkle both sides of the steaks with salt and pepper to taste. Brush with a mixture of the olive oil and garlic.
- Grill over medium-hot coals for 10 minutes or until cooked through.

To prepare the shrimp
- Peel and devein the shrimp; sprinkle with 1/8 teaspoon salt.
- Melt the butter in a skillet. Add the shrimp, lemon juice, Worcestershire sauce, water and 1 teaspoon pepper.
- Sauté over medium-high heat for 3 to 4 minutes or until the shrimp turn pink.
- Place the fish on serving plates and top with the shrimp and pan juices.

Garnish with fresh basil leaves and freshly ground pepper.

Variation: Substitute orange roughy, red snapper or grouper for the swordfish.

SERVES TWO

POMPANO EN PAPILLOTE

7 tablespoons olive oil
4 (6-ounce) pompano fillets
4 tablespoons Creole seasoning
2 large onions, sliced into rings
8 Italian plum tomatoes, cut into
  ½-inch slices

4 teaspoons minced garlic
¾ cup chopped fresh basil
1 teaspoon salt
1 teaspoon freshly ground pepper

- Preheat the oven to 425 degrees.
- Fold four 16½x24½-inch sheets of baking parchment in half. Cut the 2 open corners off in a rounded shape. Open the sheets on a work surface and brush each with 1 tablespoon of the olive oil.
- Sprinkle each fish fillet with 1 tablespoon Creole seasoning, pressing onto the fish with the hand. Place on 1 half of a parchment sheet.
- Arrange the onion rings and tomato slices over the fillets. Sprinkle with the garlic, basil, salt and pepper; drizzle each with 1 teaspoon olive oil.
- Fold the second side of the paper over the fillet and fold the bottom edge over the top. Seal the parchment into a bag by working edge over edge while folding and twisting.
- Place the packets seam side down on a baking sheet or 4 ovenproof plates. Brush with the remaining olive oil.
- Bake for 20 minutes or until the parchment is puffed and golden brown.
- Slit the bags in an X design and fold back the parchment; serve immediately.

Variation: Substitute flounder, scrod, snapper, haddock, bass, redfish, sole or grouper for the pompano in this recipe.

SERVES FOUR

ARKANSAS FISH

Arkansas is number three in the nation in the production of farm-raised catfish. These "pedigreed" catfish are very different from their bottom-feeding, river-dwelling ancestors. They prefer to consume their special diet of nutrients and natural grains at the top of the pond. The water in the ponds is monitored twenty-four hours a day for proper temperature and oxygen level. The result is a consistently mild, sweet-tasting fish that is widely available and very versatile. If you prefer to catch your fish, both the White and Little Red rivers are world famous for trout fishing. A world-record 40¼-pound trout (Salmo Trutta) was caught by Rip Collins on the Little Red River in 1992. The state record for the oldest and heaviest fish is a 215-pound alligator gar caught on the Arkansas River in 1964.

117

SALMON WITH ROSEMARY

3 cloves of garlic
1 tablespoon salt
6 to 8 salmon steaks
2 tablespoons chopped parsley
juice of 4 limes
rosemary sprigs
butter

- Mash the garlic with the salt to form a paste. Rub onto both sides of the salmon.
- Place in a shallow baking dish. Sprinkle with parsley. Drizzle with the lime juice.
- Marinate in the refrigerator for 2 hours, spooning the marinade over the fish occasionally.
- Preheat the grill. Add sprigs of fresh rosemary to the coals and brush the grill with oil.
- Place the fish on the grill and grill for 5 minutes.
- Turn the fish and dot with butter. Grill for 10 to 15 minutes longer or until the fish flakes easily.

Variation: You may also use 1 side of a 10- to 12-pound salmon in this recipe.

SERVES SIX

SMOKED TROUT

1 quart cold water
¼ cup sugar
⅓ cup kosher salt
½ teaspoon pepper
2 or 3 cleaned trout with heads

For the brine
- Combine the water, sugar, kosher salt and pepper in a plastic bowl. Add the trout. Soak in the refrigerator for 4 to 8 hours; drain.

To smoke the trout
- Prepare a smoker with moistened hickory chips and nuts.
- Place the trout on a rack directly over the chips and ignite the chips. Smoke the trout for 2 to 3 hours.
- Serve with a dill sauce (page 119).

Note: This will serve 4 to 6 as an appetizer.

SERVES TWO TO THREE

CRAB MEAT ENCHILADAS

1 medium yellow onion, chopped
2 medium tomatoes, seeded,
  chopped
1 jalapeño, seeded, minced
1 clove of garlic, minced
1/4 cup butter
1/2 teaspoon salt
1/4 teaspoon white pepper

1 pound crab meat
1/2 cup safflower oil
6 large or 12 small flour tortillas
1 cup half-and-half
1 cup shredded Havarti cheese
1 cup shredded Monterey Jack
  cheese

For the filling

- Sauté the onion, tomatoes, jalapeño and garlic in the butter in a large skillet for 8 minutes. Add the salt and white pepper. Remove to a bowl.
- Sauté the crab meat in the skillet until heated through. Stir in half the tomato mixture.
- Heat the safflower oil in a small skillet over medium heat. Soften the tortillas 1 at a time in the heated oil for 10 seconds; drain on paper towels.

For the enchiladas

- Spoon the crab meat filling onto the tortillas and roll to enclose the filling. Arrange seam side down in an 11x17-inch baking dish.
- Pour the half-and-half over the enchiladas. Let stand at room temperature for 1 hour.
- Preheat the oven to 375 degrees.
- Spoon the remaining tomato mixture over the enchiladas; top with the cheeses.
- Bake for 10 to 15 minutes or until bubbly.

Garnish with fresh cilantro.

SERVES SIX

TARTAR SAUCE

Combine 2 cups mayonnaise
with 1/4 teaspoon dillweed and
2 teaspoons each of lemon juice,
chopped olives, chopped parsley,
chopped pickle, chopped capers
and minced onion. Serve with
fish and seafood.

DILL SAUCE

Combine 1 cup mayonnaise,
1 cup sour cream, 1/3 cup chopped
parsley, 1 tablespoon chopped
chives and 2 teaspoons chopped
fresh dill or 1 tablespoon dried
dillweed in a blender container.
Add 1/2 of a 10-ounce package
thawed frozen chopped spinach if
desired. Blend at high speed for 1
minute. Chill for 2 hours or longer.
Serve with swordfish, red
snapper or salmon.

SHRIMP KABOBS

1 medium onion, chopped
3 cloves of garlic, minced
½ cup vegetable oil
6 tablespoons lemon juice
3 tablespoons soy sauce
2 teaspoons ground ginger
36 fresh shrimp, peeled
2 green, red or yellow bell peppers
2 red or purple onions

To marinate the shrimp
- Combine the chopped onion, garlic, oil, lemon juice, soy sauce and ginger in a large bowl and mix well. Add the shrimp and toss to coat well.
- Marinate, covered, in the refrigerator for 4 hours or longer; drain.

For the kabobs
- Cut the bell peppers into coarse chunks. Cut the red onions into wedges.
- Thread the shrimp through the neck and tail onto skewers, alternating with the bell peppers and onion wedges.
- Grill over medium-hot coals for 5 minutes on each side or until the shrimp are pink.
- Serve with wild rice and spinach salad.

SERVES SIX

JAMAICAN JERK SHRIMP

2 tablespoons cider vinegar
2 tablespoons olive oil
2 tablespoons minced onion
1 teaspoon brown sugar
1 teaspoon allspice
1 teaspoon ground ginger
½ teaspoon cinnamon
½ teaspoon salt
½ teaspoon pepper
1 pound large shrimp, peeled, deveined

To marinate the shrimp
- Combine the vinegar, olive oil, onion, brown sugar, allspice, ginger, cinnamon, salt and pepper in a large bowl and mix well.
- Add the shrimp. Marinate, covered, in the refrigerator for 1 to 4 hours. Drain, reserving the marinade.

For the shrimp
- Preheat the broiler.
- Thread the shrimp onto metal skewers or onto wooden skewers that have been soaked in water. Brush with the reserved marinade.
- Broil 5 inches from the heat source for 1 to 1½ minutes on each side or until the shrimp turn pink.

Note: This makes a tasty appetizer as well as an excellent entrée.

SERVES TWO

CRAWFISH ÉTOUFFÉE

1 medium white onion, chopped
½ cup butter
2 tablespoons flour
1 pound crawfish tails
1½ cups water
1 (10-ounce) can cream of
   mushroom soup
1 (8-ounce) can sliced mushrooms
   (optional)
1 large bunch green onions,
   chopped

hot sauce to taste
1 teaspoon garlic powder
¼ teaspoon thyme
¼ teaspoon paprika
¼ teaspoon tarragon (optional)
1 teaspoon salt, or to taste
¼ teaspoon red pepper
¼ teaspoon white pepper
1 teaspoon black pepper

- Sauté the onion in the butter in a large saucepan until translucent. Sprinkle with the flour. Cook for 5 minutes or until the flour is golden brown, stirring constantly.
- Add the crawfish tails, water, soup, mushrooms, green onions, hot sauce, garlic powder, thyme, paprika, tarragon, salt, red pepper, white pepper and black pepper; mix well. Simmer for 10 minutes. Adjust the seasonings and amount of water if necessary for the desired consistency. Simmer for 20 minutes longer.
- Serve over hot rice with salad and French bread.

Note: Crawfish, also known as crawdads, Arkansas lobsters or mud bugs, are raised in southeast Arkansas and shipped worldwide.

SERVES SIX TO EIGHT

For a **Cajun Shrimp Boil,** fill a large stockpot half full with water. Add 12 bay leaves, 3 quartered onions, 3 unpeeled cloves of garlic, 3 bags crab boil, 2 tablespoons Old Bay seasoning, ½ cup salt and ¼ cup cayenne. Squeeze the juice of 4 lemon halves into the stockpot and add the lemon halves. Bring to a boil. Add 18 to 22 new potatoes and boil for 10 minutes. Add 18 to 22 small ears of corn and boil for 10 minutes. Add 5 pounds large unpeeled shrimp and boil for 5 minutes. Remove from the heat and let stand, covered, for 30 minutes; drain. A Cajun shrimp boil is a great idea for a fun and casual meal. To serve, spread newspapers on the table and place the drained mixture in the center. The only thing I don't put on the table is the crab boil bags. Add French bread, cocktail sauce, squeeze margarine, salt, pepper and lots of paper towels; no forks or knives allowed! To clean up, just roll up the newspaper and throw away the whole thing. Serves 6.

Brenda Johnson Majors

Lunch at the Lake

PASTA

Corn Dip
Baked Delta Catfish
Roasted Potato Salad
Watermelon Slices
Spicy Tomato Relish
Spicy Hush Puppies
Hillary Clinton's Cookies
Long Island Tea

Lunch at the Lake

Aromatique™ has been fortunate enough to enjoy sales of its products
in many foreign countries. Even though traveling is not one of my favorite sports,
I find myself across the big water quite often. The first thing I realize when I return home
and walk in the door is ...WOW! There is no view like this anywhere in the world.

Greers Ferry Lake and Eden Isle are as much a part of the lives of my
husband, Dick, and me as they can be. Whether it is our work with the Red Apple Inn, or
just being deck potatoes, our surroundings reflect our lifestyle. When we have guests,
we purposely let the lake "be the star," and as you would expect, everyone leaves with a memory.

Lunch on the lake can be off the grill or any of dozens of combinations, and
we've done them all. A segment for Robin Leach's "Lifestyles" was shot from the deck
overlooking the lake. It was a perfect setting. The production crew had created a
beautiful scene—gazpacho, chicken salad, fruit, Italian bread, and wine. It was
a spectacular segment that has played many times over the last three years...and every time
it breaks us up...because there is Dick Upton...drinking his iced tea
with the lemon wedge still on the side of the glass.

I consider myself one of the luckiest people in the world.
Good food and good friends have been an important part of my life,
and I never forget that Arkansas has been the propagator.

PATTI UPTON

ORZO AND ARTICHOKE SALAD WITH PROSCIUTTO

1 tablespoon white wine vinegar
1 tablespoon fresh lemon juice
2 teaspoons Dijon mustard
3 tablespoons olive oil
2 tablespoons minced fresh basil
3/4 cup uncooked orzo
salt to taste
2 green onions, finely chopped

1 (6-ounce) jar artichoke hearts, drained, quartered
1/3 cup chopped sliced prosciutto
1/3 cup freshly grated Parmesan cheese
2 tablespoons chopped fresh parsley
pepper to taste

For the dressing
- Whisk the vinegar, lemon juice and mustard in a bowl until well mixed.
- Add 2 tablespoons of the olive oil gradually, whisking constantly. Whisk in the basil.

For the salad
- Cook the orzo al dente in a large saucepan of boiling salted water; drain. Rinse under cold water and drain again.
- Combine with the remaining 1 tablespoon olive oil in a large bowl. Toss to coat.
- Add the dressing and mix gently. Add the green onions, artichoke hearts, prosciutto, cheese, parsley, salt and pepper. Toss gently to mix.
- Store, covered, in the refrigerator for 1 to 24 hours. Serve chilled.

Variation: Prepare without the prosciutto for a vegetarian dish.

SERVES FOUR

LUNCH ON THE GO

Packing lunch for the lake or putting together a luscious picnic doesn't have to be a soggy mess. The following tips will help you arrive with food that is fresh, crisp, and properly chilled. When packing an ice chest, place meats and cheeses closest to the ice blocks, and vegetables and fruits farthest away. Chill foods in the refrigerator before packing the cooler. Chop vegetables and tear salad greens at home. Rinse and dry well and place in a zip-top bag. Dress salads at the last minute to keep them crisp and prevent the dressing from leaking into the cooler. Use dry ice for longer travel times. Label things in the cooler clearly. Keep the cooler in a cool shady place and cover with blankets. Keep drinks in a separate cooler, reducing the number of times the food cooler has to be opened. Fill clean plastic jugs to 1 1/2 inches from the top with water or fruit juice and freeze. The jugs will act as ice blocks in the cooler without creating a wet mess in the bottom of the cooler. As they melt, you will have a cool refreshing drink.

125

GREEK PASTA SALAD

3 tablespoons red wine vinegar
⅓ cup olive oil
1 teaspoon oregano
salt and pepper to taste
12 ounces uncooked tri-color spiral, tubular or
    shell pasta
½ cup chopped red onion
1 cucumber, sliced, quartered
1 tomato, chopped
4 ounces feta cheese, crumbled
⅓ cup kalamata olives (optional)

For the dressing
• Combine the vinegar, olive oil, oregano, salt
  and pepper in a small bowl and mix well.

For the salad
• Cook the pasta using the package directions;
  drain. Rinse under cold water and drain again.
• Combine with the onion, cucumber, tomato,
  cheese and olives in a large bowl and mix
  gently.
• Pour the dressing over the salad and toss to mix.
• Serve immediately or chill for up to several
  days.

SERVES EIGHT TO TEN

TORTELLINI CHICKEN SALAD

1 (9-ounce) package fresh cheese-filled tortellini
3 cups chopped cooked chicken or turkey
2 cups marinated deli vegetables
½ cup Caesar salad dressing
2 tablespoons chopped fresh basil, or
    2 teaspoons dried
1 tablespoon grated Parmesan cheese
1 tablespoon capers, drained (optional)

• Cook the tortellini using the package directions;
  drain. Rinse with cold water and drain again.
• Combine the chicken, undrained vegetables,
  salad dressing, basil, cheese and capers in a
  bowl and mix well.
• Add the tortellini and toss gently to mix.
• Refrigerate, covered, for 1 to 2 hours or until
  chilled through. Toss before serving.
• Serve with additional grated Parmesan cheese
  and freshly ground pepper.

*Variation: Substitute 1 cooked and drained
(16-ounce) package frozen vegetables and ⅔ cup
Italian salad dressing for the deli vegetables and
Caesar salad dressing.*

SERVES EIGHT

FIESTA PASTA

1 pound zucchini, chopped
1 medium onion, thinly sliced
¼ cup sliced jalapeños
1 large clove of garlic, crushed
2 tablespoons olive oil
½ teaspoon dried oregano

1 (14-ounce) can chopped
  tomatoes
½ teaspoon salt
8 ounces uncooked pasta
½ cup grated Parmesan cheese

- Sauté the zucchini, onion, jalapeños and garlic in the olive oil in a large skillet over medium heat until tender-crisp.
- Add the oregano, undrained tomatoes and salt. Bring to a boil.
- Reduce the heat to low. Simmer, uncovered, for 10 minutes or until the mixture thickens.
- Cook the pasta using the package directions; drain. Combine with the vegetable mixture in a large bowl and toss to mix. Sprinkle with Parmesan cheese.

Variation: Add chopped cooked chicken, cooked shrimp or other leftover meat to this salad to serve as a main dish. Add one 3-ounce can tomato paste if necessary to thicken the sauce.

SERVES FOUR

While Arkansas has many beautiful lakes and rivers, it is short on beaches, so many sun-loving Arkansans head for the northern panhandle of Florida, particularly the family-oriented Destin area, to get their yearly fix of sugar-white sand and emerald-green waves. The trip is about a ten-hour drive from Little Rock, so the question arises of how to survive the drive with children. It isn't impossible: all it takes is a little planning and creativity. Try to secure a van or utility vehicle so the kids can have plenty of room to spread out. Have a variety of things to keep the children entertained. Good ideas are books; stuffed animals; crayons and paper; electronic games; CDs and tape players with headphones; and a small TV/VCR that can be hooked up in the car. Pack lots of your children's favorite food treats and a cooler of drinks. Have a separate bag with swimsuits and towels in case your accommodations aren't ready when you arrive. You don't want to have to wait to hit the beach!

SPINACH AND TOMATO PASTA

1/4 cup sun-dried tomatoes
1 small onion, chopped
2 cloves of garlic, minced
1 to 2 teaspoons olive oil
8 ounces fresh mushrooms, sliced
2 tablespoons tamari
freshly ground pepper to taste
1 (16-ounce) can artichoke hearts, drained,
   chopped
1/4 cup kalamata olives
1/4 cup pine nuts
1 bunch fresh spinach
cooked pasta
3 ounces feta cheese, crumbled
16 ounces pasta, cooked

- Combine the sun-dried tomatoes and a small amount of hot water in a bowl. Let stand for 30 minutes and drain.
- Slice the tomatoes into thin strips.
- Sauté the onion and garlic in the olive oil in a skillet over medium heat for 2 to 3 minutes.
- Add the mushrooms, tamari and pepper. Sauté for 3 minutes longer or until the mushrooms are tender.
- Add the artichoke hearts, sun-dried tomatoes, olives and pine nuts and mix well.
- Rinse the spinach; remove and discard the stems. Add to the sauce. Cook, covered, over medium heat until heated through.
- Serve over the pasta. Top with the feta cheese.

Note: Tamari is available at specialty food stores. Substitute soy sauce if unavailable.

SERVES FOUR

♥

LOW-FAT TOMATO BASIL PASTA

3 cloves of garlic, crushed
2 tablespoons extra-virgin olive oil
1 (16-ounce) can crushed tomatoes
1 (16-ounce) can diced tomatoes
1/4 cup chopped fresh basil
2 tablespoons sugar
16 ounces tube-shaped or angel hair pasta,
   cooked

For the sauce
- Sauté the garlic in the olive oil in a skillet. Add the tomatoes, basil and sugar.
- Bring to a boil. Cook over low heat for 30 minutes, stirring occasionally.

For the pasta
- Add a small amount of the sauce to the cooked pasta and toss to mix.
- Spoon into a serving bowl and top with the remaining sauce.

Garnish with freshly grated Parmesan cheese.

Variations: For **Shrimp and Tomato Basil Pasta,** *add 1 pound fresh deveined shrimp for the last 10 minutes of cooking.*
For **Mushroom and Tomato Basil Pasta,** *add 1 cup sliced fresh mushrooms for the last 15 minutes of cooking. For* **Meat and Tomato Basil Pasta,** *add 1 pound chopped smoked beef or turkey sausage and cook for the entire 30 minutes.*

SERVES FOUR

♥

MIXED MUSHROOM PASTA

*8 ounces fresh button mushrooms,
thinly sliced*
*8 ounces fresh mixed mushrooms
such as morels, cremini and
shiitake, thinly sliced*
*2 large cloves of garlic, finely
chopped*

2 tablespoons butter
*1 teaspoon crumbled dried
tarragon*
1 cup whipping cream
3 tablespoons dry white wine
12 ounces uncooked fettuccini
salt and pepper to taste

For the sauce

- Sauté the mushrooms and garlic in the butter in a large heavy skillet over medium-low heat for 5 minutes or just until the vegetables begin to soften.
- Add the tarragon. Sauté for 2 minutes or until the mushrooms begin to release their moisture.
- Add the whipping cream and wine. Cook for 1 minute, stirring occasionally.

For the pasta

- Cook the fettuccini al dente in salted boiling water in a saucepan; drain.
- Combine the sauce and the pasta in a large bowl and toss to coat. Season with salt and pepper.

Garnish with chopped fresh parsley and freshly grated Parmesan cheese.

SERVES FOUR

LEMON CREAM PASTA SAUCE

Bring 1⅓ cups whipping cream and 1 tablespoon freshly grated lemon peel to a boil in a small heavy saucepan and boil for 3 minutes. Reduce the heat to medium-low and whisk in ½ cup chopped butter until melted. Add 2 teaspoons lemon juice, 1½ cups freshly grated Parmesan cheese, ½ teaspoon freshly grated nutmeg and salt and pepper to taste, cooking over low heat until the cheese is melted and whisking constantly. Toss with 16 ounces of cooked pasta. Serves 4.

GOURMET CHICKEN WITH PASTA

6 boneless skinless chicken breasts
salt and pepper to taste
1/2 cup flour
1/4 cup olive oil
2 cloves of garlic, minced
1/2 cup marsala wine
1 envelope Knorr's Hunter Sauce mix
1 (14-ounce) can diced tomatoes
16 ounces angel hair pasta, cooked

• Rinse the chicken and pat dry. Sprinkle with salt and pepper and coat with flour.
• Brown the chicken in the olive oil in a large skillet. Remove to a 3-quart baking dish sprayed with nonstick cooking spray.
• Drain the oil from the skillet. Add the garlic and wine to the skillet. Cook for 3 to 4 minutes, stirring frequently.
• Preheat the oven to 350 degrees.
• Prepare the Hunter Sauce using the package directions. Add the garlic and wine mixture. Add the undrained tomatoes and mix well.
• Cook for 5 minutes over medium heat, stirring occasionally. Pour the sauce over the chicken.
• Bake, covered, for 40 to 45 minutes.
• Serve over the pasta.

Variation: Serve over rice.

SERVES SIX

CHICKEN AND FETA SPINACH SAUCE

6 boneless skinless chicken breasts
salt and pepper to taste
1 teaspoon paprika
1/2 cup butter
1/2 cup flour
1 1/2 cups unsalted chicken broth or water
1 cup milk
8 ounces feta cheese, crumbled
1 1/2 cups chopped spinach
3/4 cup chopped red bell pepper
cooked pasta or rice

For the chicken
• Preheat the oven to 325 degrees.
• Rinse the chicken and pat dry.
• Season with salt, pepper and paprika. Arrange in a greased baking dish.
• Bake, covered, for 20 minutes or until cooked through. Keep warm.

For the sauce
• Melt the butter in a large skillet over low heat. Stir in the flour until well blended.
• Add the chicken broth and whisk with a wire whisk. Add the milk and whisk until well blended. Stir in the cheese.
• Cook over low heat for 30 minutes or until the liquid is reduced and the mixture is thickened, stirring frequently.
• Stir in the spinach and red pepper. Simmer for 15 minutes, stirring occasionally.
• Serve over the baked chicken with pasta or rice.

SERVES SIX

SANTA FE CHICKEN AND PASTA

1 large onion, chopped
1/2 large green or red bell pepper, chopped
2 teaspoons minced garlic
3 dried chipotle peppers
1 (16-ounce) can tomatoes, chopped
1 (4-ounce) can chopped green chiles

3 Roma tomatoes, chopped
1 teaspoon ground cumin
1 1/2 teaspoons chili powder
1 1/2 teaspoons dried oregano
hot sauce to taste
salt and pepper to taste
4 boneless skinless chicken breasts
12 ounces penne pasta, cooked

For the sauce
- Spray a 12-inch nonstick skillet with nonstick cooking spray 2 or 3 times. Sauté the onion, green pepper and garlic in the skillet until tender, covering the skillet to retain the moisture if needed.
- Soak the chipotle peppers in warm water in a bowl for several minutes. Remove the seeds and discard. Chop the peppers.
- Add the peppers, tomatoes, green chiles, Roma tomatoes, cumin, chili powder, oregano, hot sauce, salt and pepper to the skillet.
- Add water if necessary to make a thin sauce. Simmer, covered, over low heat for 20 minutes.

For the chicken
- Rinse the chicken and pat dry. Grill or roast until cooked through. Add to the sauce.
- Serve over the pasta.

SERVES FOUR

LEMON LINGUINI PARMESAN

Sauté 2 cloves of minced garlic in 2 tablespoons olive oil for 1 minute. Add 1/2 cup milk and bring to a simmer. Cook 9 ounces linguini using the package directions and drain. Toss with 1/3 cup fresh lemon juice. Add the garlic mixture, 1/2 cup freshly grated Parmesan cheese, 1/4 cup chopped parsley and pepper to taste and toss to coat well.
Serves 4.

ITALIAN COUNTRY CHICKEN PASTA

3 tablespoons olive oil
1 large onion, cut into eighths
3 cloves of garlic, minced
1 pound boneless skinless chicken breasts
1 (6-ounce) jar marinated artichoke hearts
1 (7-ounce) jar roasted red peppers
½ cup pitted small black olives
salt and cracked pepper to taste
12 ounces tri-color fusilli, cooked

- Heat the olive oil in a large heavy skillet or wok over medium heat.
- Add the onion and garlic. Sauté for 10 minutes or until translucent.
- Rinse the chicken and pat dry. Cut into ½-inch strips. Add to the skillet.
- Cook the chicken for 5 minutes or until cooked through, stirring frequently.
- Cut the artichokes into halves, reserving the liquid. Cut the roasted peppers into ½-inch strips, reserving the liquid.
- Add the artichokes, roasted peppers and reserved liquids to the skillet. Cook until heated through.
- Add the olives, salt, pepper and pasta, tossing gently to mix.
- Serve with Caesar salad and hot Parmesan toast or garlic bread for a great buffet supper.

Garnish with freshly grated Parmesan cheese.

SERVES SIX TO EIGHT

ITALIAN CHICKEN PASTA

2 pounds boneless chicken breasts
1 cup Italian salad dressing
1 (3-ounce) package sun-dried tomatoes
1 small onion, chopped
1 clove of garlic, minced
1 pound fresh mushrooms, sliced
½ cup margarine
12 ounces bow tie pasta
1 (3-ounce) jar of pesto

For the chicken
- Rinse the chicken and pat dry. Marinate in the dressing in a shallow dish in the refrigerator for several hours.
- Grill the chicken until cooked through.

For the pasta
- Soak the sun-dried tomatoes in enough boiling water to cover in a bowl for 5 minutes and drain.
- Sauté the onion, garlic and mushrooms in the margarine in a large skillet.
- Cook the pasta using the package directions.
- Combine the pasta with the sun-dried tomatoes, pesto and the sautéed vegetables in a serving bowl and toss to mix.
- Cut the chicken into slices and arrange on top of the pasta.

Garnish with crumbled feta cheese.

SERVES SIX

CHICKEN PASTA RAPHAEL

1 pound boneless skinless chicken
*   breasts*
¼ cup olive oil
2 (16-ounce) cans artichoke hearts
2 cups chopped onions
2 tablespoons minced garlic
½ teaspoon dried oregano
½ teaspoon dried basil
1 teaspoon black pepper

½ teaspoon salt
Red pepper flakes to taste
2 (16-ounce) cans tomatoes
¼ cup grated Parmesan cheese
¼ cup chopped fresh Italian
*   parsley*
16 ounces penne or tortellini,
*   cooked*

- Rinse the chicken and pat dry. Cut into bite-size pieces.
- Brown the chicken in the olive oil in a large skillet for 2 to 3 minutes.
- Drain the artichoke hearts, reserving the liquid. Add the reserved artichoke liquid, onions, garlic, oregano, basil, black pepper, salt and red pepper flakes to the chicken.
- Cook over medium-low heat for 10 minutes or until the onions are translucent, stirring frequently.
- Add the tomatoes. Simmer, covered, for 30 minutes, stirring occasionally.
- Stir in the artichokes, Parmesan cheese and parsley. Heat to serving temperature.
- Serve over pasta with bread and a salad.

SERVES SIX

CHINESE PASTA

Cut 1 pork tender into medallions and combine with 1 cup pineapple juice, 1 tablespoon minced fresh ginger and ½ cup soy sauce. Marinate in the refrigerator for 4 hours or longer. Drain, reserving the marinade. Brown the pork in olive oil. Add the reserved marinade and bring to a boil. Reduce the heat to medium-low and add snow peas, sliced fresh green beans, red bell pepper chunks and sliced water chestnuts. Cook for 5 minutes or until the vegetables are tender-crisp. Add 3 cups of vermicelli cooked al dente and toss lightly. Serves 4.

133

FETTUCCINI CARBONARA

1 carton egg substitute, or 2 eggs
⅔ cup grated Parmesan cheese
¼ cup milk
1 tablespoon chopped fresh basil, or
  1 teaspoon dried
½ teaspoon chopped fresh oregano
¼ teaspoon nutmeg
4 ounces prosciutto or bacon
1 clove of garlic, minced
2 tablespoons butter
6 ounces uncooked fettuccini, cooked al dente

- Combine the egg substitute, cheese, milk, basil, oregano and nutmeg in a bowl and mix well.
- Fry the prosciutto in a nonstick skillet until crisp. Drain and crumble.
- Sauté the garlic in the butter in a large skillet.
- Add the egg mixture and the fettuccini. Cook over low heat until the sauce coats a spoon, stirring constantly.
- Spoon into a serving bowl. Sprinkle with the prosciutto.

SERVES FOUR

BOW TIE PASTA WITH BROCCOLI

1 pound Italian sausage
3 cloves of garlic, mashed
1 small onion, chopped
florets of 1 bunch broccoli
½ cup white wine
½ cup chicken broth
12 ounces bow tie pasta, cooked
¼ cup pine nuts or walnuts, toasted
freshly grated Parmesan cheese

- Remove the casing from the sausage. Brown the sausage lightly in a skillet; drain.
- Add the garlic and onion. Sauté for 3 to 4 minutes or until the onion is translucent.
- Blanch the broccoli in boiling water; drain.
- Add the broccoli to the sausage with the wine and chicken broth. Cook for several minutes, stirring frequently. Stir in the pasta.
- Spoon into a serving bowl. Top with the pine nuts.
- Serve with the Parmesan cheese.

SERVES FOUR TO SIX

Penne Pasta with Italian Sausage

1 pound Italian sausage
1 red or yellow bell pepper
2 pounds (4 medium) zucchini
4 cloves of garlic, minced
1 cup chopped onion
2 tablespoons olive oil
1 teaspoon salt
¼ teaspoon black pepper

½ teaspoon red pepper flakes
2 tablespoons chopped basil
1 teaspoon oregano
½ teaspoon sugar
3 large tomatoes, chopped
½ cup red wine
16 ounces uncooked penne pasta

For the sauce

- Remove the casing from the sausage. Brown the sausage in a heavy skillet and drain.
- Chop the bell pepper. Cut the zucchini into ½-inch rounds and cut the rounds into quarters.
- Sauté the bell pepper, garlic and onion in the olive oil in a heavy skillet over low heat for 2 minutes.
- Add the zucchini. Cook over medium heat for 3 minutes or until brown, stirring frequently.
- Stir in the salt, black pepper, red pepper flakes, basil, oregano and sugar. Add the tomatoes, sausage and wine. Simmer over low heat for 30 minutes, stirring occasionally.

For the pasta

- Cook the penne using the package directions. Spoon into a serving dish. Add the sauce and toss to mix well.

Garnish with Parmesan cheese.

Variations: Substitute 1 (28-ounce) can tomatoes for fresh tomatoes. Substitute eggplant for the zucchini or use half eggplant and half zucchini.

Note: The sauce may be prepared the day before and reheated just before serving. It is also good combined with mozzarella cheese as a pizza topping.

SERVES SIX

Pesto! Pesto!

Pesto is a wonderful uncooked sauce made with fresh basil, garlic, pine nuts, Parmesan cheese, and olive oil. It can be found in the refrigerated or deli section of most large grocery stores. It will add a zesty flavor to pasta and a variety of other foods.
For a super salad, just stir pesto into cooked tortellini that has been rinsed in cold water and toss with chopped Roma tomatoes. It is wonderful with any pasta.
For dinner in minutes, toss pesto with hot cooked pasta and sprinkle with freshly grated Parmesan cheese. Top grilled chicken breasts with a dollop of pesto and serve on hot cooked fettuccini.

SCALLOP PASTA PROVENÇALE

3 tablespoons light olive oil
3 tablespoons unsalted butter
1 pound sea scallops, cut into quarters
8 green onions, minced
8 shallots, minced
1 clove of garlic, minced
2 teaspoons dried basil
1 teaspoon dried tarragon
¼ teaspoon dried thyme
½ cup dry white wine
4 cups canned tomatoes, crushed, drained
½ cup whipping cream
2 teaspoons sugar
salt and pepper to taste
1 pound linguini, cooked
1 large avocado, peeled, chopped

- Heat the olive oil and butter in a large nonaluminum skillet over medium heat.
- Add the scallops. Sauté for 2 minutes or just until firm. Remove the scallops to a bowl with a slotted spoon.
- Increase the heat to medium-high and add the green onions and shallots to the skillet.
- Sauté until tender. Add the garlic, basil, tarragon and thyme. Cook for 1 minute.
- Add the wine and cook for 2 minutes. Stir in the tomatoes.
- Increase the heat to high and boil until the sauce is thickened, stirring constantly.
- Stir in the cream and sugar. Cook for 20 seconds. Season with salt and pepper.
- Add the scallops and mix gently.
- Toss with the pasta in a bowl. Spoon onto serving plates. Top with the avocado.
- Serve with a fresh green salad tossed with a light vinaigrette.

SERVES FOUR

GREEK SHRIMP PASTA

¼ cup olive oil
4 cloves of garlic, minced
1 to 2 pounds medium shrimp, peeled and deveined
1 red bell pepper, thinly sliced
2 cups chunky salsa
1 (15-ounce) can small artichoke hearts, drained
½ to 1 cup crumbled feta cheese
1 pound fettuccini, cooked

- Heat 2 tablespoons of the olive oil in a large skillet. Sauté the garlic and the shrimp in the oil until the shrimp turn pink. Remove to a bowl with a slotted spoon.
- Add the remaining 2 tablespoons oil. Sauté the bell pepper for 3 minutes or until tender.
- Add the salsa. Simmer for 2 to 3 minutes.
- Cut the artichokes into halves. Add the artichokes, shrimp, garlic and ½ of the feta cheese to the skillet. Cook over medium heat for 2 to 3 minutes or just until the shrimp are cooked through.
- Spoon over the fettuccini in a serving bowl. Sprinkle with the remaining feta cheese and serve immediately.

SERVES FOUR

SEASIDE PASTA

1½ ounces sun-dried tomatoes, chopped
½ cup boiling water
10 fresh asparagus spears
¼ cup olive oil
8 ounces shrimp, peeled, deveined
1 bunch green onions, chopped

2 tablespoons pine nuts
¼ cup sliced black olives
basil to taste
4 ounces linguini, cooked, drained
¼ cup grated Parmesan cheese
salt and pepper to taste

For the sauce
- Soak the sun-dried tomatoes in the boiling water in a bowl for several minutes; drain. Snap the asparagus into 1½-inch pieces.
- Heat the oil in a 10-inch skillet over medium heat. Sauté the shrimp in the oil for 2 minutes.
- Add the asparagus, ½ of the green onions, sun-dried tomatoes, pine nuts, black olives and basil. Cook for 2 minutes, stirring frequently.

For the pasta
- Combine the linguini, shrimp mixture and ½ of the Parmesan cheese in a bowl and toss to mix. Season with salt and pepper. Top with the remaining Parmesan cheese and green onions.
- Serve with tossed salad and hard rolls.

Variation: Prepare without the shrimp to serve as a side dish.

SERVES TWO

There is nothing finer than a delicious wine with a meal, particularly if it is selected by a true connoisseur of wine. My brother-in-law knows wines and gave us one of his top choices as a gift. Unfortunately, it found its way to the shelf with several other bottles the day I needed a wine for a slow-cooker beef tip recipe, so I inadvertently used the expensive wine. Needless to say, the beef tips were a real palate pleaser, yet not a recipe I expect to replicate!

Beth Hatfield Cousins

SHRIMP AND CHEESE CASSEROLE

3 medium eggs
1 cup evaporated milk
1 cup plain yogurt
8 ounces feta cheese, crumbled
8 ounces shredded Swiss cheese
1/3 cup fresh parsley, chopped
1 teaspoon dried basil
1 teaspoon dried oregano
4 cloves of garlic, minced
8 ounces angel hair pasta, cooked
1 (16-ounce) jar chunky salsa
1 pound uncooked peeled shrimp
1 pound mozzarella cheese, shredded

- Preheat the oven to 350 degrees.
- Coat the bottom and sides of an 8x10-inch baking dish with nonstick cooking spray.
- Combine the eggs, evaporated milk, yogurt, feta cheese, Swiss cheese, parsley, basil, oregano and garlic in a bowl and mix well.
- Layer 1/2 of the pasta, salsa and 1/2 of the shrimp in the prepared baking dish.
- Layer the remaining pasta, egg mixture, remaining shrimp and mozzarella cheese over the top.
- Bake, covered, for 30 to 40 minutes or until hot and bubbly. Let stand at room temperature for 10 minutes before serving.

SERVES EIGHT TO TEN

SPINACH FETTUCCINI WITH SHRIMP

2 medium jalapeño peppers
2 large cloves of garlic, minced
1/4 cup butter
1/4 cup chicken broth
2 cups whipping cream
salt and pepper to taste
32 medium shrimp, peeled, deveined
2 tablespoons butter
12 ounces spinach fettuccini
freshly grated Parmesan cheese

- Remove the seeds from the jalapeño peppers and chop the peppers very fine.
- Sauté the peppers and garlic in 1/4 cup butter in a skillet for 1 minute.
- Add the chicken broth. Simmer over low heat until reduced to about 1 tablespoon.
- Add the cream. Bring to a boil. Reduce the heat to low. Simmer until thickened, stirring frequently. Add salt and pepper.
- Sauté the shrimp in 2 tablespoons butter in a skillet for 2 minutes or until cooked through. Tent with foil and set aside to keep warm.
- Cook the fettuccini using the package directions.
- Spoon onto serving plates. Top with the shrimp and jalapeño pepper sauce. Sprinkle with Parmesan cheese.

SERVES FOUR

SHRIMP AND ARTICHOKE PASTA

½ pound mushrooms, sliced
2½ tablespoons margarine
2 (14-ounce) cans artichoke
  hearts, drained, chopped
1½ to 2 pounds shrimp, cooked,
  peeled
4½ tablespoons margarine
4½ tablespoons flour

¾ cup milk
¾ cup whipping cream
½ cup cooking sherry
1 tablespoon Worcestershire sauce
salt and pepper to taste
½ cup freshly grated Parmesan
  cheese
cooked angel hair pasta or rice

- Preheat the oven to 375 degrees.
- Sauté the mushrooms in 2½ tablespoons margarine in a skillet.
- Layer the mushrooms, artichokes and shrimp in a greased 2-quart casserole.
- Combine 4½ tablespoons margarine and flour in a saucepan. Cook over medium heat until the margarine is melted, stirring constantly to blend.
- Add the milk, whipping cream, sherry, Worcestershire sauce, salt and pepper. Cook until thickened, stirring constantly.
- Pour the sauce over the layers. Sprinkle with the Parmesan cheese.
- Bake for 20 to 30 minutes or until hot and bubbly.
- Serve over pasta.

Variation: Substitute chopped cooked chicken for the shrimp.

SERVES SIX TO EIGHT

PASTA TIPS

Don't rinse cooked pasta unless you are using it for a cold pasta dish or it needs to be cool enough to be handled right away or a casserole.

Freeze leftover pasta to serve again. Just plunge it, still frozen, into rapidly boiling water until the strands separate, then drain and serve.

If pasta must wait a bit before serving, toss it with a little butter or oil to prevent sticking.

Four ounces of uncooked pasta per person is considered a main-dish serving. Two ounces is enough for a first course or side dish.

Add salt to pasta only after it comes to a boil. Coarse salt is preferable to table salt because it salts the water better and heightens the pasta's face. Use a heaping tablespoon to every 4 quarts of water.

Traditional Southern Thanksgiving

VEGETABLES AND SIDE DISHES

Relish Tray

Chicken-Wild Rice Soup

Ambrosia Salad

Tossed Salad with Vinaigrette

Roast Turkey and Corn Bread Dressing

Giblet Gravy

Sweet Potato-Apple Bake

Spinach-Artichoke Casserole

Corn Casserole

Cranberry-Ginger Chutney

Buttermilk Rolls

Pumpkin Cake Roll

Raspberry Cream Pie

American Thanksgiving

Over the river and through the rain-jammed traffic Dad fetched his children's Grandmother,
a trip that stretched to six legs in a week, four hours each way, 1300 miles total.
All because Dad's older son, just moved to Houston from Boston,
insisted on bringing his new "puppy." Until then, Dad, Mom, Stepdaughter,
Younger Son (home from college in Maryland), and Miniature Schnauzer
were simply going to Tupelo, once over and once back,
a snap of a drive. But when pup turned out to be an 80-pound Yellow Lab,
Grandmother put her boney foot down. Oh, for the grit of old ladies.

The family stayed in Little Rock. Younger Son arrived Monday night,
Dad left to get Mother/Gram on Tuesday, the two returned Wednesday in time
to greet Older Son and witness the first snarling battle between Lab and Schnauzer,
the latter determined to hold his turf. It was soon clear that Older Son
and Lab had to stay in one room while the Schnauzer brooded in another.
Dad gravitated between the two, with frequent stops at the bar.

The big day dawned with 70 percent cloud cover, intermittent surliness,
and all the trimmings. Mom produced a miracle meal, preceded by
mood-enhancing Milk Punch. Friday, Dad and Younger Son left to take Mother/Gram
home to make way for Mom's friend and her five-year-old daughter, coming
to spend Saturday night. But just this side of the river, in blinding rain and merging traffic,
the transmission blew. Eighteen wheelers swerved in the rear-view mirror, missing by inches.
The car couldn't be fixed till Monday. Mother/Gram was delivered by rental car.

Sunday everyone left, by Tuesday the car was back, the Lab hair swept.
Dogs, kids, moms, pals, automobiles all in their rightful places. One extra
Jack Daniel's to celebrate. At long last, Thanksgiving.

JAMES MORGAN

GLAZED CARROTS WITH GRAPES

2 pounds carrots
¼ cup plus 1 tablespoon
  cornstarch
½ cup water
1¾ cups orange juice

¼ cup fresh lime juice
⅔ cup sugar
¼ cup dry white wine
1 pound seedless green or red
  grapes

- Cut the carrots into diagonal slices. Place in a small amount of boiling water in a saucepan.
- Cook for 12 to 15 minutes or until tender-crisp; drain.
- Blend the cornstarch with ½ cup water in a small bowl.
- Combine the orange juice, lime juice, sugar and wine in a saucepan. Bring to a boil over medium heat. Stir in the cornstarch mixture.
- Cook over low heat until smooth and thickened, stirring constantly. Remove from the heat. Stir in the carrots and grapes.

SERVES EIGHT TO TEN

FRIED OKRA

After the death of my grandmother, I realized how much I missed her fried okra. I talked with folks who had known her, then my wife and I began the trial and error process to develop THE BEST fried okra recipe ever produced . . . well, with the exception of Grandmother Ola's original. Prepare the coating in a zip-top bag, using just over ½ cornmeal and just under ½ cornmeal mix, adding salt, pepper and garlic salt. Wash the okra and cut it into ¾- to ⅞-inch nuggets. Soak in water for 1 to 3 minutes. Shake gently in the bag. Cover the bottom of a skillet with less than ¼ inch oil. Add the okra to HOT oil, spread evenly, and cover. After 2 to 3 minutes, stir/flip/turn the okra and cover again. Do this several times for 6 to 7 minutes, always replacing the lid. Stab or gouge the okra with the edge of a metal spatula to eliminate excess coating; the perfect blend should be part crispy and part semi-chewy, some pieces still intact and some pieces a little smashed up. As to when it's done, you're on your own!

Brent Bumpers

SOUTHWESTERN STUFFED CHILES

3 (4-ounce) cans whole green chiles
1 (15-ounce) can black beans
¼ cup chopped onion
3 cloves of garlic, minced
1 tablespoon vegetable oil
1 cup chopped canned tomatoes
¼ teaspoon ground cloves
1 cup whipping cream
½ cup shredded Cheddar cheese
½ cup shredded Monterey Jack cheese

To stuff the chiles

- Rinse the chiles and remove the seeds. Rinse the black beans and drain.
- Stuff the chiles loosely with the black beans. Place side by side down the center of a 9x13-inch baking dish.

For the sauce

- Sauté the onion and garlic in the oil in a skillet. Stir in the tomatoes and cloves. Simmer over low heat for 10 minutes, stirring occasionally.
- Preheat the oven to 375 degrees.
- Pour the whipping cream over the chiles and spoon the tomato sauce down the center. Sprinkle half of each cheese along each side of the dish.
- Bake for 20 minutes.

SERVES FOUR TO SIX

CORN CASSEROLE

1 large onion, chopped
1 (17-ounce) can whole kernel corn
1 (17-ounce) can cream-style corn
2 eggs, beaten
1 teaspoon seasoned salt
2 cups shredded cheese of choice
1 green bell pepper, chopped
1 (4-ounce) jar chopped pimentos
1 cup cracker crumbs
salt and pepper to taste
Tabasco sauce to taste

- Preheat the oven to 300 degrees
- Sauté the onion in a nonstick skillet.
- Add the whole kernel corn, cream-style corn, eggs, seasoned salt, cheese, green pepper, pimentos, cracker crumbs, salt, pepper and Tabasco sauce and mix well.
- Spoon into a baking dish sprayed with nonstick cooking spray. Bake for 1 hour.

SERVES EIGHT TO TEN

ITALIAN EGGPLANT

1 red bell pepper, chopped
1 green bell pepper, chopped
1 yellow bell pepper, chopped
2 tablespoons olive oil
1 eggplant, unpeeled, chopped
1½ onions, chopped
4 cloves of garlic, chopped

1 teaspoon salt
1 teaspoon pepper
10 fresh basil leaves, finely
  chopped
1 cup tomato sauce
¼ cup freshly grated Parmesan or
  Romano cheese

- Preheat the oven to 375 degrees.
- Sauté the bell peppers in the olive oil in a large skillet just until tender.
- Add the eggplant, onions, garlic, salt, pepper and basil. Sauté for 10 minutes or until the eggplant is tender.
- Spoon into a shallow 10x12-inch baking dish. Spread the tomato sauce over the top. Sprinkle with the Parmesan cheese.
- Bake for 20 minutes.
- Serve with grilled pork tenderloin or chicken.

SERVES SIX

CAPER MAYONNAISE

Combine 1 cup mayonnaise,
1 tablespoon capers, 1 teaspoon caper
juice, 2 cloves of minced garlic,
1 tablespoon Dijon mustard,
1 tablespoon fresh lemon juice, ⅛
teaspoon dried oregano and pepper to
taste in a blender container; blend
until smooth. Serve over steamed
fresh asparagus. Serves 4 to 6.

BLACK-EYED PEAS CREOLE

2 slices bacon
1 cup chopped onion
1 cup chopped green bell pepper
1 cup chopped celery
1 (20-ounce) can stewed tomatoes
1/2 teaspoon basil
1 tablespoon sugar
1 large bay leaf
salt and pepper to taste
1 (16-ounce) package frozen black-eyed peas

• Fry the bacon in a large skillet until crisp. Drain and crumble the bacon, reserving the drippings.
• Sauté the onion, green pepper and celery in the reserved bacon drippings.
• Add the crumbled bacon, tomatoes, basil, sugar, bay leaf, salt and pepper. Simmer over low heat for 5 minutes.
• Add the black-eyed peas. Simmer for 1 1/2 to 2 hours, adding water as necessary.
• Discard the bay leaf before serving.

SERVES EIGHT

BLEU CHEESE BACON POTATOES

4 baking potatoes
shortening
1/2 cup sour cream
1/4 cup butter
2 ounces bleu cheese, crumbled
1/4 cup milk
4 slices bacon, crisp-fried, crumbled
salt and pepper to taste

• Preheat the oven to 400 degrees.
• Grease the potatoes with the shortening and place on a baking sheet.
• Bake for 1 hour or until tender. Reduce the oven temperature to 350 degrees.
• Cut the potatoes into halves lengthwise. Scoop the pulp into a mixer bowl, reserving the shells. Beat potato pulp until fluffy.
• Add the sour cream, butter, 1/2 of the bleu cheese and milk and mix well. Stir in the bacon. Season with salt and pepper.
• Spoon into the reserved shells. Place on a baking sheet.
• Bake for 10 minutes. Top with the remaining cheese. Bake for 5 minutes longer.

SERVES FOUR TO EIGHT

SPECIAL POTATO CASSEROLE

8 large potatoes
salt and pepper to taste
8 ounces cream cheese
2 cups shredded Cheddar cheese
   (optional)
2 eggs, beaten

2 tablespoons flour
2 tablespoons parsley flakes
2 tablespoons chopped chives
1 (6-ounce) can French-fried
   onions

- Preheat the oven to 325 degrees.
- Cook the potatoes in water to cover in a saucepan. Drain and cool slightly.
- Peel the potatoes and place in a bowl. Beat with a hand mixer until the potatoes are mashed. Add the salt, pepper, cream cheese, Cheddar cheese, eggs, flour, parsley and chives. Beat until well mixed. Stir in the onions.
- Spoon into a buttered 1-quart baking dish. Bake for 30 minutes.
- Serve with grilled steaks.

SERVES EIGHT

Sometimes I forget that I am a noncook and venture into the kitchen. One particular Fourth of July, I grilled corn on the cob along with chicken and burgers for a traditional holiday dinner. I placed the corn from the grill in the oven to keep it warm for "just a little while." We rediscovered the corn over Labor Day when we preheated the oven and the smoke alarm went off. My friends still ask for my home-cooked corn each Fourth of July.

Joyce Bradley Babin

GRUYÈRE POTATOES

3 cups milk
1/4 cup butter
salt and pepper to taste
6 medium baking potatoes

2 teaspoons minced garlic
1 cup shredded Gruyère or
   Swiss cheese

- Preheat the oven to 325 degrees.
- Combine the milk, butter, salt and pepper in a saucepan. Bring to a boil over medium heat, stirring occasionally.
- Peel the potatoes and cut into 1/8-inch slices. Add to the milk mixture. Stir in the garlic.
- Cover the saucepan partially and bring to a boil. Simmer over low heat for 15 minutes, stirring occasionally.
- Spoon into a buttered 1 1/2-quart baking dish. Sprinkle with the cheese.
- Bake for 30 to 45 minutes or until bubbly and brown around the edge.

SERVES EIGHT

147

HERBED MASHED POTATOES

6½ cups cubed peeled baking potatoes
2 cloves of garlic, cut into halves
½ cup milk
½ cup sour cream
2 tablespoons minced fresh parsley
2 tablespoons minced fresh oregano
1 tablespoon minced fresh thyme
1 tablespoon butter
¾ teaspoon salt
⅛ teaspoon pepper

- Cook the potatoes and garlic in water to cover in a large saucepan for 20 minutes or until very tender; drain.
- Return the potatoes and garlic to the saucepan and add the milk and sour cream; beat until smooth.
- Add the parsley, oregano, thyme, butter, salt and pepper and beat at medium speed until smooth.

Variation: Substitute 2 percent milk, low-fat or nonfat sour cream and low-fat margarine for a lighter version.

SERVES SIX

SPINACH-ARTICHOKE CASSEROLE

1 (8-ounce) can artichoke hearts
2 (10-ounce) packages frozen chopped spinach
8 ounces cream cheese
½ cup butter or margarine
8 ounces bacon, crisp-fried, crumbled
grated Parmesan cheese

- Preheat the oven to 350 degrees.
- Drain the artichokes and cut into quarters. Cook the spinach using the package directions and drain.
- Combine the cream cheese and butter in a saucepan. Cook over low heat until melted, stirring constantly.
- Layer the artichokes, spinach, cream cheese mixture and bacon in an 8x8-inch casserole. Sprinkle with Parmesan cheese.
- Bake for 30 minutes or until bubbly.

SERVES FOUR TO SIX

SPINACH MADELAINE

2 (10-ounce) packages frozen
  chopped spinach
1/4 cup butter
2 tablespoons flour
2 tablespoons chopped onion
1/2 cup evaporated milk

1/2 teaspoon black pepper
3/4 teaspoon celery salt
3/4 teaspoon garlic salt
red pepper to taste
1 teaspoon Worcestershire sauce
1 (6-ounce) roll jalapeño cheese

- Cook the spinach using the package directions. Drain and reserve 1/2 cup of the liquid.
- Melt the butter in a saucepan over low heat. Stir in the flour until smooth. Add the onion. Cook until soft, stirring constantly.
- Stir in the reserved spinach liquid and evaporated milk gradually. Cook until thickened, stirring constantly.
- Stir in the black pepper, celery salt, garlic salt, red pepper and Worcestershire sauce.
- Cut the cheese roll into small pieces. Add to the mixture. Cook until the cheese is melted, stirring constantly.
- Add to the spinach and mix well. Serve immediately.

Variation: Pour the spinach mixture into a buttered baking dish and top with buttered bread crumbs. Chill for 8 hours or longer to improve the flavor. Bake at 350 degrees for 30 minutes or until brown and bubbly.

Note: This can be served from a chafing dish as a hot appetizer.

SERVES SIX

Perhaps the spirit and flavor of Arkansas, known as "The Natural State," can best be illustrated by the crops produced: Alma claims the title of "Spinach Capital of the World." Most varieties of spinach used for canning in the United States were developed at the University of Arkansas. Dr. James N. Moore of the University has developed or co-developed numerous varieties of fruits. The University also has the largest blackberry breeding program in the world. Atkins, known as "Pickle City USA," is home to the fried dill pickle. Hope claims to be the watermelon capital of the world and, in 1985, produced a world-record 260-pound watermelon. Arkansas is the number-one producer of rice, with the largest rice mill in the world found in Stuttgart. Arkansas is the largest producer of commercial broilers, produces 5 percent of the nation's soybean crop, and produces most of the beets used for baby food in the United States.

SWEET POTATO-APPLE BAKE

1 cup shredded coconut (optional)
1 cup chopped pecans
1 cup packed brown sugar
1/3 cup flour
1/3 cup melted butter or margarine
1 (32-ounce) can sweet potatoes, sliced
1 (15-ounce) can apples
1 cup sugar
1/2 cup milk
1/3 cup butter or margarine
2 eggs, lightly beaten
1 teaspoon vanilla extract
2 tablespoons frozen orange juice concentrate

- Preheat the oven to 375 degrees.

For the topping
- Combine the coconut, pecans, brown sugar, flour and melted butter in a bowl and mix until crumbly.

For the casserole
- Combine the sweet potatoes, apples, sugar, milk, 1/3 cup butter, eggs, vanilla and orange juice concentrate in a bowl and mix well. Pour into a buttered 2-quart baking dish.
- Sprinkle the topping over the sweet potatoes.
- Bake for 20 to 30 minutes or until golden brown and bubbly.

Variation: Substitute 2 teaspoons grated orange peel for the orange juice concentrate.

SERVES TEN TO TWELVE

SUMMER TOMATO TART

1 recipe basic pastry dough
8 ounces mozzarella cheese, shredded
2 1/2 tablespoons chopped fresh basil
4 to 5 ripe tomatoes
3/4 teaspoon salt
1/2 teaspoon cracked pepper
1/4 cup extra-virgin olive oil

- Preheat the oven to 400 degrees.
- Line a 10-inch springform tart pan with the pastry dough. Layer the cheese and basil over the dough.
- Cut the tomatoes into 1/2-inch slices. Arrange in the pan, covering as evenly as possible. Sprinkle with salt and pepper; drizzle with the olive oil.
- Bake for 30 minutes. Slice into wedges and serve warm.

Garnish with chopped fresh basil.

SERVES EIGHT

TOMATOES WITH BACON

1 pound bacon
1 large purple onion, chopped
8 ounces Gruyère cheese, grated

1/2 cup minced fresh parsley
6 large tomatoes
salt and pepper to taste

- Preheat the broiler.
- Fry the bacon in a skillet until crisp. Drain and crumble, reserving 1/4 cup bacon drippings.
- Sauté the onion in the bacon drippings in the skillet for 10 minutes or just until tender. Combine the onion with the bacon, cheese and parsley in a bowl and mix well.
- Cut the tomatoes into 1/2-inch slices. Arrange in a baking dish, over-lapping the tomatoes slightly. Season with salt and pepper. Sprinkle with the cheese mixture.
- Broil until the cheese melts and browns slightly.
- Serve warm with grilled chicken for a summertime treat.

Garnish with fresh basil.

SERVES EIGHT

TERIYAKI GRILLED VEGETABLES

1/3 cup soy sauce
3 tablespoons rice wine or dry
    sherry
1 1/2 tablespoons sugar

1 tablespoon minced ginger
2 cloves of garlic, minced
8 cups sliced vegetables

- Mix the soy sauce, rice wine, sugar, ginger and garlic in a large bowl. Add the vegetables and toss to coat. Let stand for 30 minutes.
- Preheat the grill or broiler.
- Grill 6 inches from the heat source for 5 minutes on each side or until brown and slightly charred on the outside and tender-crisp on the inside.

Note: Vegetables that are good prepared in this manner are bell peppers, onions, zucchini, yellow squash, carrots, mushrooms and tomatoes.

SERVES FOUR TO EIGHT

VEGETABLES ON THE GRILL

Good choices for grilling include cabbage wedges, new potatoes, thick squash and onion slices, broccoli florets and cauliflowerets. Wash the vegetables, leaving as much water as possible on them. Place enough for one serving on a 12x14-inch piece of foil sprayed with nonstick cooking spray and season with salt and pepper. Top with butter and seal the foil tightly. Grill over medium coals for 15 to 30 minutes or until the vegetables reach desired tenderness.

ZUCCHINI CASSEROLE

3 medium zucchini
3 medium yellow squash
1 medium red onion, thinly sliced
2 tablespoons olive oil
2 ripe tomatoes
2 tablespoons chopped parsley
salt and pepper to taste
1 teaspoon Italian seasoning
¼ to ½ cup grated Parmesan cheese
⅓ cup Italian bread crumbs

- Preheat the oven to 350 degrees.
- Cut the squash into ¼-inch slices. Steam over boiling water in a saucepan just until tender-crisp.
- Sauté the onion in the oil in a skillet for 3 minutes. Peel the tomatoes and cut into thin slices.
- Layer the zucchini, tomatoes, yellow squash, onion and parsley in a greased 3-quart baking dish. Sprinkle with salt, pepper, Italian seasoning, Parmesan cheese and bread crumbs.
- Bake for 30 to 40 minutes or until hot and bubbly.

Note: This very pretty low-fat dish can be prepared a day in advance and stored in the refrigerator until baking time.

SERVES SIX

OVEN-ROASTED WINTER VEGETABLES

2 pounds rutabagas, peeled
1 pound sweet potatoes
2 pounds red and yellow onions
1½ pounds carrots
6 tablespoons olive oil
15 cloves of garlic
15 fresh sage leaves, or 1 tablespoon dried
8 sprigs of fresh rosemary, or 1 tablespoon dried
pepper to taste

- Preheat the oven to 450 degrees.
- Cut the rutabagas and sweet potatoes into 1-inch cubes. Cut the onions into 1-inch chunks. Cut the carrots into 2-inch pieces.
- Place 2 large heavy roasting pans in the oven and heat for 15 minutes. Remove the pans and drizzle 1 tablespoon oil on each.
- Layer half of the vegetables in each pan. Sprinkle the unpeeled garlic, sage, rosemary and pepper over each. Drizzle the remaining 4 tablespoons oil over the vegetables.
- Roast for 1 hour or until tender when pierced with a fork, stirring occasionally.

SERVES EIGHT

CORN BREAD AND MUSHROOM DRESSING

1 medium onion, finely chopped
*4 ounces mushrooms, finely
  chopped*
1 cup finely chopped celery
½ cup butter
*1 (16-ounce) package corn bread
  stuffing*
*1 (16-ounce) package herb-
  seasoned stuffing mix*

1 cup coarsely chopped pecans
½ teaspoon salt, or to taste
*½ teaspoon freshly ground
  pepper*
½ tablespoon dried thyme
2 teaspoons chopped sage
*1 egg, or equivalent amount of
  egg substitute*
1 cup (or more) chicken stock

- Preheat the oven to 325 degrees.
- Sauté the onion, mushrooms and celery in the butter in a skillet over medium heat for 7 minutes.
- Combine with the stuffing, stuffing mix, pecans, salt, pepper, thyme, sage and egg in a large bowl and mix well. Add enough chicken stock to moisten.
- Spoon into a 9x13-inch baking dish sprayed with nonstick cooking spray.
- Bake for 30 minutes or until brown, adding additional chicken stock during baking as needed to keep the dressing moist.

SERVES TWELVE TO SIXTEEN

POLENTA

Polenta has become a very popular dish, largely because it is tasty and quite versatile. Polenta can be found in most markets in the rice and pasta section, and is usually packaged like rice. If true polenta cannot be found, cornmeal can be substituted, although most cornmeal is more finely ground. Polenta can be served as a main dish or as a side dish. For these variations, prepare the polenta using the package directions.

*For **Grilled Polenta,** pour prepared polenta into a 9-inch pie plate and chill. Cut into slices and grill for several minutes on each side or until slightly charred and heated through.*

*For **Fried Polenta,** pour prepared polenta into a pan and let set. Cut into desired portions and fry in heated oil in a skillet.*

*For **Creamy Polenta,** substitute milk for the water called for in the preparation step. Stir in Parmesan or other cheese until melted.*

*For **Marinara Polenta,** prepare any of the above variations and serve topped with marinara sauce and sprinkled with Parmesan cheese.*

SQUASH DRESSING

1 (7-ounce) package corn bread mix
3 cups sliced yellow squash
1 white onion, sliced
1 teaspoon salt
1/2 cup butter
1 (10-ounce) can cream of chicken soup
2 eggs, beaten
1/3 cup milk
pepper to taste
Tabasco sauce to taste

- Preheat the oven to 350 degrees.
- Prepare and bake the corn bread using the package directions. Cool slightly and crumble.
- Combine the squash, onion, salt and a small amount of water in a saucepan. Cook over medium heat for 20 minutes or just until tender; drain well.
- Heat the butter and chicken soup in a saucepan over medium heat just until the butter is melted, stirring frequently. Remove from the heat. Add the eggs, milk and pepper and mix well.
- Combine the soup mixture, squash mixture, corn bread crumbs and Tabasco sauce in a bowl and mix well.
- Pour into a greased 8x8-inch baking dish. Bake for 35 minutes or until golden brown.

SERVES FOUR

LEMON RICE

2 1/2 cups canned chicken broth
1 clove of garlic, slightly crushed
salt to taste
1 cup uncooked long grain rice
1 tablespoon grated lemon or orange peel
2 tablespoons chopped fresh dill
2 tablespoons chopped fresh parsley
2 tablespoons unsalted butter
pepper to taste
1/4 cup chopped pecans

- Bring the chicken broth, garlic and salt to a boil in a heavy saucepan over medium heat. Stir in the rice. Simmer, covered, for 20 minutes or until the liquid is absorbed. Remove from the heat.
- Stir in the lemon peel. Let stand, covered, for 5 minutes. Remove the garlic and discard.
- Stir in the dill, parsley, butter, pepper and pecans.

SERVES SIX

RICE AND GREEN CHILES

1 cup chopped onion
1/4 cup butter
4 cups cooked rice
2 cups sour cream
1 cup cream-style cottage cheese
1 large bay leaf, crumbled

1/2 teaspoon salt
1/8 teaspoon pepper
3 (4-ounce) cans green chiles,
   chopped
2 cups shredded sharp Cheddar
   cheese

- Preheat the oven to 375 degrees.
- Sauté the onion in the butter in a skillet for 5 minutes or until golden brown. Remove from the heat.
- Add the rice, sour cream, cottage cheese, bay leaf, salt, pepper and green chiles and mix well.
- Layer the rice mixture and the cheese 1/2 at a time in a greased 8x12-inch baking dish.
- Bake, uncovered, for 25 minutes or until hot and bubbly.

Garnish with chopped parsley.

SERVES EIGHT TO TEN

QUICK AND EASY RICE

Combine 1 cup of uncooked rice,
1 can each of consommé and French
onion soup, and 1 small can of
sliced mushrooms in a 2 1/2-quart
baking dish. Bake at 350 degrees
for 1 hour or until the liquid has
been absorbed and the rice
is tender. Serves 6.

LIME PEANUT RICE

1 cup basmati rice
1 green bell pepper
½ red bell pepper
¼ cup peanut oil
1 tablespoon mustard seeds
1 cup raw peanuts
⅛ teaspoon turmeric
¼ cup flaked coconut
juice of 2 limes
½ tablespoon dried cilantro

• Cook the rice using the package directions. Chop the green and red peppers into ½-inch pieces.
• Heat the peanut oil in a 10-inch skillet over medium heat. Add the mustard seeds.
• Cook, covered, for 10 minutes or until the seeds begin to pop. Add the peanuts and turmeric. Sauté for 5 minutes or until the peanuts are light brown, stirring constantly.
• Add the bell peppers and coconut. Cook until the oil is absorbed, stirring occasionally.
• Add the lime juice. Simmer, covered, for 1 minute. Stir in the rice and cilantro. Heat to serving temperature.
• Serve as a side dish with chicken and fresh pineapple or as a meatless main course.

Garnish with additional coconut.

SERVES FOUR

BREAD AND BUTTER PICKLES

6 quarts sliced cucumbers
4 medium white onions, chopped
1 green bell pepper, chopped
3 cloves of garlic, peeled
⅓ cup noniodized salt
5 cups sugar
3 cups white vinegar
3 tablespoons mustard seeds
1½ teaspoons turmeric seeds
1½ teaspoons celery seeds
1 (7-ounce) jar pimentos

• Combine the cucumbers, onions, green pepper, garlic and salt in a large container. Cover with ice.
• Let stand for 3 hours. Drain well and discard the garlic.
• Combine the sugar, vinegar, mustard seeds, turmeric seeds, celery seeds and pimentos in a large stockpot.
• Bring to a boil over medium heat, stirring occasionally. Add the cucumber mixture. Bring to a boil, stirring occasionally.
• Pour into hot sterilized jars, leaving ½-inch headspace. Seal with 2-piece lids.

YIELDS FIVE TO SIX QUARTS

SQUASH PICKLES

*4 quarts thinly sliced small yellow
  squash*
6 medium white onions, chopped
1/3 cup salt

5 cups sugar
1 1/2 teaspoons turmeric
1 1/2 teaspoons celery seeds
3 cups cider vinegar

- Mix the squash, onions and salt in a large bowl. Cover with ice.
- Let stand for 3 hours to overnight. Drain well.
- Combine the sugar, turmeric, celery seeds and vinegar in a large saucepan. Bring to a boil.
- Add the squash mixture. Bring just to a simmer, but do not boil.
- Pour into hot sterilized jars, leaving 1/2-inch headspace. Seal the jars with 2-piece lids.
- Process in a hot water bath for 15 minutes. Test the jars for complete seal.

YIELDS THREE TO FOUR QUARTS

SPICY TOMATO RELISH

12 to 14 ripe tomatoes
5 jalapeños
2 onions, chopped
1/2 cup packed brown sugar
1/2 cup white vinegar

1 teaspoon salt
1/2 teaspoon pepper
1/4 teaspoon ground cinnamon
1/4 teaspoon ground cloves
1/4 teaspoon allspice

- Peel and chop the tomatoes and jalapeños, discarding the pepper seeds.
- Combine the tomatoes and jalapeños with the onions, brown sugar, vinegar, salt, pepper, cinnamon, cloves and allspice in a large stockpot.
- Bring to a boil over high heat. Reduce the heat to medium. Simmer until slightly thickened, stirring occasionally.
- Pour into hot sterilized jars, leaving 1/2-inch headspace. Seal the jars with 2-piece lids.
- Process in a hot water bath for 15 minutes. Test the jars for complete seal.

Note: To peel fresh tomatoes, plunge in boiling water for 10 to 15 seconds and slip skins off.

YIELDS TWO QUARTS

One Thanksgiving my ability to remain a calm and gracious hostess was stretched to the limit. The dining table was carefully set with the china, crystal, and silver, and I was dressed to receive the twenty-nine guests who were coming for Thanksgiving dinner. What a time for roots to attack the plumbing in my home, but attack they did, and my pipes were spewing water all over the kitchen floor. My guests arrived just in time to witness the Roto Rooter™ man under my sink and all his equipment spread out on the kitchen floor. There was nothing to do but carry on. We continued with our Thanksgiving meal, being careful to step over and around the Roto Rooter™ man, even giving him nibbles of turkey while in the kitchen. What did I learn from this? The best thing a hostess can ever do is RELAX! If anything goes wrong, it is never reason enough to ruin an evening.

Evlyn (Sissy) McDade Clinton

SALSA

2 to 3 jalapeños, seeded
¼ (or more) Vidalia or red onion
6 cups peeled fresh tomatoes
3 tablespoons fresh cilantro
¼ teaspoon sugar
¼ to ½ teaspoon minced garlic
cumin powder to taste

- Process the jalapeños and onion in a food processor or blender until puréed.
- Add the tomatoes. Process to a slightly chunky consistency. Add the cilantro, sugar, garlic and cumin powder. Process to the desired consistency.
- Store, covered, in the refrigerator.

Note: Substitute 2 (28-ounce) cans good quality tomatoes when fresh tomatoes are not in season. Scallions may be substituted for the onion.

YIELDS TWO QUARTS

SALSA VERDE

10 tomatillos
½ onion
2 to 4 jalapeños
3 green tomatoes
4 cloves of garlic
leaves of ½ bunch cilantro
½ tablespoon salt
3 avocados, peeled, seeded
¼ cup sour cream

- Rinse the tomatillos and peel. Chop the onion and peppers. Remove the cores of the green tomatoes.
- Combine the tomatillos, onion, peppers, green tomatoes, garlic, cilantro and salt in a food processor container. Process until puréed.
- Pour into a 4-quart saucepan. Heat to a boil over medium heat, stirring occasionally. Remove from the heat. Adjust the seasoning.
- Process the avocados and sour cream in a food processor until puréed.
- Add the tomatillo mixture. Process until well mixed.
- Chill, covered, in the refrigerator.
- Serve with corn chips or tacos.

Variation: Substitute canned tomatoes if fresh tomatillos are not available.

SERVES TEN TO FIFTEEN

PIZZA SAUCE

1 onion, grated
1/3 cup vegetable oil
2 (12-ounce) cans whole tomatoes
1 (12-ounce) can tomato paste
1/4 cup sugar
1 tablespoon oregano
1 tablespoon salt

1 tablespoon pepper
1 teaspoon garlic salt
2 teaspoons MSG
1 teaspoon basil
3 tablespoons grated Parmesan
   cheese

- Sauté the onion in the oil in a heavy cast-iron skillet until translucent.
- Add the tomatoes, tomato paste, sugar, oregano, salt, pepper, garlic salt, MSG, basil and Parmesan cheese.
- Cook over low heat for 10 to 15 minutes or until thick, stirring frequently.
- Serve on traditional pizza crusts or on English muffins for mini-pizzas, or freeze in an airtight container for later use.

YIELDS SAUCE FOR THREE LARGE PIZZAS

PINEAPPLE SALSA

Combine 1 tablespoon brown sugar, 1/4 cup unsweetened pineapple juice, 1/3 cup finely chopped red or green bell pepper and 1/4 cup sliced green onions. Add 1 cup diced fresh pineapple or one 8-ounce can diced unsweetened sliced pineapple. Chill until serving time. This is delicious with pork or seafood.

Sunday at Grandmother's

BREADS

Eggs au Gratin
Bean and Tomato Salad
Pork Loin Roast-
Blueberry Sauce
Herbed Mashed Potatoes
Zucchini Casserole
Spinach Madelaine
Bread and Butter Pickles
Old-Fashioned Yeast Rolls
Peach Jam
Sour Cream Apple Pie
Baked Fudge
Iced Tea

I Remember Lily

I was asked to write about grandmothers. This initially stumped me. I rarely saw one grandmother, who lived and died far away. She didn't cook much. Cabbage mostly. She passed her talent on to my mother. (She became a hospital dietitian.) My other grandmother, Lily Jane Brantley, died around my sixth birthday. What could I possibly remember, all these years later, about Lily and food?

Food memories endure, I discovered. They resonate as lyrically as the music that played the night I met the woman I married. Recollections of my short time with Lily turned out to be a feast, a celebration of her own love of food and family.

In the huge backyard of her South Louisiana house, I remembered, she stooped to harvest papershell and Stuart pecans from towering trees. "I'm squeezing my liver," she'd say of this and all toil. What pecans she didn't sell, she'd put into her baking and my divinity (do I have to explain that divinity is a feather-light, divinely sweet candy of egg whites and sugar and pecans?).

Her pears went into preserves; the figs, too. She'd slather a thick and sticky spoonful of fig jam on my ice cream. Spring was strawberry season. She'd lead me out among the tiny hills in the dewy morning. I'd pluck fat ones and drop them in her apron, then eat them, with sugar and cream, at the old metal table on her back porch. Come evening, about the time the bats fluttered back to their roosts in the live oaks, we'd take the same seat for home-grown cantaloupe halves, with a scoop of Watson's vanilla in the hollowed-out center. I loved the back porch. It was shaded by trees and smelled of earth and the newspaper-wrapped amaryllis bulbs she sold. In my memory, that porch is cool.

It certainly was by comparison to Lily's kitchen, an inferno in the days before air conditioning. I remember Lily, sweat beaded on her lip, mopping her brow as she turned chicken in the spitting fat of a smoking iron skillet. Or maybe she was sprinkling backyard herbs on stewing chicken cacciatore. It wasn't much cooler on Louisiana mornings—not when the oven was baking the morning biscuits. She'd let me roll them. I'd cut them, too, using the metal cutter with the red wooden knob. Best of all, she'd give me scraps of dough to make snakes and other bits of fancy. Her friends often dropped by for coffee then. They poured the inky black liquid from a French drip pot into demitasse cups, all stirred with tiny silver spoons. That gentle ritual and the smell of chicory, are with me today as sharply as the bitter coffee she splashed in my little cup of sugared milk. As close as her soft, kindly face.

Food memories about my grandmother? I'm glad you asked.

MAX BRANTLEY

ANGEL BISCUITS

5 cups flour
¼ cup sugar
1 tablespoon baking soda
1 teaspoon salt
1 cup shortening

1 envelope dry yeast
2 tablespoons warm water
2 cups buttermilk
½ cup melted butter

- Preheat the oven to 400 degrees.
- Sift the flour, sugar, baking soda and salt into a bowl. Add the shortening and cut in until crumbly.
- Dissolve the yeast in the warm water and stir in the buttermilk. Add to the dry mixture and mix lightly.
- Pat out on a floured surface. Cut with a biscuit cutter.
- Dip into the butter and fold in half. Place on a baking sheet.
- Let rise for 30 to 40 minutes before baking. Bake for 15 minutes or until golden brown.

YIELDS TWO DOZEN

CORN BREAD

½ cup melted butter
1 cup cream-style corn
1 cup sour cream

2 eggs, beaten
½ medium onion, finely minced
1 cup self-rising cornmeal

- Preheat the oven to 350 degrees.
- Combine the butter, corn, sour cream, eggs, onion and cornmeal in a bowl and mix well.
- Spoon into a greased 9-inch cast-iron skillet.
- Bake for 20 to 25 minutes or until the edge is brown.

SERVES SIX TO EIGHT

One of my most treasured memories is that of Sunday meals at Grandma's house, where we all had lunch AND dinner at one table. When guests joined us, Grandma would extend the table into the living room with a sewing table or old door added for length. The makeshift table was then camouflaged with a beautiful linen and lace tablecloth.

Her menu was always highlighted with vegetables from the garden and homemade rolls. Before each meal, the same blessing was prayed by the grandchildren: "God is great, God is good . . ." I can't remember when I found out the correct words: I always said "Goddess great, goddess good . . ." The grandchildren were always served milk, but my PaPa would add sugar and lemon to his tea glass and pass it over to me to "make sure it was okay" before he drank. This tradition went on until 1990, when, with over 30 years of Sunday family meals to her credit, my grandma died at the age of 84. Fortunately, we have her recipes, which we treasure and will pass along to our children.

Carolyn Brabston Gunn

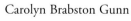

163

BROCCOLI CORN BREAD

1 (10-ounce) package frozen chopped broccoli
2 (7-ounce) packages corn bread mix
½ cup melted butter or margarine
1 cup cottage cheese
2 eggs
1 cup chopped onion

- Cook the broccoli using the package directions; drain well.
- Preheat the oven to 400 degrees.
- Combine the corn bread mix and melted butter in a bowl and mix well.
- Add the cottage cheese, eggs, onion and broccoli and mix well. Spoon into a greased 9x13-inch baking pan or muffin cups.
- Bake for 30 minutes.

Note: Serve hot or cold. This is especially good with black-eyed peas.

SERVES FIFTEEN

CORN CAKES

¼ cup flour
¼ cup yellow cornmeal
1 teaspoon sugar
½ teaspoon baking powder
¼ teaspoon baking soda
⅛ teaspoon garlic powder
¼ teaspoon salt
¼ teaspoon black pepper
cayenne to taste
½ cup plain low-fat yogurt
1 egg
1 (11-ounce) can no-salt-added whole kernel corn, drained

- Mix the flour, cornmeal, sugar, baking powder, baking soda, garlic powder, salt, black pepper and cayenne in a bowl.
- Combine the yogurt and egg in a bowl and mix well. Stir in the corn.
- Add the corn mixture to the dry ingredients and mix just until moistened.
- Coat a griddle or skillet with nonstick cooking spray and preheat over medium heat.
- Spoon ¼ cup of the batter onto the griddle for each corn cake. Bake on each side for 2 to 3 minutes or until brown.
- Serve with chili or hearty vegetable or bean soup.

SERVES FOUR TO SIX

SPOON BREAD

³/₄ cup yellow cornmeal
2 cups milk
3 tablespoons melted unsalted
   butter

4 large egg yolks
½ teaspoon salt
4 large egg whites

- Combine the cornmeal and milk in a large metal bowl.
- Place the bowl over simmering water and whisk until the mixture is thickened and smooth.
- Remove from the heat and whisk in the butter, egg yolks and salt.
- Let stand until cool.
- Preheat the oven to 350 degrees. Butter a 6-cup soufflé dish.
- Beat the egg whites in a large bowl until stiff peaks form.
- Fold ⅓ of the beaten egg whites into the cooled mixture; fold in the remaining egg whites gently.
- Spoon into the prepared soufflé dish. Bake for 40 to 45 minutes or until puffed, golden brown and just set in the center.

SERVES SIX

Having been born above the Mason-Dixon line, I was not exposed to true southern food until I attended the University of Arkansas as a freshman in 1938. My enlightenment began when I pledged Kappa Kappa Gamma and moved into the sorority house. The first night I sat down for a meal in the large dining room, the house boys brought by a bowl of what I thought was the most tasteless dish I had ever seen. "What is this? Mush?" I asked. "It's spoon bread," my astonished server replied. Since we never ate our bread with a spoon in Kansas, you can imagine my apprehension at trying this new dish. But I did and I loved it, and spoon bread continues today to be one of my favorites. Another rite of passage into the land of southern cooking was occasioned by a large bowl of steaming black-eyed peas. "We feed that to the hogs in Kansas," I screamed. That comment not only brought down the house, but brought out the cook, who informed me in a very indignant tone that by "growing up a Yankee" I had obviously "missed a lot of good food." She was right, and I have been making up for it ever since.

Willie Long Oates

165

SPICY HUSH PUPPIES

1 cup cornmeal
½ cup corn flour (masa)
½ cup all-purpose flour
1 tablespoon baking powder
½ teaspoon thyme
¼ teaspoon oregano
½ teaspoon salt
1 teaspoon cayenne
⅓ cup finely chopped green onions
2 teaspoons minced garlic
1 jalapeño, chopped
2 eggs, beaten
2 tablespoons vegetable oil
1 cup milk
vegetable oil for deep-frying

- Mix the cornmeal, corn flour, all-purpose flour, baking powder, thyme, oregano, salt and cayenne in a bowl.
- Add the green onions, garlic and jalapeño. Add the eggs and mix well.
- Bring 2 tablespoons oil and milk to a boil in a saucepan. Add the flour mixture.
- Cook until thickened, stirring constantly.
- Chill for 1 hour.
- Heat vegetable oil to 350 degrees in a large skillet or deep fryer.
- Drop the batter by tablespoonfuls into the hot oil. Deep-fry until dark brown. Drain on paper towels.

YIELDS THREE DOZEN

RAISIN BRAN MUFFINS

2 cups raisin bran flakes
1 cup whole wheat flour
¾ cup packed brown sugar
1¼ teaspoons baking soda
¼ teaspoon salt
1 cup buttermilk
¼ cup melted butter
1 egg, or ¼ cup egg substitute
1 teaspoon vanilla extract

- Preheat the oven to 400 degrees.
- Mix the bran flakes, flour, brown sugar, baking soda and salt in a bowl.
- Add the buttermilk, butter, egg and vanilla; stir just until moistened. Spoon into muffin cups sprayed with nonstick cooking spray.
- Bake for 15 to 20 minutes or until golden brown.

Variation: Stir in 2 tablespoons sliced almonds and ¼ cup chocolate chips.

YIELDS SIXTEEN

SCONES

¼ *cup dried currants or raisins*
¼ *cup boiling water*
2 *cups flour*
2 *tablespoons sugar*
2½ *teaspoons baking powder*
½ *teaspoon salt*

⅓ *cup shortening*
½ *cup milk*
1 *egg, lightly beaten*
2 *tablespoons milk*
1 *tablespoon sugar*

- Preheat the oven to 450 degrees.
- Combine the currants and boiling water in a bowl. Let stand for 10 minutes; drain.
- Mix the flour, 2 tablespoons sugar, baking powder and salt in a large bowl.
- Cut in the shortening with a pastry blender until the mixture resembles coarse meal.
- Stir in the currants.
- Combine ½ cup milk and the egg in a small bowl and mix well. Add to the dry ingredients and mix just until moistened.
- Knead lightly 4 or 5 times on a lightly floured surface.
- Divide the dough into 2 equal portions. Roll each portion to a circle ¼ to ½ inch thick.
- Cut each circle into 6 wedges.
- Place the wedges on a lightly greased baking sheet; brush with 2 tablespoons milk and sprinkle with 1 tablespoon sugar.
- Bake for 10 to 12 minutes or until light brown.
- Serve warm with butter, jam and clotted cream (at right).

YIELDS ONE DOZEN

CLOTTED CREAM

For a southern-style version of clotted cream, whip 1 cup whipping cream until soft peaks form. Add ⅓ cup sour cream and 4 teaspoons confectioners' sugar. Beat until the mixture is very thick. Chill for 1 to 6 hours. Serve with scones.

ALMOND LEMON YOGURT BREAD

3 cups flour
½ teaspoon baking powder
1 teaspoon each baking soda and salt
1 cup finely chopped toasted almonds
3 eggs
1 cup vegetable oil
1¾ cups sugar
2 cups lemon yogurt
1 tablespoon finely grated lemon peel
2 tablespoons lemon extract
1 teaspoon almond extract
3 to 4 tablespoons lemon juice
⅔ cup sifted confectioners' sugar
2 teaspoons finely grated lemon peel

For the bread
- Preheat the oven to 325 degrees.
- Sift the flour, baking powder, baking soda and salt together. Stir in the almonds.
- Beat the eggs in a large mixer bowl. Add the oil and sugar and beat until smooth.
- Add the yogurt, 1 tablespoon lemon peel and flavorings and mix well.
- Add to the dry ingredients and mix well.
- Spoon into 2 greased and floured 5x9-inch loaf pans.
- Bake for 1 hour or until a wooden pick inserted in the center comes out clean.
- Cool in the pans for 10 minutes. Remove to a wire rack to cool completely.

For the glaze
- Combine the lemon juice, confectioners' sugar and 2 teaspoons lemon peel in a bowl and mix well. Drizzle over the cooled bread.

YIELDS TWENTY-FOUR SERVINGS

BANANA BREAD

2 large ripe bananas, chopped
1 cup sugar
3 large eggs
½ cup unsalted butter, softened
½ cup buttermilk
1½ teaspoons vanilla extract
2 cups flour
1 teaspoon baking powder
1 teaspoon baking soda
½ teaspoon salt

- Preheat the oven to 350 degrees.
- Process the bananas in a food processor for 1 minute or until puréed.
- Add the sugar and eggs and process for 1 minute. Add the butter and process for 1 minute.
- Add the buttermilk and vanilla gradually, processing constantly.
- Mix the flour, baking powder, baking soda and salt in a bowl.
- Add to the food processor and pulse 3 to 5 times or just until moistened; do not overprocess.
- Pour into a buttered and floured 7-cup loaf pan.
- Bake for 1 hour or until a wooden pick inserted in the center comes out clean.
- Cool in the pan for several minutes and remove to a wire rack to cool completely.

Note: This recipe can also be prepared using a mixer.

YIELDS ONE LOAF

HERBED BREAD

2¼ teaspoons dry yeast
1 tablespoon sugar
1 cup warm water
3 cups bread flour
¼ cup dry milk powder
¾ teaspoon celery seeds
¾ teaspoon caraway seeds

¾ teaspoon sage
¾ teaspoon nutmeg
1½ teaspoons garlic salt
1 large egg, beaten
1 teaspoon lemon juice
2 tablespoons melted margarine

- Dissolve the yeast and sugar in the warm water in a bowl.
- Mix the bread flour, dry milk powder, celery seeds, caraway seeds, sage, nutmeg and garlic salt in a large bowl.
- Add the yeast mixture and mix well. Add the egg and lemon juice and mix to form a dough.
- Knead the dough on a floured surface for 8 to 10 minutes or until smooth and elastic.
- Shape into a ball and place in a greased bowl. Brush with 1 tablespoon of the melted margarine.
- Let rise, covered, in a warm place until doubled in bulk. Punch the dough down.
- Shape the dough into a loaf and place in a greased loaf pan. Brush with the remaining 1 tablespoon margarine. Let rise until doubled in bulk.
- Preheat the oven to 350 degrees. Bake the bread for 45 to 55 minutes or until golden brown.

Variation: To prepare in a bread machine, have all ingredients at room temperature. Add to the machine in the order directed by the manufacturer. Most specify placing the dry ingredients in the machine and then adding the liquids. Set the machine for basic/standard bread and select the normal baking cycle.

YIELDS SIXTEEN

WORDS OF WISDOM FROM GRANDMOTHER

You can eat fried chicken with your fingers as long as both feet are on the floor.
"Thank you" and "please" are two little keys that open the door to happiness.
Don't ever prepare any recipe until you have read it thoroughly and assembled all the ingredients and utensils required.
Never tell the cook that you are "stuffed"; instead say you are "comfortable."
Save the "wish bite," the point of the pie slice, until last!
Never use the butter knife in the jelly or jam.
Serve from the left and remove from the right.
Never begin to clear the table if someone is still eating— even if they are slow!
Never wipe your hands on a kitchen towel at the same time as another, or you will have a disagreement.
After cutting meat, rest the knife on the plate before taking a bite— the food is not going to run away from you!
If you can read a recipe, you can cook!

SOFT PRETZELS

½ cake yeast, crumbled
¾ cup warm water
¾ teaspoon sugar
⅜ teaspoon salt
1¾ cups (about) flour
2 tablespoons melted butter
coarse salt (optional)

- Preheat the oven to 400 degrees.
- Dissolve the yeast in the warm water in a large bowl. Stir in the sugar and salt.
- Add enough flour to make a soft dough.
- Knead on a floured surface. Divide into 4 equal portions.
- Flatten each portion to a 4x4-inch rectangle on a lightly greased surface. Cut into 2x2-inch pieces for 16 medium pretzels, or cut into smaller or larger pieces if preferred.
- Roll each piece into a long rope and bend into a pretzel shape.
- Place on a lightly greased and floured baking sheet. Brush with melted butter and sprinkle with coarse salt.
- Bake for 15 to 20 minutes or until golden brown, turning once if necessary.
- Broil for 2 minutes if necessary to brown.
- Serve with Mustard Butter or Herb Butter.

Variation: For **Herb Pretzels,** *add 1 crushed clove of garlic, 2 teaspoons basil and 2 teaspoons parsley with the flour. You can also brush with a mixture of 1 egg yolk and 2 tablespoons water instead of butter, or sprinkle with sesame seeds, cinnamon or Parmesan cheese in place of salt.*

YIELDS SIXTEEN

PRETZEL BUTTERS

For mustard butter
- Soften ½ cup butter and beat until smooth. Add 2 tablespoons Dijon mustard and mix well. Spoon into a serving bowl and chill until serving time.

Variation: Add 2 to 3 cloves of minced garlic.

YIELDS ONE-HALF CUP

For herb butter
- Soften ½ cup butter and beat until smooth. Add 2 tablespoons minced fresh or 2 teaspoons dried whole basil, oregano, tarragon or chervil, or a combination of the herbs; mix well. Spoon into a serving bowl and chill until serving time.

Variation: Add 2 to 3 cloves of minced garlic.

YIELDS ONE-HALF CUP

BUTTERMILK ROLLS

1 envelope dry yeast
1/2 cup warm water
1 cup buttermilk, scalded
2/3 cup sugar
2/3 cup shortening
1/2 teaspoon baking soda

1 teaspoon salt
1 cup prepared instant mashed
  potatoes
2 eggs, beaten
6 to 8 cups flour

- Dissolve the yeast in the warm water. Pour the scalded buttermilk into a large bowl. Add the sugar, shortening, baking soda, salt and mashed potatoes and mix well. Cool to lukewarm. Stir in the yeast and eggs.
- Add enough flour to form a stiff dough. Knead on a floured surface until smooth and elastic. Place in a greased bowl, turning to coat the surface.
- Let rise, covered, in a warm place for 1 1/2 hours or until doubled in bulk. Punch the dough down.
- Roll on a floured surface and cut out as desired. Place on a greased baking sheet. Let rise, covered, for 1 to 1 1/2 hours or until doubled in bulk.
- Preheat the oven to 350 degrees.
- Bake the rolls for 12 to 15 minutes or until golden brown.

YIELDS THREE DOZEN

CINNAMON ROLLS

1 recipe Buttermilk Roll dough
1/2 cup melted margarine
3/4 cup packed brown sugar

1 cup chopped pecans
cinnamon to taste
1/2 cup dark corn syrup

- Roll the dough into a circle and brush with the melted margarine.
- Sprinkle with the brown sugar, pecans and cinnamon. Drizzle the corn syrup around the outer edge.
- Slice into wedges 3 inches wide at the outer edge. Roll up the wedges from the wide end and shape into crescents in a greased baking pan.
- Let rise for 1 to 1 1/2 hours or until doubled in bulk.
- Preheat the oven to 350 degrees.
- Bake the cinnamon rolls for 12 to 15 minutes or until golden brown.

YIELDS TWO DOZEN

GLORIFIED BUTTERS

Herb butters are a good way to liven up breads, meats and vegetables. They can be made days in advance, spooned into molds or ramekins and stored in the refrigerator.
*For **Firecracker Butter,** mix 1 cup softened unsalted butter with 1/4 cup minced scallions, 1 teaspoon ground cumin, 1 teaspoon crumbled dried oregano leaves, 1/8 teaspoon red pepper flakes and black pepper to taste.*
*For **Garlic Butter,** mix 1/2 cup softened butter with 2 to 3 cloves of minced garlic.*
*For **Chive Butter,** mix 1/2 cup softened butter with 2 tablespoons minced fresh or frozen chives. Add 2 to 3 cloves of minced garlic if desired.*
*For **Parsley Butter,** mix 1/2 cup softened butter with 1/4 cup minced fresh parsley. Add 2 to 3 cloves of minced garlic if desired.*
*For **Lemon Butter,** blend 1/2 cup lemon juice with 1 cup clarified butter.*

OLD-FASHIONED YEAST ROLLS

2 envelopes dry yeast
1/3 cup warm water
1 cup butter
1 1/2 cups milk
5 cups unsifted flour
1/2 cup sugar
1 teaspoon salt
2 eggs, beaten

- Dissolve the yeast in the warm water.
- Melt the butter in the milk in a saucepan over low heat.
- Mix the flour, sugar and salt in a bowl. Stir in the milk mixture gradually.
- Add the eggs and mix well. Add the yeast mixture and mix to form a dough.
- Knead on a floured surface until smooth and elastic.
- Place in a greased bowl, turning to coat the surface.
- Let rise, covered, in a warm place until doubled in bulk. Punch the dough down.
- Shape into rolls and arrange in buttered and floured baking pans.
- Let rise, covered, until doubled in bulk.
- Preheat the oven to 400 degrees.
- Bake the rolls for 15 to 20 minutes or until golden brown. Brush with butter if desired.

YIELDS THREE DOZEN

TRADITIONAL YEAST ROLLS

1 cup boiling water
1 cup butter
2/3 cup sugar
2 teaspoons salt
3 envelopes dry yeast
1 tablespoon sugar
1 cup warm water
2 eggs
6 cups flour
1/2 cup melted butter

- Pour the boiling water over 1 cup butter, 2/3 cup sugar and salt in a mixer bowl. Let stand until cool.
- Dissolve the yeast and 1 tablespoon sugar in the warm water in a bowl. Beat in the eggs.
- Add the yeast mixture to the cooled butter mixture and mix well.
- Add the flour and mix to form a dough.
- Let rise, covered, in the refrigerator for 8 hours or longer.
- Roll 1/2 inch thick on a floured surface. Cut into 2-inch circles.
- Fold the circles in half and place in a greased baking pan.
- Let rise, covered, for 2 hours. Brush with the melted butter.
- Preheat the oven to 425 degrees.
- Bake the rolls for 12 minutes.

Variation: Sprinkle rolls with sesame seeds or poppy seeds or shape the dough into small balls for **Cloverleaf Rolls** *and place 3 in each greased muffin cup and bake as above.*

YIELDS FIVE DOZEN SMALL ROLLS

FOCACCIA

2 teaspoons dry yeast
1 cup flour
1 teaspoon dried oregano
1/2 teaspoon salt
3/4 cup warm (120- to 130-degree)
    water
1 cup flour

1 tablespoon olive oil
1 clove of garlic, minced
2 tablespoons olive oil
1/3 cup grated Parmesan cheese
3 tablespoons chopped fresh
    parsley

- Combine the yeast, 1 cup flour, oregano and salt in a large mixer bowl.
- Add the warm water gradually, beating constantly at low speed.
- Add 1 cup flour gradually, mixing to form a soft dough.
- Knead on a floured surface for 10 minutes or until smooth and elastic.
- Place in a greased bowl, turning to coat the surface.
- Let rise, covered, in an 85-degree place for 1 hour or until doubled in bulk. Punch the dough down.
- Oil a 12- or 14-inch pizza pan with 1 tablespoon olive oil. Stretch and press the dough to fit the pan.
- Let rise, covered, in a warm place for 30 to 40 minutes or until doubled in bulk.
- Preheat the oven to 400 degrees.
- Mix the garlic and 2 tablespoons olive oil in a small bowl. Poke holes in the dough with 2 fingers.
- Drizzle with the garlic mixture. Sprinkle with the cheese and parsley.
- Bake for 25 to 30 minutes or until brown. Cool on a wire rack.
- Cut into serving pieces and serve warm. Wrap any remaining focaccia in plastic wrap and store at room temperature for up to 3 days.

Variation: Prepare the dough in a bread machine, placing the ingredients in the machine in the order suggested by the manufacturer. Set for Dough or Manual setting and proceed as above when the cycle is complete.

SERVES EIGHT

DINNER CRACKERS

Combine 1/2 cup melted butter with 1 teaspoon garlic powder and 1 tablespoon minced chives. Cut an 18-inch loaf of French bread diagonally into thin slices. Brush the butter mixture over both sides of the bread and coat with 2 cups grated Parmesan cheese. Arrange on a baking sheet and broil until light brown on both sides. Drain on paper towels. Yields 10 servings.

BREADSTICKS

1 envelope dry yeast
¼ cup warm water
1 tablespoon honey
2 tablespoons olive oil
¾ cup cool water
¼ cup Italian seasoning
1 teaspoon salt
3 cups flour
melted butter

• Preheat the oven to 500 degrees.
• Dissolve the yeast in ¼ cup warm water and let stand for 10 minutes.
• Combine the honey, olive oil, ¾ cup cool water, Italian seasoning and salt in a bowl and mix well.
• Combine with the flour in a food processor and mix well. Add the yeast and mix well.
• Roll the dough on a floured surface; cut into strips.
• Brush lightly with butter and place on a baking sheet.
• Bake for 15 minutes or until golden brown.

Variation: For **Pizza Crust,** *place rolled dough on an oiled pizza pan and top as desired. Bake at 500 degrees for 15 minutes or until the crust is golden brown.*

SERVES EIGHT

ITALIAN BREAD

1 loaf French bread
½ cup butter, softened
½ cup chopped fresh parsley
1 clove of garlic, minced
1 tablespoon olive oil
½ cup grated Parmesan cheese
½ teaspoon basil
½ teaspoon oregano

• Preheat the oven to 375 degrees.
• Slice the French bread into halves horizontally.
• Combine the butter, parsley, garlic, olive oil, cheese, basil and oregano in a bowl and mix well.
• Spread on the cut sides of the bread. Wrap the bread with foil.
• Bake for 20 minutes or until heated through. Serve warm.

SERVES TWELVE

TOOTIE BREAD

1 loaf French bread
8 slices Swiss cheese
1/2 cup margarine, softened
1/4 cup finely chopped onion

1 tablespoon prepared mustard
1 tablespoon poppy seeds
4 slices bacon, crisp-fried,
  crumbled

- Preheat the oven to 400 degrees.
- Slice the bread into 16 pieces, slicing to but not through the bottom.
- Cut the cheese slices diagonally into halves. Place the cheese between the slices of bread.
- Place the bread on a foil-covered baking sheet.
- Mix the margarine, onion, mustard and poppy seeds in a bowl.
- Spread the margarine mixture over the top and sides of the bread. Sprinkle with the bacon.
- Bake the bread for 20 minutes. Serve hot.

SERVES SIX TO EIGHT

TOASTED CHEESE BREAD

1/2 cup butter, softened
3 tablespoons grated Parmesan
  cheese
1/8 teaspoon Tabasco sauce

1/2 teaspoon celery seeds, paprika
  and caraway seeds
1 (1-pound) loaf Italian or
  French bread

- Preheat the oven to 350 degrees.
- Combine the butter, cheese, Tabasco sauce, celery seeds, caraway seeds and paprika in a bowl and mix well.
- Slice the bread, cutting to but not through the bottom.
- Spread the butter mixture on the cut sides of the bread. Wrap with foil.
- Bake for 30 to 45 minutes or until heated through.

Note: Double the butter mixture for a long loaf of bread.

SERVES EIGHT TO TEN

PESTO BREAD

Cut a 1-pound loaf of French bread into halves lengthwise. Combine 1/2 cup softened butter, 1/4 cup mayonnaise, 2 tablespoons grated Parmesan cheese, 1/4 cup pesto and 2 or 3 crushed cloves of garlic in a bowl and mix well. Spread on the cut sides of the bread and place on a baking sheet. Bake at 375 degrees for 10 to 15 minutes or until bubbly. Cut into 1-inch slices to serve.

Sweet Childhood Memories

DESSERTS

Peach Ice Cream
Fudge Melt-Aways
Sour Cream Blueberry Pie
Pink Lemonade

Just Desserts

Desserts, the least essential part of the meal, exist strictly to pleasure and express fondness toward ourselves and those for whom we cook. Oh, certainly, a case can be made for the sweet balancing the other flavors of the meal, or providing one last indulgence to linger over for conversation, but nobody really needs dessert...although most of us want it.

My mother, although she was not a baker and had very little sweet tooth herself, understood this. One of the original working women, she took the train from Manhattan every day to the Hudson River bedroom community in which I was raised. Often, when my father and I met her at the Hastings Station, she was carrying, in addition to a purse and one or two enormous bulging canvas tote bags of paperwork, a small white bakery box, tied with string.

Those white boxes: I have to confess I felt a huge surge of pleasure at the sight of a box in my mother's hand as she stepped from the train. Since my brother had already moved away from home and my father didn't care much for sweets, it was clearly in the line of a small gift-wrapped present for me. I regarded it as such, with the propriety and selfish pleasure of a secure childhood. I'm sure I said "Thank you" and, later, "Mmmm, these are really good"...my mother was a Southerner by birth, and politeness was inculcated in her, and by her in us.

Here are some of the things I might anticipate being in that box: eclairs, meringue cookies, tiny diamond-shaped petit fours, or individual fruit tarts. I don't remember ever asking her, "What did you pick out?" Part of the pleasure was getting home, cutting through that shiny, sturdy, double-wrapped length of string, and being surprised by whatever was there.

Where we as a culture are now about desserts is in some ways an old, old story; we've mixed up pleasure with guilt, and come up with sin. "This rich icing is positively wicked." "I'm going to atone for this later at the gym." "I think I'll be bad and have dessert." "Ooooh, that cheesecake looks sinful." While moral and ethical questions are essential in giving balance and meaning to a life, we trivialize such questions by applying them to whether or not we should have a slice of apple pie!

So go ahead. Slit the string. Open that box. See what's inside. Have at it. I carried it home, really, for both our pleasure. And pleasure's what dessert is about.

CRESCENT DRAGONWAGON

CARAMEL-GLAZED APPLE CAKE

3 eggs
1¼ cups vegetable oil
2 cups sugar
2 cups flour
1 teaspoon baking soda
1 teaspoon salt
3 cups chopped peeled apples
1 cup chopped pecans or walnuts
2 teaspoons vanilla extract

3 tablespoons butter
3 tablespoons whipping cream
3 tablespoons sugar
3 tablespoons brown sugar
½ cup confectioners' sugar
¼ teaspoon vanilla extract

For the cake
- Preheat the oven to 350 degrees.
- Beat the eggs in a large mixer bowl. Add the oil and beat until thick and light yellow. Beat in the sugar.
- Mix the flour, baking soda and salt together.
- Add to the egg mixture and mix well. Stir in the apples, pecans and 2 teaspoons vanilla; do not overmix.
- Spoon into a greased and floured bundt pan. Bake for 1 hour or until set; the cake will be very moist.
- Cool in the pan for several minutes. Remove to a serving plate.

For the glaze
- Combine the butter, whipping cream, sugar and brown sugar in a heavy skillet.
- Bring to a boil and boil for 1 minute. Cool to room temperature.
- Add the confectioners' sugar and ¼ teaspoon vanilla; beat until smooth.
- Drizzle over the top and side of the cake.

Garnish servings with whipped cream.

SERVES SIXTEEN

My grandmother, fondly known as Big Mom, was the epitome of a true southern cook. She made almost everything from scratch. Sweets were among her special gifts. She would make angel food cakes with fresh strawberries for me, and continued this delectable tradition by making them for my children.

Still, I can't remember Big Mom's cooking without mentioning what she called her "Better Cakes." She would take a package of cake mix and improve—better—it.

*For Big Mom's **Sour Cream Cake**, start with a package of yellow cake mix and add ½ cup sugar, ¾ cup vegetable oil, 4 eggs, 1 cup sour cream and 2 teaspoons vanilla.*

*For her **Apricot Nectar Cake**, start with a package of lemon cake mix and add 1 package of lemon gelatin, 6 ounces apricot nectar, ⅔ cup vegetable oil, 4 eggs and 1 teaspoon vanilla. Glaze with a mixture of 1½ cups confectioners' sugar and 6 tablespoons lemon juice; spoon over the cake while it is still hot.*

Mimi Myer Hurst

APRICOT LEMON CAKE

1 (2-layer) package lemon cake mix
1/2 cup sugar
4 eggs, at room temperature
1 to 2 cups apricot nectar
1/2 cup vegetable oil
1 cup confectioners' sugar
Juice of 1 lemon

For the cake
- Preheat the oven to 350 degrees.
- Combine the cake mix, sugar, eggs, apricot nectar and vegetable oil in a mixer bowl and beat for 2 minutes.
- Spoon into a greased and floured tube pan. Bake for 45 to 55 minutes or until the cake tests done.
- Cool in the pan for several minutes. Remove to a serving plate and let cool.

For the glaze
- Combine the confectioners' sugar and lemon juice in a microwave-safe bowl and mix well.
- Microwave until heated through; stir to blend well.
- Drizzle over the cake.

Garnish the top with mint leaves and fresh raspberries.

SERVES SIXTEEN

CHOCOLATE CUPCAKES

8 ounces cream cheese, softened
1 egg, beaten
1/2 cup sugar
1 cup semisweet chocolate chips
1 1/2 cups flour
1 cup water
1 cup sugar
1/4 cup baking cocoa
1 teaspoon baking soda
1/2 cup vegetable oil
1 tablespoon white vinegar
1 teaspoon vanilla extract

For the filling
- Combine the cream cheese, egg and 1/2 cup sugar in a bowl and mix well.
- Stir in the chocolate chips. Set aside.

For the cupcakes
- Preheat the oven to 350 degrees.
- Mix the flour, water, 1 cup sugar, baking cocoa and baking soda in a bowl.
- Add the oil, vinegar and vanilla and beat until smooth.
- Fill paper-lined muffin cups 1/2 full with the chocolate batter.
- Spoon 1 tablespoon of the filling into each cup.
- Bake for 25 minutes. Remove to a wire rack to cool.

SERVES SIXTEEN

FIVE-FLAVOR POUND CAKE

1 cup butter, softened
1/2 cup shortening
3 cups sugar
5 eggs, beaten
3 cups flour
1/2 teaspoon baking powder
1 cup milk

2 teaspoons coconut extract
2 teaspoons lemon extract
2 teaspoons butter flavoring
2 teaspoons almond extract
2 teaspoons vanilla extract
1 cup sugar
1/2 cup water

For the cake
- Preheat the oven to 325 degrees.
- Cream the butter, shortening and 3 cups sugar in a mixer bowl until light and fluffy. Beat in the eggs.
- Mix the flour and baking powder together. Combine the milk with 1 teaspoon of each of the flavorings in a bowl.
- Add the flour mixture to the creamed mixture alternately with the milk, mixing well after each addition.
- Spoon into a greased and floured bundt pan. Bake for 1 1/2 hours.

For the glaze
- Combine the remaining 1 teaspoon of each flavoring with 1 cup sugar and water in a saucepan. Bring to a boil.
- Pour half the glaze over the cake as soon as it is removed from the oven. Let stand for 10 minutes.
- Remove the cake to a serving plate. Spoon the remaining glaze over the top.

SERVES SIXTEEN

Most southern cooks have a trademark recipe that is their identifying item at potlucks. My mother's marker was a pineapple chiffon cake. She made this cake to commemorate all life occasions— births, deaths, illnesses, or special days. She must have taken great pride in the lightness and height achieved by this masterpiece. Mama was a woman of few words. In reflecting back, I believe this cake represented what she was unable to express in words, because its beautiful yellow color always looked like a circle of sunshine on whatever table it graced.

Ann Pendleton Ellen

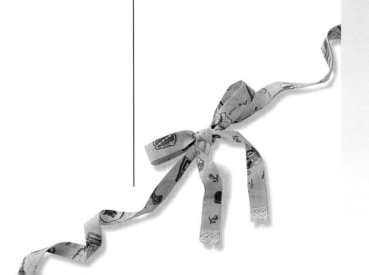

SOUR CREAM POUND CAKE

1 cup butter, softened
3 cups sugar
1 cup sour cream
2 tablespoons light rum
1 tablespoon vanilla extract
1 teaspoon almond extract
3 cups flour
½ teaspoons baking soda
6 eggs
1 teaspoon cinnamon
confectioners' sugar

- Preheat the oven to 325 degrees.
- Cream the butter and sugar in a mixer bowl until light and fluffy.
- Add the sour cream, rum and flavorings and beat until smooth.
- Mix the flour and baking soda together. Add to the creamed mixture alternately with the eggs, mixing well after each addition.
- Spoon half the mixture into a greased and floured bundt pan. Sprinkle with the cinnamon. Cut through the batter to marbleize. Top with the remaining batter.
- Bake for 1 hour or longer. Cool in the pan for several minutes.
- Remove to a serving plate. Sprinkle with confectioners' sugar.

SERVES TWELVE

KAHLÚA CAKE

1 (2-layer) package yellow cake mix
1 (3.4-ounce) package chocolate instant
   pudding mix
4 eggs
1 cup vegetable oil
⅓ cup Kahlúa
⅓ cup vodka
½ cup sugar
¾ cup water
¼ cup Kahlúa
½ cup confectioners' sugar

For the cake
- Preheat the oven to 350 degrees.
- Combine the cake mix, pudding mix, eggs and oil in a mixer bowl and beat until smooth.
- Add ⅓ cup Kahlúa, vodka, sugar and water and mix well; batter will be thin.
- Spoon into a greased and floured bundt pan. Bake for 50 minutes or until a wooden pick inserted in the center comes out clean.
- Cool in the pan for several minutes. Remove to a serving plate.

For the glaze
- Mix ¼ cup Kahlúa and confectioners' sugar in a bowl. Spoon over the warm cake.
- Let stand until cool.

SERVES SIXTEEN

PUMPKIN CAKE ROLL

1 cup confectioners' sugar
2 to 3 ounces cream cheese,
   softened
1/4 cup butter or margarine,
   softened
1/2 teaspoon vanilla extract
3 eggs
1 cup sugar
2/3 cup pumpkin

1 teaspoon lemon juice
3/4 cup flour
1 teaspoon baking powder
2 teaspoons cinnamon
1 teaspoon ginger
1/2 teaspoon nutmeg
1/2 teaspoon salt
1 cup chopped walnuts or pecans

For the filling
- Combine 1 cup confectioners' sugar, cream cheese, butter and vanilla in a mixer bowl and mix until smooth; set aside.

For the cake
- Preheat the oven to 375 degrees.
- Beat the eggs in a mixer bowl at high speed for 5 minutes.
- Add the sugar gradually, beating constantly at high speed.
- Stir in the pumpkin and lemon juice.
- Mix the flour, baking powder, cinnamon, ginger, nutmeg and salt together. Fold gently into the pumpkin mixture.
- Spread in a greased and floured 10x15-inch baking pan. Sprinkle with the walnuts.
- Bake for 15 minutes or until dry on top.
- Invert onto a towel sprinkled with additional confectioners' sugar. Roll in the towel from the narrow end.
- Let stand until cool. Unroll the cake.
- Spread the filling over the cake. Roll to enclose the filling.
- Chill until serving time.

SERVES EIGHT

I have reason to know that the "secret's in the sauce." Once I served an overly-soaked rum cake to a tee-totaler. She kept asking over and over again for the recipe—especially that wonderful sauce!

Claudia Heath Howe

BUTTER TIPS

Butter and margarine are interchangeable in recipes if both are listed in the ingredients list. Do not use low-fat spreads, soft margarine, or tub margarine unless the recipe specifically calls for these ingredients, especially in baking. They may react differently and yield less than desirable results.

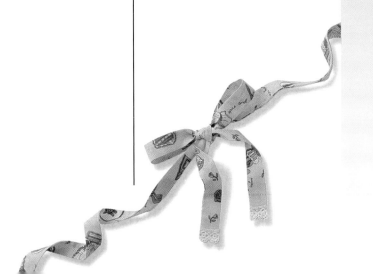

BAKED FUDGE

2 cups sugar
½ cup flour
½ cup baking cocoa
4 eggs
1 cup butter, softened
2 teaspoons vanilla extract
1 cup chopped toasted pecans
1 cup whipping cream, whipped

- Preheat the oven to 300 degrees.
- Mix the sugar, flour and baking cocoa in a bowl. Add the eggs and mix until smooth.
- Add the butter, vanilla and pecans and mix well.
- Spoon into a 9x9-inch baking pan. Set in a larger pan of hot water.
- Bake for 45 minutes or until it has the texture of a custard when tested with a knife; fudge will become more firm as it cools.
- Cool on a wire rack. Cut into squares.
- Serve with the whipped cream.

SERVES EIGHT TO TEN

MICROWAVE PRALINES

1 (1-pound) package light brown sugar
1 cup whipping cream
2 tablespoons margarine
1 cup pecan halves

- Combine the brown sugar and whipping cream in a 3-quart microwave-safe bowl.
- Microwave on High for 13 minutes.
- Stir in the margarine and pecans.
- Drop by spoonfuls onto foil. Let stand until cool.
- Store in an airtight container.

YIELDS TWO DOZEN

COCOA BONBONS

6 ounces cream cheese, softened
2 cups confectioners' sugar
½ cup baking cocoa
2 tablespoons melted butter
1 teaspoon vanilla extract
12 ounces milk chocolate chips

4 teaspoons shortening
6 tablespoons butter
3 cups confectioners' sugar
¼ cup milk
1 teaspoon vanilla extract
red, green or yellow food coloring

For the centers
- Beat the cream cheese in a small mixer bowl until light. Add 2 cups confectioners' sugar, baking cocoa, melted butter and 1 teaspoon vanilla and blend until smooth.
- Chill, covered, for several hours or until firm enough to handle.
- Shape into 1-inch balls and place on a waxed-paper-covered tray. Chill, uncovered, for 3 hours or until dry.

For the chocolate coating
- Fill a large bowl to a depth of 1 inch with 100- to 110-degree water.
- Place the chocolate chips and shortening in a medium bowl and place the bowl in the water bath.
- Stir with a spatula to blend as the shortening and chocolate melt, replacing the water if necessary as it cools; do not let any water touch the chocolate. Keep warm.

For the pastel coating
- Combine 6 tablespoons butter, 3 cups confectioners' sugar, milk and 1 teaspoon vanilla in a medium microwave-safe bowl.
- Microwave on High for 1 to 2 minutes or until smooth, stirring occasionally to blend well. Tint pastel as desired with food coloring.

To assemble the bonbons
- Place the centers in the freezer for 10 minutes. Dip 1 at a time into either the chocolate or pastel coating, using a fork and tapping the fork gently on the side of the bowl to remove the excess coating.
- Place on a waxed-paper-covered tray to stand until firm. Drizzle with a small amount of the coating not used to decorate if desired.
- Store chocolate bonbons in an airtight container in a cool place. Store pastel bonbons in the refrigerator.

SERVES TWENTY-FOUR

MINTS

Combine 1 pound of confectioners' sugar with 5 to 6 ounces softened cream cheese and ½ teaspoon mint flavoring in a food processor. Add food coloring as desired and process until smooth. Press into candy molds or pipe onto waxed paper with a confectioners' tube fitted with a baker's tip. Freeze if necessary to hold the shape.

COCOA SUBSTITUTION

Baking cocoa may be used in place of unsweetened baking chocolate in most recipes. Three tablespoons of baking cocoa plus 1 tablespoon of shortening or oil is equal to 1 ounce of unsweetened baking chocolate.

FUDGE BROWNIES

¾ cup butter, softened
1½ cups sugar
3 eggs
1 cup flour
¼ cup baking cocoa
⅛ to ¼ teaspoon salt
1 cup coarsely chopped pecans
1 teaspoon vanilla extract
¼ cup butter
2 tablespoons baking cocoa
2 tablespoons milk
1¼ cups confectioners' sugar
¼ cup coarsely chopped pecans

For the brownies
- Preheat the oven to 350 degrees.
- Cream ¾ cup butter and sugar in a mixer bowl until light and fluffy.
- Beat in the eggs 1 at a time.
- Sift the flour, ¼ cup baking cocoa and salt together. Add to the creamed mixture and mix well.
- Stir in 1 cup pecans and vanilla.
- Spoon into a greased 9x9-inch baking pan. Bake for 35 minutes or until a wooden pick inserted in the center comes out clean.

For the frosting
- Melt ¼ cup butter in a saucepan over low heat. Stir in 2 tablespoons baking cocoa and milk.
- Remove from the heat. Beat in the confectioners' sugar and ¼ cup pecans.
- Spread evenly over warm brownies. Cool on a wire rack and cut into squares.

SERVES SIXTEEN

SAUCEPAN BROWNIES

4 (1-ounce) squares unsweetened chocolate
⅔ cup margarine
2 cups sugar
4 eggs
1 teaspoon vanilla extract
1½ cups flour
½ teaspoon salt
1 cup chopped pecans

- Preheat the oven to 375 degrees.
- Melt the chocolate with the margarine in a saucepan over low heat, stirring constantly to blend. Remove from the heat.
- Stir in the sugar, eggs, vanilla, flour, salt and pecans in the order listed.
- Spoon into a greased 9x13-inch baking pan.
- Bake for 15 to 20 minutes or until the brownies test done.
- Cool on a wire rack. Cut into squares.

Garnish with confectioners' sugar sifted over the top.

SERVES SIXTEEN

DELICIOUS COOKIES

1 cup sugar
1 cup packed brown sugar
1 cup margarine, softened
1 cup vegetable oil
1 egg
2 teaspoons vanilla extract
3½ cups flour
1 teaspoon baking soda

1 teaspoon cream of tartar
1 teaspoon salt
1 cup shredded coconut
1 cup rolled oats
½ cup cornflakes
½ cup crisp rice cereal
1 cup chocolate chips
½ cup chopped pecans

- Preheat the oven to 350 degrees.
- Mix the sugar and brown sugar in a mixer bowl. Add the margarine and oil and beat until smooth.
- Add the egg and vanilla and mix well.
- Sift the flour, baking soda, cream of tartar and salt together.
- Add to the sugar mixture and mix well.
- Stir in the coconut, rolled oats, cornflakes and rice cereal.
- Stir in the chocolate chips and pecans.
- Drop by teaspoonfuls onto ungreased cookie sheets.
- Bake for 12 to 15 minutes or until light brown.
- Cool on the cookie sheets for several minutes. Remove to a wire rack to cool completely.

Note: Because this recipe makes a large quantity and they freeze well, it is a good choice for a cookie swap or fund raiser.

YIELDS FIVE DOZEN

AMARETTO BROWNIES

Combine 1 package brownie mix with 3 tablespoons vegetable oil, 2 eggs and scant ½ cup amaretto. Spoon into a greased and floured 9x13-inch baking pan and bake at 350 degrees for 30 to 35 minutes or until the brownies test done.

BROWNIE TIPS

Shiny pans are best for baking brownies, as well as cakes and other cookies, because they reflect heat and produce lighter, more delicate crusts. Dull metal or glass pans produce crisp, brown crusts. Brownies and other sticky bar cookies and desserts will slice more easily with a plastic knife.

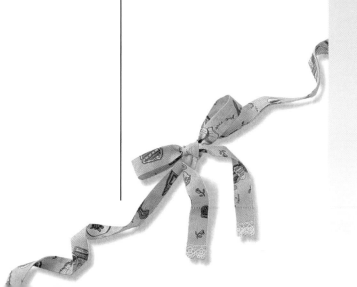

HILLARY CLINTON'S COOKIES

1 cup shortening
½ cup sugar
1 cup packed light brown sugar
1 teaspoon vanilla extract
2 eggs
1½ cups flour
1 teaspoon baking soda
1 teaspoon salt
2 cups rolled oats
2 cups semisweet chocolate chips

- Preheat the oven to 350 degrees.
- Cream the shortening, sugar, brown sugar and vanilla in a large bowl until light and fluffy.
- Add the eggs and beat until smooth.
- Mix the flour, baking soda and salt together. Add to the creamed mixture gradually and mix well.
- Stir in the oats and chocolate chips.
- Drop by rounded teaspoonfuls onto greased cookie sheets.
- Bake for 8 to 10 minutes or until golden brown.
- Cool on the cookie sheets for 2 minutes. Remove to a wire rack to cool completely.

YIELDS THREE DOZEN

SUGAR COOKIES

1 cup butter or margarine, softened
1 cup sugar
1 cup confectioners' sugar
2 eggs
1 cup vegetable oil
4½ cups flour
1 teaspoon cream of tartar
1 teaspoon baking soda
1 teaspoon salt
1 tablespoon vanilla extract
1 teaspoon almond extract
white or tinted sugar

- Preheat the oven to 350 degrees.
- Combine the butter, 1 cup sugar, confectioners' sugar and eggs in a mixer bowl and beat until smooth. Add the oil gradually, beating constantly.
- Add the flour, cream of tartar, baking soda, salt and flavorings and mix well.
- Shape into small balls and place on greased cookie sheets.
- Dip the bottom of a glass in additional sugar and press each ball to flatten.
- Bake for 10 minutes.
- Cool on the cookie sheets for several minutes. Remove to a wire rack to cool completely.

Note: To tint sugar, mix with several drops of food coloring to achieve the desired shade.

YIELDS FOUR DOZEN

TEA COOKIES

1 cup butter, softened
1 cup vegetable oil
1 cup sugar
1 cup sifted confectioners' sugar
2 large eggs

1 teaspoon vanilla extract
4 cups flour
1 teaspoon baking soda
1 teaspoon cream of tartar
1 teaspoon salt

- Combine the butter and oil in a mixer bowl and beat at medium speed until smooth.
- Add the sugar and confectioners' sugar gradually, beating constantly. Beat in the eggs and vanilla.
- Mix the flour, baking soda, cream of tartar and salt together.
- Add to the butter mixture and mix well.
- Chill in the refrigerator.
- Preheat the oven to 350 degrees.
- Shape into 1-inch balls and place 2 to 3 inches apart on cookie sheets.
- Chill for 5 to 10 minutes longer. Press with the end of a plastic thread spool to make a decorative design if desired.
- Bake for 9 to 12 minutes or until the edges are light brown.
- Sprinkle with additional sugar while warm if desired. Cool on the cookie sheets for several minutes. Remove to wire racks to cool completely.
- Freeze in airtight containers for up to 1 month.

Note: Chilling the shaped cookies keeps them from sticking to the spoon and from spreading too much as they bake. They may be dropped onto the cookie sheet without chilling if preferred.

YIELDS FOUR DOZEN

My dad has perfected certain culinary specialties—including the most delicious, melt-in-your-mouth sugar cookies. One day I decided to make these cookies. I had not made a lot of cookies before, but I was armed with Dad's wonderful recipe, and all I had to do was follow directions. I measured all the ingredients carefully, made the cookie dough, and rolled it into small balls. However, the next step in the directions really stumped me. So I gave Dad a quick call. "Dad, how much water do you need to put in the water glass? The recipe says to place the balls of cookie dough onto a baking sheet and to lightly press them down with a water glass." My dad, quite the jokester, said, "Oh, about half a glass of water should do." When he could no longer contain his laughter, I realized that my predisposition to literal thinking had led to a rather stupid assumption—that there had to be water in the water glass that pressed the cookie dough down.

Michelle Howard

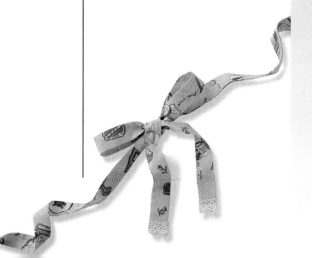

189

LEMON WAFERS

1 cup butter, softened
1 cup sugar
1 large egg
1 teaspoon vanilla extract
2 cups cake flour
2 tablespoons grated lemon peel
sliced almonds

- Preheat the oven to 350 degrees.
- Cream the butter and sugar in a large mixer bowl until light and fluffy.
- Beat in the egg and vanilla.
- Add the flour gradually. Stir in the lemon peel.
- Drop by heaping half-teaspoonfuls 2 inches apart onto ungreased cookie sheets.
- Press several almonds gently into the center of each cookie.
- Bake for 8 to 10 minutes or until the edges are golden brown.
- Cool on the cookie sheets for 2 minutes. Remove to a wire rack to cool completely.

YIELDS TWO DOZEN

MOLASSES COOKIES

³/4 cup shortening
1 cup sugar
1 egg
2 teaspoons baking soda
¹/4 cup molasses
2 cups flour
1 teaspoon ginger
1 teaspoon cinnamon
¹/2 teaspoon salt
sugar

- Preheat the oven to 375 degrees.
- Cream the shortening and 1 cup sugar in a mixer bowl until light and fluffy. Beat in the egg.
- Blend the baking soda into the molasses in a small bowl.
- Add the molasses mixture, flour, ginger, cinnamon and salt to the creamed mixture and mix well.
- Shape teaspoonfuls into balls. Roll in additional sugar.
- Place on cookie sheets and press with a fork.
- Bake for 8 to 9 minutes or until golden brown.
- Cool on the cookie sheets for several minutes. Remove to a wire rack to cool completely.

YIELDS TWO DOZEN

OATMEAL MACAROON COOKIES

½ cup shortening
½ cup margarine, softened
1 cup sugar
1 cup packed brown sugar
2 eggs
1 teaspoon vanilla extract

½ teaspoon almond extract
1¼ cups flour
1 teaspoon baking soda
½ teaspoon salt
3 cups quick-cooking oats
1 cup shredded coconut

- Preheat the oven to 350 degrees.
- Cream the shortening, margarine, sugar and brown sugar in a mixer bowl until light and fluffy.
- Beat in the eggs and flavorings.
- Mix the flour, baking soda and salt together. Add to the creamed mixture and mix well.
- Stir in the oats and coconut. Drop by spoonfuls onto cookie sheets.
- Bake for 8 to 10 minutes or until golden brown.
- Cool on the cookie sheets for 2 or 3 minutes. Remove to a wire rack to cool completely.

Variation: For Oatmeal Cookies, *omit the coconut.*

Note: *These are very moist cookies. If they are stacked before they cool completely, they will stick together.*

YIELDS FOUR DOZEN

I always loved my grandmother's kitchen. It was a magical place for me as a child—smelling of coffee and cookies baking. In fact, some of my fondest memories of "Nana" are of her making cookies. At one of my bridal showers, Nana gave me a gift with a note attached that read "To a real sweet cookie. Love, Nana." In the box was her own cookie jar. It was cream-colored with the word "Cookies" written on both the front and the back, along with painted gingerbread men and little men in baker's hats. Little did Nana know that this was the key to so many of my precious childhood memories. Above all the exquisite crystal and silver pieces I received, that ceramic cookie jar was my favorite wedding gift. Whenever I see it, thoughts of Nana and all her sweetness come back to me.

Sheila McCown Hartzell

191

SYMPHONY® COOKIES

1 cup unsalted butter, softened
1 cup sugar
1 cup packed light brown sugar
2 eggs
2 teaspoons vanilla extract
2½ cups flour
1 teaspoon baking powder
1 teaspoon baking soda
½ teaspoon salt
3 cups rolled oats
1 Symphony® candy bar with toffee and
  almonds, chopped
2 cups semisweet chocolate chips
1½ cups chopped English walnuts (optional)

- Preheat the oven to 350 degrees.
- Combine the butter, sugar, brown sugar, eggs and vanilla in a bowl and beat until smooth.
- Mix the flour, baking powder, baking soda, salt and oats together.
- Add to the sugar mixture gradually, beating constantly.
- Stir in the candy, chocolate chips and walnuts.
- Drop by spoonfuls 2 inches apart onto ungreased cookie sheets.
- Bake for 10 to 12 minutes or until golden brown.
- Serve with cold milk.

YIELDS FOUR DOZEN

BANANA PUDDING

⅓ cup flour
⅔ cup sugar
2 cups milk
3 egg yolks, beaten
¼ teaspoon salt
2 tablespoons butter
1 teaspoon vanilla extract
1 package vanilla wafers
5 or 6 bananas, sliced
3 egg whites
3 tablespoons sugar
¼ teaspoon vanilla extract

For the pudding
- Combine the flour, ⅔ cup sugar, milk, egg yolks and salt in a saucepan. Cook over medium heat until thickened, stirring constantly.
- Remove from the heat and add the butter and 1 teaspoon vanilla. Cool slightly.
- Layer the vanilla wafers, bananas and pudding mixture ½ at a time in a deep baking dish.

For the meringue
- Beat the egg whites with 3 tablespoons sugar and ¼ teaspoon vanilla in a mixer bowl until stiff peaks form.
- Spread over the pudding, sealing to the edge.
- Bake for 15 minutes or just until the meringue is light brown.
- Serve warm.

SERVES SIX

FRUIT COBBLER

¹/₄ cup butter, softened
¹/₂ cup sugar
1 cup flour
2 teaspoons baking powder
¹/₂ cup milk

2¹/₂ cups fresh or frozen berries
¹/₄ cup sugar
¹/₄ teaspoon cinnamon
2 tablespoons bourbon
1¹/₂ cups fruit juice or water

- Preheat the oven to 375 degrees.
- Cream the butter and ¹/₂ cup sugar in a mixer bowl until light and fluffy.
- Mix the flour and baking powder together. Add to the creamed mixture alternately with the milk, mixing well after each addition.
- Spoon into a lightly greased shallow 2-quart baking dish. Spoon the berries over the batter.
- Mix ¹/₄ cup sugar and cinnamon in a small bowl. Sprinkle over the berries. Mix the bourbon with the fruit juice. Pour over the fruit.
- Bake for 45 to 50 minutes or until the top is golden brown.
- Serve warm with ice cream.

SERVES SIX

Blackberry cobbler with vanilla ice cream represents all the best memories of my childhood. My family often spent Sunday afternoons picking wild blackberries at my grandfather's farm. Our stomachs usually held more blackberries than our buckets, but we were always able to bring home enough for a cobbler. In an old yellow bowl, my mom would create a work of art with berries and pie crust woven into a beautiful lattice top. She would place it in the oven and set the timer to complete the baking process as we returned from evening services. Our home always welcomed friends, and these Sunday evenings were incomplete without another family or two sharing our treasure. It was the perfect ending to a weekend. The fruit cobbler that I make now is a much easier version. My favorite variation uses fresh blackberries with cranberry/apple juice as the liquid.

Beth Ann Waldrup

CHOCOLATE BUTTER GOOEY

1 (2-layer) package butter-recipe chocolate cake mix
10 tablespoons butter, melted
1 egg, lightly beaten
8 ounces cream cheese, softened
1 (1-pound) package confectioners' sugar
2 eggs
½ cup chocolate chips

- Preheat the oven to 350 degrees.
- Combine the cake mix, butter and 1 lightly beaten egg in a mixer bowl and mix well.
- Press into a greased and floured 9x13-inch baking pan.
- Beat the cream cheese and confectioners' sugar in a mixer bowl until light.
- Add 2 eggs and mix well. Stir in the chocolate chips.
- Spread over the layer in the prepared baking pan.
- Bake for 30 to 40 minutes or until light brown.
- Cut into squares to serve.

Variation: For **Vanilla Butter Gooey,** *use a yellow cake mix and omit the chocolate chips.*

SERVES TWENTY-FOUR

CHOCOLATE POTS DE CRÈME

1 cup semisweet chocolate chips
¼ cup sugar
1 egg, or equivalent amount of egg substitute
¾ cup milk, scalded
⅛ teaspoon salt
1 teaspoon vanilla extract

- Combine the chocolate chips, sugar, egg, milk, salt and vanilla in a blender container.
- Blend at high speed for 1 minute or until smooth.
- Pour immediately into 6 small dessert glasses.
- Chill in the refrigerator.

Garnish with whipped cream, a fresh strawberry and a sprinkle of nutmeg.

SERVES SIX

CHOCOLATE SOUFFLÉ

1½ cups milk
6 tablespoons cornstarch
2 tablespoons butter
2 tablespoons sugar
2 teaspoons cocoa mix
3 ounces semisweet chocolate

2 tablespoons rum
6 egg yolks
6 egg whites
6 tablespoons sugar
St. Cecelia Sauce

- Preheat the oven to 375 degrees.
- Combine the milk, cornstarch, butter, 2 tablespoons sugar and cocoa mix in a saucepan. Cook until very thick, whisking constantly.
- Microwave the chocolate just until melted. Add to the saucepan and mix well. Remove from the heat and place on a damp folded cloth to cool.
- Beat in the rum and egg yolks.
- Beat the egg whites until soft peaks form. Add 6 tablespoons sugar gradually, beating constantly until stiff peaks form.
- Fold ⅓ of the egg whites gently into the chocolate mixture with a wire whisk. Fold in the remaining egg whites.
- Butter six 8-ounce soufflé dishes and sprinkle with additional sugar. Spoon the custard into the dishes.
- Bake for 20 minutes or until the soufflés rise.
- Serve with St. Cecelia Sauce.

Note: This may be prepared up to the baking step and frozen.

ST. CECELIA SAUCE

2 cups whipping cream
1 egg yolk, or equivalent amount
  of egg substitute

2¼ cups confectioners' sugar
Grand Marnier to taste

- Beat the whipping cream in a mixer bowl until soft peaks form.
- Combine the egg yolk, confectioners' sugar and Grand Marnier in a bowl and mix well.
- Fold into the whipped cream.
- Store in the refrigerator.

SERVES SIX

When I was six years old, my mother planned an important dinner party and had been cooking all week. The day before the party, she carefully prepared twelve pots de crème and put them in the refrigerator to chill. At the end of three very successful dinner courses, Mom prepared to present the pièce de résistance—her pots de crème. In great anticipation, the guests lifted the antique tops of the pots only to find that they had been scraped clean. I had eaten every last one of them the night before and replaced the tops so that I wouldn't be caught!

On a serious note, my grandmother died in 1993, and somehow, when cleaning out her house, her recipe box was lost. I would do anything to have the recipes for her fried chicken, homemade rolls, boiled custard, and her wonderful homemade pies: pies that had been baked early in the morning long before I got up, so I never got the chance to see exactly how she made them so special.

Andria Nowlin Beckham

CHOCOLATE CRÈME BRÛLÉE

2 cups whipping cream
2 cups half-and-half
8 ounces semisweet chocolate, chopped
1/3 cup sugar
8 large egg yolks
8 tablespoons sugar

• Preheat the oven to 300 degrees.
• Bring the cream and half-and-half to a boil in a heavy saucepan and reduce the heat to low.
• Add the chocolate and cook until melted, whisking constantly. Remove from the heat.
• Whisk 1/3 cup sugar and egg yolks into the mixture. Strain into 8 custard cups.
• Place the custard cups in a baking pan and add enough hot water to reach halfway up the sides. Bake for 50 minutes. Remove from the water.
• Cool for 2 hours. Chill, covered, for 8 hours or longer.
• Preheat the broiler. Sprinkle the top of each custard with 1 tablespoon sugar. Broil for 3 minutes or until golden brown.
• Chill for 1 to 2 hours.

SERVES EIGHT

FUDGE MELT-AWAYS

1/2 cup butter
1 square unsweetened chocolate
1/4 cup sugar
2 cups graham cracker crumbs
1 cup shredded coconut
1/2 cup chopped pecans or almonds
1 teaspoon vanilla extract
1/4 cup butter, softened
1 tablespoon milk or cream
2 cups confectioners' sugar
1 teaspoon vanilla extract
1 1/2 squares unsweetened chocolate

• Melt 1/2 cup butter and 1 square chocolate in a saucepan and mix well.
• Stir in the sugar, cracker crumbs, coconut, pecans and 1 teaspoon vanilla.
• Press into a 9x9-inch or 7x11-inch dish. Chill in the refrigerator.
• Mix 1/4 cup butter, milk, confectioners' sugar and vanilla in a mixer bowl.
• Spread over the crumb layer. Chill in the refrigerator.
• Melt 1 1/2 squares chocolate in a double boiler over simmering water.
• Spread over the chilled layers. Chill until nearly firm.
• Cut into small squares. Chill until firm.

Variation: Add 1 beaten egg with the cracker crumbs.

YIELDS FOUR DOZEN

TURTLE-PECAN SWIRL CHEESECAKE

2 cups crushed chocolate wafers
¼ cup melted butter
20 ounces cream cheese, softened
1 cup sugar
1½ tablespoons flour
salt to taste

1 teaspoon vanilla extract
3 eggs
2 tablespoons whipping cream
Caramel Topping
Chocolate Topping
1 cup toasted chopped pecans

- Preheat the oven to 450 degrees.
- Combine the cookie crumbs and melted butter in a bowl and mix well. Press over the bottom of a 9-inch springform pan.
- Beat the cream cheese in a mixer bowl until light. Add the sugar, flour, salt and vanilla and mix well. Beat in the eggs 1 at a time. Blend in the whipping cream. Pour into the prepared pan. Bake for 10 minutes.
- Reduce the oven temperature to 200 degrees. Bake for 35 to 40 minutes longer or until set.
- Loosen the cheesecake from the side of the pan with a knife. Cool on a wire rack. Place on a serving plate and remove the side of the pan.
- Drizzle with Caramel Topping and Chocolate Topping.
- Chill for several hours. Sprinkle with the pecans just before serving.

CARAMEL TOPPING

7 ounces caramels   ¾ cup whipping cream

- Melt the caramels with the whipping cream in a small saucepan over low heat, stirring constantly.

CHOCOLATE TOPPING

1 (4-ounce) package German's
  sweet chocolate

1 teaspoon butter
2 tablespoons whipping cream

- Melt the chocolate and butter with the whipping cream in a small saucepan over low heat, stirring constantly.

SERVES TWELVE

197

CHOCOLATE SPOONS

Melt 8 ounces semisweet chocolate and 4 ounces white chocolate in separate saucepans. Dip 16 heavy plastic spoons into the dark chocolate and drizzle with the white chocolate. Place on waxed paper and let stand at room temperature until firm. Serve with coffee for a great after-dinner treat.

LIGHT CHEESECAKE

Neufchâtel cheese can be substituted for cream cheese to reduce the fat content in cheesecake but will result in a slightly different taste and texture.

ICE CREAM PARTY SQUARES

1 cup vanilla wafer crumbs
4 (1-ounce) squares unsweetened chocolate
1⅓ cups butter or margarine
3 cups sifted confectioners' sugar
¼ cup water
1 cup toasted chopped pecans
2 teaspoons vanilla extract
8 egg whites
½ teaspoon cream of tartar
½ gallon butter-pecan ice cream in a
   rectangular container

- Sprinkle the cookie crumbs in a buttered 9x13-inch dish.
- Melt the chocolate and butter in a small saucepan over low heat, stirring to blend well. Remove from the heat.
- Add the confectioners' sugar, water, pecans and vanilla and mix well.
- Beat the eggs whites with the cream of tartar in a mixer bowl until stiff peaks form. Fold into the chocolate mixture.
- Spread in the prepared dish. Freeze for 3 hours.
- Cut the ice cream into ½-inch slices. Arrange over the frozen layer. Smooth the top.
- Freeze, covered, until firm.
- Let stand at room temperature for 5 minutes. Cut into squares.

Garnish servings with toffee chips, shaved chocolate and/or pecans.

SERVES TWELVE TO FIFTEEN

ORANGE-BASIL SORBET

¾ cup sugar
¾ cup water
2 cups freshly squeezed orange juice
3 tablespoons Grand Marnier
3 tablespoons freshly grated orange zest
1 cup lightly packed chopped basil

- Combine the sugar and water in a small saucepan. Cook over medium-high heat for 5 minutes or until the sugar dissolves and the mixture is simmering. Remove from the heat.
- Measure ¾ cup of the syrup and combine it with the orange juice, Grand Marnier, orange zest and basil.
- Let stand for 1 hour.
- Strain into ice cube trays or an ice cream machine. Freeze until firm; stir the mixture in ice cubes trays occasionally to break up crystals.
- Process in a food processor until smooth. Return to the freezer and freeze for 15 minutes longer.
- Let stand in the refrigerator long enough to soften slightly.

Garnish with fresh basil flowers.

Note: This is delicious as a palate cleanser between courses.

SERVES SIX

ISLAND FRUIT TRIFLE

½ cup sugar
3 tablespoons cornstarch
¼ teaspoon salt
3 cups milk
½ cup coconut- or pineapple-
   flavored rum
3 egg yolks, beaten
3 tablespoons margarine or butter
1 tablespoon vanilla extract

4 bananas, sliced
1 quart strawberries, sliced
coconut- or pineapple-flavored
   rum or liqueur
2 packages Keebler Sparkling
   Sugar Cookies, crushed
1 cup whipping cream
2 tablespoons sugar
½ cup toasted almonds

For the custard

- Combine ½ cup sugar, cornstarch and salt in a saucepan. Stir in the milk and ½ cup rum gradually.
- Bring to a boil over medium heat, stirring constantly. Cook for 1 minute, stirring constantly.
- Blend ½ of the hot mixture into the egg yolks; blend the egg yolks gradually into the hot mixture in the saucepan.
- Cook for 1 minute, stirring constantly. Remove from the heat.
- Stir in the margarine and vanilla. Chill, covered, for 3 hours or longer.

For the trifle

- Sprinkle the bananas and strawberries with additional rum and let stand for several minutes.
- Layer half the cookies in a 2-quart trifle bowl or glass serving bowl. Sprinkle with rum.
- Layer half the fruit and half the custard in the bowl. Repeat the layers.
- Chill, covered, in the refrigerator.
- Beat the whipping cream with 2 tablespoons sugar in a mixer bowl until soft peaks form. Spread over the trifle.
- Sprinkle with the almonds.

Variation: Use other fruits in season in this recipe and use the amount of rum to suit individual tastes. For a **Quick Trifle**, *substitute instant pie filling mix made with milk and rum for the custard.*

SERVES TEN

PEACH ICE CREAM

Peel and slice 8 to 10 peaches, discarding the pits. Process with sugar to taste in the blender. Combine with 1 large package vanilla instant pudding mix, 1 large can evaporated milk and 2 cans sweetened condensed milk in an ice cream freezer container. Fill with milk to the fill line and freeze using the manufacturer's directions.

FOOD PROCESSOR PIE PASTRY

3 cups flour
1 cup shortening, chilled
1½ teaspoons salt
1 egg
½ cup cold water
1 teaspoon white vinegar

- Combine the flour, shortening and salt in a food processor container fitted with a metal blade.
- Pulse for 15 seconds.
- Add the egg, water and vinegar. Process until the mixture forms a dough.
- Chill, covered, for 1 hour.
- Roll on a floured surface and proceed with recipe instructions.

YIELDS THREE PIE SHELLS

SOUR CREAM APPLE PIE

⅓ cup slivered almonds
⅓ cup sugar
¼ cup butter
4 cups sliced peeled Granny Smith apples
1 tablespoon lemon juice
2 tablespoons flour
¾ cup sugar
2 eggs, lightly beaten
1 cup sour cream
½ teaspoon almond extract
¼ teaspoon salt
1 unbaked (9-inch) pie shell

For the topping

- Mix the almonds and ⅓ cup sugar in a bowl.
- Cut in the butter with 2 knives or a pastry blender until the mixture resembles coarse crumbs. Set aside.

For the pie

- Preheat the oven to 350 degrees.
- Toss the apples with the lemon juice in a bowl.
- Mix the flour and ¾ cup sugar in a bowl. Add the eggs, sour cream, almond extract and salt and mix until smooth.
- Add the apples. Spoon into the pie shell.
- Bake for 30 minutes.
- Sprinkle with the topping. Bake for 15 to 18 minutes longer or until golden brown.
- Serve warm or chilled.

SERVES SIX TO EIGHT

SOUR CREAM BLUEBERRY PIE

3 tablespoons flour
3 tablespoons unsalted butter, softened
¼ cup chopped pecans or walnuts
1 cup sour cream
2 tablespoons flour

¾ cup sugar
1 large egg, beaten
1 teaspoon vanilla extract
¼ teaspoon salt
2½ cups fresh blueberries
1 unbaked (9-inch) pie shell

For the topping
- Combine 3 tablespoons flour, butter and pecans in a bowl and mix until crumbly. Set aside.

For the pie
- Preheat the oven to 400 degrees.
- Combine the sour cream, 2 tablespoons flour, sugar, egg, vanilla and salt in a bowl and mix until smooth.
- Fold in the blueberries. Spoon into the pie shell.
- Bake for 25 minutes.
- Sprinkle with the topping. Bake for 10 minutes longer.
- Cool to room temperature. Chill until serving time.

SERVES EIGHT

CHOCOLATE CURLS

Melt semisweet, white or milk chocolate in a double boiler. Spread the melted chocolate in a thin layer on a cookie sheet. Cool for 5 to 10 minutes or until firm but still slightly malleable; this stage is very important. Scrape the chocolate into strips with an upside-down spatula, pushing slowly but evenly from one end to the other. Let stand until completely firm before using to decorate.

BROWNIE FUDGE PIE

½ cup butter, softened
1 cup sugar
2 ounces unsweetened chocolate, melted
¼ cup flour
2 eggs, beaten
1 teaspoon vanilla extract
⅛ teaspoon salt
1 unbaked (9-inch) pie shell

- Preheat the oven to 325 degrees.
- Cream the butter and sugar in a mixer bowl until light and fluffy.
- Add the chocolate, flour, eggs, vanilla and salt and mix well.
- Spoon into the pie shell.
- Bake for 30 minutes.

Variation: For **Miniature Brownie Fudge Tarts,** *spoon the filling into prepared miniature tart shells and bake for 15 to 20 minutes or until set.*

SERVES EIGHT

PECAN PIE

1 cup white corn syrup
½ cup sugar
3 eggs
2 tablespoons butter
salt to taste
1 cup pecans
1 tablespoon vanilla extract
1 unbaked (9-inch) pie shell

- Preheat the oven to 350 degrees.
- Combine the corn syrup, sugar, eggs, butter and salt in a bowl and mix well.
- Stir in the pecans and vanilla.
- Spoon into the pie shell.
- Bake for 30 to 40 minutes or until firm to the touch.

SERVES EIGHT

RASPBERRY CREAM PIE

*1½ cups vanilla wafer crumbs, or
33 cookies, crushed*
⅓ cup chopped pecans
¼ cup melted butter
8 ounces cream cheese, softened
⅔ cup confectioners' sugar
*2 tablespoons Grand Marnier or
Triple Sec*
1 teaspoon vanilla extract

1 cup whipping cream
1 cup sugar
*2½ cups fresh or frozen
raspberries*
1 tablespoon water
*2 tablespoons (heaping)
cornstarch*
2 tablespoons water

For the pastry
• Preheat the oven to 350 degrees.
• Combine the cookie crumbs, pecans and butter in a food processor fitted
  with a metal blade. Pulse until well mixed.
• Press over the bottom and side of an 8-inch pie plate.
• Bake for 5 to 7 minutes. Cool completely.

For the filling
• Blend the cream cheese and confectioners' sugar in a mixer bowl until
  light and fluffy. Scrape the side of the bowl.
• Add the liqueur and vanilla and mix well.
• Beat the whipping cream in a bowl until soft peaks form. Fold the
  whipped cream into the cream cheese mixture. Spoon into the cooled
  pie shell and spread evenly. Chill in the refrigerator.

For the topping
• Combine the sugar, raspberries and 1 tablespoon water in a heavy
  medium saucepan. Bring to a full boil, stirring occasionally. Remove from
  the heat.
• Dissolve the cornstarch in 2 tablespoons water in a small bowl. Stir into
  the raspberry mixture.
• Cook over medium heat for 3 to 5 minutes or until thickened, stirring
  constantly; mixture should be smooth and glossy.
• Cool to room temperature.
• Spread over the pie. Chill until serving time.

SERVES SIX TO EIGHT

*Every time we went to Mamaw's
house, she would prepare her
special coconut cream pie. The pie
was always loaded with coconut,
and the meringue was piled high,
with more coconut sprinkled on top.
I would watch in awe as she made
them. She used no recipe, just
opened the cabinets, grabbed the
ingredients, and mixed without
measuring. Yet the pies always tasted
the same—mouthwatering delicious!
My husband says that really good
cooks just use a recipe as a guide,
and measuring is for rookies. He
may be right. His cooking is always
wonderful, and just like my
Mamaw, he just grabs ingredients
and throws them together. What
about me? Well, I just sell—and
use—cookbooks.*

Angela Newsom Hopkins

Holiday Brunch

BRUNCH

Pecan Praline Crunch
Fresh Fruit Salad
Baked French Toast
Canadian Bacon
Savory Cheese Strata
Muddy Blarys
Coffee

A Holiday Meal Memory

Granny Ramey didn't know about the word brunch. In her home, breakfast was followed by
the noontime meal, which was dinner. Nobody could have reduced "breakfast-dinner"
to anything sounding appealing, even if they had a week to think about it.

What she could reduce, Luna Ramey could, was cabbage, onions, peppers, some tiny red things,
and who knew what else. She cooked everything down in vinegar and sugar until...until more than half
a century later it remains impossible not to salivate at the thought of this delicious concoction.
In any publication less elegant and widely acclaimed as this, the word would have
come out slobber. "Choss, you are excused from the table."

In those days, say the Thanksgiving or Christmas I was eight, the trip from our home in McGehee
to Granny Ramey's in Mountain Home was an all-day exercise in child torture. This was largely thanks
to the man behind the wheel. Our dad drove like he was piloting a glacier, one foot on the brake
going up mountains. It took a thousand naps to get there, each nap emerged from into a thought-picture
of a white cloth covering items in the middle of Granny's dining table. Underneath the cloth,
protected from whatever, were the sugar bowl, the salt and pepper shakers,
and a dish of what I have tried to describe.

Chomp and smack. Grownups put it on their peas, but I never had time for that.
Spoon it and eat it. Luna Ramey went to sleep in 1965 and has not yet had enough
rest for somebody who worked 80-some years. But, one of these holidays,
I'm going to rouse her long enough to get the recipe. On purpose, she'll leave something out.
I'll just have to make do until I can catch up with her and get the real thing.
They'll all be eating it there.

CHARLES ALLBRIGHT

Eggs au Gratin

8 hard-cooked eggs
salt and pepper to taste
8 medium fresh mushrooms,
    chopped
8 teaspoons chopped onion
3 to 4 tablespoons butter

3 to 4 tablespoons flour
1/4 cup butter
1 1/2 cups milk
1/2 cup cream
1 cup shredded Cheddar cheese
paprika to taste

- Preheat the oven to 350 degrees.
- Cut the eggs into halves lengthwise. Remove the yolks to a bowl and mash. Add salt and pepper.
- Sauté the mushrooms and onion in 3 to 4 tablespoons butter in a skillet. Cool.
- Add to the egg yolks and mix well.
- Fill the egg whites with the mixture. Place the eggs in a greased shallow baking dish.
- Blend the flour into 1/4 cup melted butter in a saucepan. Cook over low heat for 4 minutes, stirring constantly.
- Stir in the milk and cream gradually. Cook until smooth and thickened, stirring constantly.
- Pour the white sauce over the eggs. Sprinkle with the cheese and paprika.
- Bake for 30 minutes.

Note: The casserole may be prepared in advance and stored in the refrigerator. Bring to room temperature before baking.

SERVES EIGHT

My grandmother died four years ago, so all I have now are memories of her. A surprising number of these memories are linked to special meals. Grandmother was from Hardy, a small town in northeast Arkansas, and, until this past year, my family still had the tiny three-room cottage where she spent her summers near the Spring River. When I was growing up, we would go to Hardy for several weeks during the summer. In the mornings, I would awaken to the smell of fried green tomatoes, buttered toast, ham, grits, and red-eye gravy. Of course, I'd have to swim nearly all day to work those delicious calories off!

Another favorite food memory is associated with my mother. Whenever she made pies, she would take the leftover pastry and make "stick me's." She would roll out the extra pie pastry into a rectangle, spread it with butter, and sprinkle sugar and cinnamon on top. Then she would roll it up and bake it until crispy and light brown. I still remember how, as a child, I looked forward to this yummy treat.

Betsey Crow Mowery

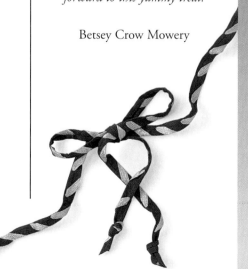

CLASSIC BRUNCH CASSEROLE

16 ounces sharp Cheddar cheese, shredded
1 (4-ounce) can chopped mild green chiles
3 eggs, beaten
3 cups milk
1 cup baking mix
1 teaspoon salt
Tabasco sauce to taste

- Preheat the oven to 350 degrees.
- Layer half the cheese, green chiles and remaining cheese in a buttered 7x11-inch baking dish.
- Combine the eggs and milk in a bowl and mix well. Add the baking mix, salt and Tabasco sauce and mix well.
- Pour over the layers, covering the cheese completely.
- Bake for 40 to 45 minutes or until brown and bubbly.

SERVES EIGHT

SAVORY CHEESE STRATA

1 large onion, chopped
2 tablespoons unsalted butter
1 (8-ounce) baguette
1 pound Monterey Jack cheese, shredded
¼ cup minced fresh rosemary
3 cups whipping cream
10 eggs
1 teaspoon salt
pepper to taste

- Sauté the onion in the butter in a skillet over medium heat until golden brown.
- Cut the baguette into 1-inch-thick slices and toast.
- Layer the bread slices, cheese, onion and rosemary ½ at a time in a buttered 9x13-inch baking dish.
- Whisk the cream, eggs, salt and pepper in a bowl. Pour over the layers.
- Chill, covered, in the refrigerator for 8 to 10 hours.
- Preheat the oven to 375 degrees.
- Bake the strata, uncovered, for 40 minutes or until golden brown and bubbly.
- Serve at breakfast with fresh fruit and muffins or for brunch with marinated asparagus and popovers.

SERVES TEN

CRAB MEAT BRUNCH SCRAMBLE

1 (6-ounce) package frozen ready-
  to-serve crab meat
2 tablespoons sliced green onions
1/4 cup butter or margarine
8 eggs, lightly beaten
1/2 cup reduced-fat sour cream

2 tablespoons grated Parmesan
  cheese
1/2 teaspoon salt
1/8 teaspoon pepper
3 English muffins, split
butter

- Thaw the crab meat and drain. Cook the crab meat and green onions in 1/4 cup butter in a skillet over medium-high heat until the green onions are tender, stirring constantly.
- Combine the eggs, sour cream, cheese, salt and pepper in a bowl and mix well. Add to the crab meat.
- Cook, without stirring, until the mixture begins to set on the bottom.
- Stir gently from the bottom until soft curds form. Cook until the eggs are thickened but still moist, stirring only occasionally.
- Spread the English muffins with additional butter and toast.
- Serve the egg mixture over the muffin halves.

SERVES SIX

When I was growing up, my mother would prepare breakfast for my brother, my sister, and me every morning. We would sit around the family table, and just before the school bus came to pick us up, my dad would make his appearance, half asleep, with his robe on and his hair all mussed. He wanted to be sure to send us off with a word of encouragement, so he would take his fist and hit the crack between the leaves in the table and say, "Hit the line hard. Don't foul, don't flinch." The breakfast dishes would bounce up in the air, reverberating his sentiments. We always went to school with a full tummy, thanks to Mom, and determination, thanks to Dad.

Marge Anna Mosley Ray

SOUTHWESTERN HUEVOS

2 tablespoons sour cream
12 eggs
½ large jar picante sauce
1 pound sausage
1 medium onion, chopped
8 ounces fresh mushrooms, sliced
8 ounces Monterey Jack cheese, shredded
8 ounces Cheddar cheese, shredded

• Preheat the oven to 350 degrees.
• Combine the sour cream and the eggs in a mixer bowl and beat well. Pour into a greased 9x12-inch baking dish.
• Bake for 15 minutes or until set. Pour the picante sauce over the eggs and cool.
• Reduce the oven temperature to 300 degrees.
• Brown the sausage in a skillet, stirring until crumbly; drain. Layer the sausage, onion and mushrooms over the picante sauce. Top with the cheeses.
• Bake for 30 minutes longer. Serve warm or cool.

Garnish with tomato slices and green bell pepper.

Variation: Substitute chopped red and green bell peppers, steamed asparagus and cooked chopped ham for the picante sauce, sausage, mushrooms and onion.

SERVES TEN TO TWELVE

CANADIAN BACON QUICHE

1 onion, chopped
1 cup chopped Canadian bacon
2 tablespoons butter
½ cup nonfat dry milk powder
4 eggs
2½ cups milk
salt and pepper to taste
Tabasco sauce to taste
2 cups shredded Cheddar cheese
2 unbaked (9-inch) pie shells

• Preheat the oven to 350 degrees.
• Sauté the onion and Canadian bacon in the butter in a skillet.
• Combine the dry milk powder, eggs, milk, salt, pepper and Tabasco sauce in a mixer bowl and beat until frothy.
• Layer half of the Canadian bacon mixture and cheese into each pie shell. Pour half of the egg mixture over each.
• Bake for 45 minutes or until the centers are firm.

Variation: Add 1 cup cooked mixed vegetables such as broccoli, squash, bell peppers or mushrooms.

Variation: Substitute your cheese of choice for the Cheddar cheese.

SERVES TWELVE

MEXICAN GREEN CHILE QUICHE

8 ounces ground chicken or turkey
$^1\!/_3$ cup chopped onion
$1^1\!/_2$ teaspoons ground cumin
$^1\!/_4$ teaspoon crushed red pepper
$^1\!/_8$ teaspoon salt
1 (4-ounce) can chopped green
   chiles, drained
5 (6-inch) corn tortillas

$^1\!/_2$ cup shredded sharp Cheddar
   cheese
1 cup evaporated skim milk
$1^1\!/_2$ teaspoons cornstarch
$^1\!/_8$ teaspoon salt
2 eggs
1 egg white

- Preheat the oven to 350 degrees.
- Coat a large nonstick skillet with nonstick cooking spray. Heat over medium-high heat.
- Brown the ground chicken with the onion in the skillet, stirring until the chicken is crumbly.
- Stir in the cumin, red pepper and $^1\!/_8$ teaspoon salt. Add the green chiles and mix well.
- Cut the corn tortillas into halves. Coat a 9-inch pie plate with nonstick cooking spray. Arrange 2 tortilla halves in the bottom of the pie plate and the remaining around the side, overlapping slightly and extending 1 inch above the rim of the plate.
- Spoon the chicken mixture into the pie plate. Sprinkle with the cheese.
- Combine the evaporated milk, cornstarch, $^1\!/_8$ teaspoon salt, eggs and egg white in a blender container. Process until smooth and well mixed.
- Pour over the top.
- Bake for 45 minutes or until a knife inserted 1 inch from the center comes out clean. Let stand for 10 minutes before serving.

Note: This is delicious as a lunch or dinner entrée, as well as for brunch.

SERVES SIX

MARBLED EGGS

Marbled eggs make special gifts or a beautiful centerpiece. They are fun and easy to make, even for children. To make three marbled eggs, trim the ends from 1 large red or yellow onion and cut it into halves. Remove the skins carefully, keeping the large pieces. Wrap each egg completely with a single layer of onion skin. Cover each egg with foil to keep the onion skin in place. Combine with 1 teaspoon vinegar and enough water to cover in a small saucepan. Bring to a boil over high heat. Reduce the heat and simmer for 15 minutes. Combine 3 cups cold water and 1 cup ice cubes in a large bowl. Place the eggs carefully in the ice water and let stand for 5 minutes. Remove the foil and onion skins and pat the eggs dry. Store in the refrigerator until needed.

CHEESE AND SPINACH PIE

1 (10-ounce) package frozen chopped spinach
16 ounces small curd cottage cheese
3 eggs, or equivalent amount of egg substitute
3 tablespoons flour
1/4 cup melted margarine
6 slices Old English cheese

- Preheat the oven to 350 degrees.
- Thaw the spinach and drain, squeezing out excess liquid. Combine with the cottage cheese, eggs, flour and margarine in a bowl; mix well.
- Tear the Old English cheese into small pieces and add to the mixture, mixing well.
- Spoon into a greased 10-inch pie plate. Bake for 1 hour; do not overcook.

SERVES SIX

FRESH TOMATO AND BASIL PIZZA

1 can refrigerator pizza dough
1/4 cup extra-virgin olive oil
2 cloves of garlic, minced
3 cups shredded mozzarella cheese
4 Roma tomatoes, thinly sliced
10 to 15 fresh basil leaves
grated Parmesan cheese

- Preheat the oven to 425 degrees.
- Unroll the pizza dough and press onto a greased 12-inch pizza pan.
- Bake for 6 to 7 minutes or just until the dough begins to brown.
- Brush with a mixture of the olive oil and garlic. Layer with mozzarella cheese and tomato slices.
- Bake for 8 to 12 minutes longer or until the crust is golden brown and the cheese is bubbly.
- Sprinkle with basil leaves and Parmesan cheese.

SERVES FOUR

CHIQUITA FAJITAS

½ cup butter
6 (8-inch) flour tortillas
3 large ripe bananas, sliced
6 tablespoons light brown sugar

1½ teaspoons cinnamon
8 ounces caramel sauce
whipped cream topping
⅓ cup finely chopped pecans

- Preheat the oven to 350 degrees.
- Melt the butter in a skillet over medium-low heat. Remove from the heat. Dip each tortilla in the butter.
- Arrange the bananas in a single row in the center of each tortilla.
- Sprinkle each row of bananas with 1 tablespoon brown sugar and drizzle with the remaining butter. Sprinkle with cinnamon.
- Fold over each side of the tortilla to enclose the bananas and place seam side down on a greased baking sheet. Repeat the process with the remaining tortillas.
- Bake for 10 to 15 minutes or until light golden brown.
- Warm the caramel sauce in a saucepan until of pouring consistency. Drizzle part of the sauce onto 6 plates.
- Slice the tortillas diagonally and arrange in the sauce. Drizzle with the remaining sauce and top with whipped cream topping. Sprinkle with the pecans.

SERVES SIX

I remember growing up at a time when you didn't make many long-distance telephone calls. Consequently, my mother and grandmother wrote many letters to each other. Often a letter would share a recipe that one or the other had tried. To this day, my favorite recipes are the ones surrounded by bits and pieces of the letters from my mother and grandmother.

Virginia Hamman Porta

CRANBERRY AND APPLE BAKE

3 cups chopped unpeeled apples
2 cups whole fresh cranberries
1½ cups sugar
1½ cups rolled oats
⅓ cup flour
½ cup melted butter
½ cup chopped nuts

- Preheat the oven to 350 degrees.
- Combine the apples and cranberries in a bowl and mix well. Spread in a greased 9x13-inch baking dish.
- Combine the sugar, oats, flour, butter and nuts in a bowl and mix well. Sprinkle over the fruit.
- Bake for 1 hour.

SERVES EIGHT

HOT FRUIT COMPOTE

12 macaroons, crumbled
4 cups drained canned peaches, pears, apricots, pineapple and cherries
½ cup slivered almonds, toasted
¼ cup packed brown sugar
¼ cup sherry
¼ cup melted butter

- Preheat the oven to 350 degrees.
- Sprinkle ⅓ of the macaroon crumbs in a buttered 2½-quart baking dish.
- Layer the fruit and remaining macaroons ½ at a time in the prepared baking dish.
- Sprinkle with the almonds and brown sugar. Drizzle with the sherry.
- Bake for 30 minutes or until hot and bubbly. Drizzle with the melted butter.

SERVES EIGHT

GARLIC CHEESE GRITS

4 cups water
1 teaspoon salt
1 cup uncooked grits

1 (6-ounce) roll jalapeño cheese
1 (6-ounce) roll garlic cheese
¼ cup butter

- Preheat the oven to 350 degrees.
- Bring the water and salt to a boil in a saucepan. Stir in the grits gradually. Bring to a boil and reduce the heat.
- Cook over medium heat for 4 to 5 minutes, stirring frequently.
- Slice the jalapeño cheese and garlic cheese into small pieces. Add to the grits with the butter and stir until melted.
- Spoon into an ungreased 1½-quart baking dish.
- Bake, uncovered, for 30 minutes.

SERVES SIX

SWEET BACON

1 cup packed brown sugar
1 tablespoon cinnamon

¼ teaspoon nutmeg
1 pound bacon, sliced

- Preheat the oven to 350 degrees.
- Combine the brown sugar, cinnamon and nutmeg in a bowl.
- Coat the bacon slices generously on both sides with the brown sugar mixture. Arrange on a broiler pan.
- Bake for 15 to 20 minutes or until the bacon is crisp.
- Serve warm or at room temperature.

SERVES EIGHT

STRAWBERRY JAM

Combine 2 cups sliced strawberries and 4 cups puréed strawberries in a saucepan. Add 1 package of Sure-Jell and ½ teaspoon butter. Bring to a boil. Add 7 cups sugar, bring to a rolling boil, and boil for 1 minute, stirring constantly. Remove from the heat and skim off any foam. Pour into sterilized jars, leaving ½-inch headspace. Seal with 2-piece lids. Process in a boiling water bath for 15 minutes. Check lids for seal. Yields 8 cups.

EASY CHEESE DANISH

16 ounces cream cheese, softened
½ teaspoon vanilla extract
½ cup sugar
2 cans crescent roll dough
½ cup raspberry jam
1 egg, beaten

- Preheat the oven to 350 degrees.
- Combine the cream cheese, vanilla and sugar in a mixer bowl and beat well.
- Unroll the crescent roll dough from 1 of the cans. Place on a greased 9x13-inch baking sheet, sealing the perforations.
- Spread the cream cheese filling over the dough. Top with the raspberry jam.
- Unroll the remaining crescent roll dough. Place over the top, sealing the edges with a fork. Brush with the egg.
- Bake for 25 minutes or until golden brown.

Variation: Substitute your favorite flavor of jam for the raspberry.

SERVES SIX TO EIGHT

BAKED FRENCH TOAST

2 eggs, beaten
2 egg whites
½ cup skim milk
1½ tablespoons orange juice
1 tablespoon brown sugar
½ teaspoon cinnamon
½ teaspoon vanilla extract
8 (¾-inch) slices French bread
2 tablespoons confectioners' sugar

- Preheat the oven to 425 degrees.
- Coat a shallow baking pan with nonstick cooking spray. Heat in the oven for 15 minutes.
- Combine the eggs, egg whites, milk, orange juice, brown sugar, cinnamon and vanilla in a bowl and beat well.
- Dip the bread slices into the mixture, coating completely. Place the bread in the heated baking pan.
- Bake for 5 to 7 minutes. Turn the bread. Bake for 5 to 6 minutes longer or until golden brown.
- Sprinkle with confectioners' sugar. Serve hot.

SERVES FOUR

DANISH ÆBLESKIVER

3 egg yolks
2 cups buttermilk
2 tablespoons sugar
½ teaspoon salt
2 cups flour

1 teaspoon baking powder
1 teaspoon baking soda
3 egg whites, stiffly beaten
shortening
applesauce, apple slices or prunes

- Beat the egg yolks in a bowl until light. Add the buttermilk, sugar and salt and mix well.
- Sift the flour, baking powder and baking soda together. Add to the egg mixture; mix well.
- Beat the egg whites in a mixer bowl until stiff peaks form. Fold into the batter.
- Place a small amount of shortening in each depression of an æbleskiver pan and heat over high heat. Spoon the batter into the depressions, filling ⅔ full.
- Cook until the æbleskiver begin to bubble like a pancake. Spoon fruit onto the top and spread with additional batter. Turn with a fork. Cook until brown on the bottom.
- Serve warm with melted butter and syrup.

SERVES TWELVE

My Scandinavian grandmother was an excellent cook. She was in her seventies by the time I came along and wasn't cooking nearly as much as in her earlier years. But my mother tells tales of coming home from school to wonderful homemade cinnamon rolls. I suspect that she was the type of cook who made everything from scratch, even when modern mixes became available. She passed to her children and grandchildren a cooking tradition that I continue to enjoy today and celebrate with my own family. On Christmas morning, we make a treat called æbleskiver for breakfast. Æbleskiver are like tiny pancakes, sometimes filled with applesauce or other fruit and served with syrup. Making them requires a special pan and a watchful eye, but the result is delicious and unusual.

Stacy Johnson Hurst

OVEN-PUFFED PANCAKE

½ cup flour
2 tablespoons sugar
¼ teaspoon salt
½ cup milk
2 eggs
2 tablespoons margarine or butter
currant jelly or seedless red raspberry preserves
fruit juice, fruit syrup or fruit liqueur
chopped fresh fruit

For the pancake
- Preheat the oven to 425 degrees. Combine the flour, sugar, salt, milk and eggs in a bowl and beat with a whisk until smooth.
- Place the margarine in a 9-inch pie pan. Heat in the oven for 2 to 4 minutes or until the margarine is sizzling. Rotate the pie pan to spread evenly over the bottom.
- Pour the batter into the hot pan.
- Bake for 14 to 18 minutes or until puffed and golden brown. Cut into wedges.

For the topping
- Heat jelly in a saucepan over low heat. Stir in a small amount of fruit juice.
- Add chopped fresh fruit such as berries, kiwifruit, pineapple, mango or papaya just before serving.
- Serve over the pancake.

SERVES TWO OR THREE

POTATO PANCAKES

4 large potatoes
2 eggs
1 teaspoon grated onion
½ teaspoon baking powder
1 teaspoon salt
2 tablespoons flour
pepper to taste

- Peel the potatoes and grate on a fine grater or in a food processor. Pour off the liquid.
- Beat the eggs in a large bowl. Add the potatoes, onion, baking powder, salt, flour and pepper and mix well.
- Drop by spoonfuls onto a hot oiled griddle or skillet. Bake until the top appears dry. Turn and bake until golden brown. Drain on paper towels and keep warm.
- Serve with apple sauce or sour cream.

SERVES EIGHT TO TEN

LAYERED APPLE COFFEE CAKE

5 tablespoons sugar
2 teaspoons cinnamon
2 cups sugar
1 cup vegetable oil
4 eggs
3 cups flour

1 teaspoon salt
1 tablespoon baking powder
¼ cup orange juice
2 teaspoons vanilla extract
4 to 6 apples, peeled, thinly sliced

- Preheat the oven to 350 degrees.
- Grease a bundt or tube pan. Combine the 5 tablespoons sugar and cinnamon in a small bowl and mix well.
- Combine 2 cups sugar and oil in a mixer bowl and beat until smooth. Beat in the eggs 1 at a time.
- Mix the flour, salt and baking powder together. Add to the egg mixture alternately with the orange juice and vanilla, beating well after each addition.
- Layer the batter, apples and cinnamon mixture ½ at a time in the prepared pan.
- Bake for 1½ hours or until the coffee cake tests done. Cool in the pan until lukewarm. Invert onto a serving plate.
- Serve with whipped cream and grated pecans or walnuts.

SERVES TEN

FRENCH TOAST

The French term for French toast is pain perdu, *or lost bread. This refers to the technique of dipping stale French bread into a milk and egg mixture and using it for a delicious breakfast treat rather than wasting it.*
French toast can be made with any type of bread, as well as with French bread, and each type will lend a different texture and flavor. Thin sandwich bread will soak up the egg mixture to create a moist, custard-like texture. Unsliced bakery bread can be cut thicker and will produce a light, spongy texture. Whole-grain breads, such as whole wheat and oatmeal, are dense and will result in a moist, heavier French toast with a slightly nutty flavor. Cinnamon bread offers a spicy swirl, and often includes raisins.
Experiment with the different types of bread available at the market and bakery to determine the flavor and texture you like best.

FRESH BLUEBERRY COFFEE CAKE

⅓ cup sugar
¼ cup flour
½ teaspoon cinnamon
2 tablespoons melted butter
1 cup blueberries
1 tablespoon lemon juice
1 cup flour
1½ teaspoons baking powder
½ teaspoon salt
⅓ cup sugar
1 egg
½ cup milk
⅓ cup melted butter

For the topping
- Combine ⅓ cup sugar, ¼ cup flour, cinnamon and 2 tablespoons melted butter in a bowl and mix well.

For the coffee cake
- Preheat the oven to 375 degrees.
- Sprinkle the blueberries with the lemon juice in a bowl and set aside.
- Sift 1 cup flour, baking powder, salt and ⅓ cup sugar into a mixer bowl.
- Add the egg, milk and ⅓ cup melted butter and beat until smooth.
- Pour into a greased 8-inch square pan. Sprinkle the blueberries over the top.
- Sprinkle with the topping.
- Bake for 45 minutes or until the coffee cake tests done.

SERVES EIGHT

LOW-FAT ORANGE BREAD

1 teaspoon flour
2 teaspoons baking powder
1¾ cups flour
¼ teaspoon salt
¾ cup sugar
1 tablespoon grated orange peel
⅔ cup fresh orange juice
¼ cup vegetable oil
4 egg whites, stiffly beaten

- Preheat the oven to 350 degrees.
- Spray the bottom of a 4x8-inch loaf pan with nonstick cooking spray. Sprinkle with 1 teaspoon flour.
- Combine the baking powder, 1¾ cups flour, salt and sugar in a mixer bowl.
- Mix the orange peel, orange juice and oil in a small bowl. Add to the flour mixture and beat at medium speed just until smooth.
- Fold in ⅓ of the egg whites, then fold in the remaining egg whites.
- Pour the batter into the prepared loaf pan. Bake for 55 minutes or just until a wooden pick inserted in the center comes out clean; do not overbake.
- Cool in the pan for 10 minutes; remove to a wire rack to cool completely.

SERVES TEN OR TWELVE

Good-For-You Cinnamon Rolls

1 cup skim milk
3 tablespoons sugar
1 tablespoon margarine
1 envelope dry yeast
1/4 cup warm (110-degree) water
1 egg, beaten
1/2 teaspoon salt
3 3/4 cups plus 2 tablespoons bread
  flour

2 tablespoons melted margarine
1/4 cup plus 2 tablespoons packed
  brown sugar
2 teaspoons ground cinnamon
1/2 teaspoon ground nutmeg
1/2 cup sifted confectioners' sugar
1 tablespoon skim milk
1/2 teaspoon vanilla extract

For the rolls

- Heat 1 cup milk in a saucepan over medium heat to 180 degrees or until tiny bubbles form around the edge; do not boil. Remove from the heat.
- Add the sugar and 1 tablespoon margarine, stirring until the margarine melts. Cool to 105 to 115 degrees.
- Dissolve the yeast in the warm water. Let stand for 5 minutes. Combine the milk mixture and the yeast in a large bowl. Stir in the egg and salt.
- Add 3 1/2 cups of the bread flour gradually, stirring until a soft dough forms.
- Knead on a floured surface for 5 to 8 minutes or until smooth and elastic, adding the remaining flour 1 tablespoon at a time to prevent sticking.
- Coat a large bowl with nonstick cooking spray. Place the dough in the bowl, turning to coat the surface.
- Let rise, covered, for 1 hour or until doubled in bulk.
- Punch the dough down. Roll into an 8x20-inch rectangle on a lightly floured surface. Brush with 2 tablespoons melted margarine.
- Mix the brown sugar, cinnamon and nutmeg in a bowl. Sprinkle over the dough. Roll from the long side as for a jelly roll. Pinch the seam to seal but do not seal the ends. Cut into twenty 1-inch slices. Place the slices cut side down on a 9x13-inch baking pan coated with nonstick cooking spray. Let rise, covered, for 30 minutes or until doubled in bulk.
- Preheat the oven to 350 degrees. Bake for 20 to 25 minutes or until brown.

For the glaze

- Combine the confectioners' sugar, 1 tablespoon milk and vanilla in a bowl and mix well. Drizzle over the hot rolls.

SERVES TWENTY

221

KWANZAA

Kwanzaa, a seven-day nonreligious ritual celebrating the African-American heritage, was created by Dr. Maulana Karenga, a philosopher and social activist, in 1966. The word means first fruits and symbolizes the collective harvest. Kwanzaa was born of curiosity about the past and a longing for community, along with a positive portrayal of Africa and her people. Kwanzaa provides families a base from which to share experiences that are unique to their heritage.

The seven principles that are celebrated from December 26 to January 1 are unity, self-determination, collective work and responsibility, cooperative economics, purpose, creativity, and faith. Decorations often include many colorful dried fruits and vegetables and are trimmed with the Kwanzaa colors of black to celebrate the African race, red to symbolize the blood shed in its struggles, and green to symbolize fruitful harvests and hope for the future.

Pat Gray

ORANGE MUFFINS

1 cup sugar
½ cup unsalted butter
2 eggs
1 teaspoon baking soda
1 cup buttermilk
2 cups sifted flour
½ teaspoon salt
1 cup raisins
peel and juice of 1 orange
½ cup sugar

- Preheat the oven to 400 degrees. Spray 30 miniature muffin cups with vegetable cooking spray.
- Cream 1 cup sugar and the butter in a mixer bowl until light and fluffy. Beat in the eggs 1 at a time.
- Mix the baking soda and the buttermilk together. Sift the flour and salt together.
- Add the flour mixture and buttermilk mixture to the creamed mixture alternately, blending well after each addition.
- Process the raisins and orange peel in a food processor until finely chopped. Stir into the batter.
- Spoon into the prepared muffin cups. Bake for 12 minutes or until golden brown and firm to the touch.
- Place the muffin tins on wire racks. Brush the tops of the warm muffins with the orange juice and sprinkle with ½ cup sugar.
- Let stand for 5 minutes. Remove from the muffin cups.

YIELDS THIRTY MUFFINS

PEACH MUFFINS

1½ cups flour
¾ teaspoon salt
½ teaspoon baking soda
1 cup sugar
2 eggs, beaten
½ cup vegetable oil
2 cups finely chopped peaches
½ teaspoon vanilla extract
½ teaspoon almond extract
½ cup toasted chopped pecans or almonds

- Preheat the oven to 350 degrees.
- Combine the flour, salt, baking soda and sugar in a bowl and mix well.
- Make a well in the center and add the eggs and oil, stirring just until the dry ingredients are moistened.
- Stir in the peaches, extracts and pecans. Fill greased muffin cups ²/₃ full.
- Bake for 20 to 25 minutes or until golden brown.

SERVES TWELVE

BANANA WHIRL

1 banana
1½ cups milk
¼ cup frozen orange juice
   concentrate

1 teaspoon vanilla extract
4 teaspoons sugar
¼ teaspoon cinnamon
6 ice cubes

- Combine the banana, milk, orange juice concentrate, vanilla, sugar, cinnamon and ice cubes in a blender container.
- Process on high until frothy. Serve immediately.

SERVES TWO

PEACH FUZZIES

3 ripe peaches
1 banana
1 (6-ounce) can frozen pink
   lemonade concentrate

6 ounces lemon-lime soda, vodka
   or gin
ice cubes

- Remove the pits from the peaches but do not peel.
- Combine the peaches, banana, lemonade concentrate and lemon-lime soda in a blender container.
- Add ice cubes to the liquid mark. Process until the ice is crushed.
- Serve immediately.

Note: This mixture can be frozen, covered, in a plastic container for up to 4 days. Let stand at room temperature to soften, and stir before serving.

SERVES SIX

PEACH JAM

Combine 5 cups chopped peaches and 1 drained 10-ounce can of crushed pineapple with 7 cups sugar in a large saucepan. Bring to a full rolling boil and boil for 15 minutes, stirring constantly. Remove from the heat and stir in two 3-ounce packages strawberry gelatin until dissolved. Pour into hot sterilized glasses. Top with melted paraffin.

223

Gourmet Supper Club

ENTERTAINING

Caponata with Pita Wedges
Almond Soup
Hearts of Palm Salad
Seaside Pasta
Herbed Bread
Chocolate Soufflé
St. Cecelia Sauce
Chardonnay

Currying Favor with Our Friends

When my husband, Griffin, and I entertain, we often prepare Indian food...perhaps a spicy vindaloo or a grilled Tandoori chicken, ginger-and-red-pepper-laced vegetables, and sweet rice with stick cinnamon. We also like a yogurt raita made with bananas and jalapeños that helps "cool" the hot food and tasty Indian breads like naan and paratha.

For many years, Indian food was not a very well-known cuisine in the South. On a visit to Washington, D.C. some 20 years ago, I first tasted it at a little Georgetown restaurant called Apana. The blend of spices and textures was so delicate and yet aggressive, and I was hooked.

Returning home, I quickly purchased "Introduction to Indian Cooking" by Madhur Jaffrey, who had a cooking program on Indian television. Using her family recipes, I duplicated several of the dishes I had enjoyed at Apana, and gradually expanded my repertoire. It's now become a specialty at our house.

But sometimes specializing in a cuisine can get you into trouble.

Several years ago, I worked in a political campaign and donated an Indian dinner in a silent auction at the annual Jefferson-Jackson Day dinner. The fellow who purchased the dinner called me to discuss the arrangements and, in a heavily-accented voice, gently grilled me about the menu and where I learned to prepare Indian food. My answers seemed to satisfy his curiosity, and I asked him how he became interested in the cuisine. "Oh, my dear, I am from Bombay," he replied. Needless to say, the night of his party, the intimidation level was running pretty high.

LIBBY SMITH

Working with a Caterer

There are many good reasons to use a caterer when having a party. The primary reason is that, with a caterer, the host can relax and enjoy the party as a guest. It is easy, otherwise, to get too bogged down with kitchen duty and last-minute preparations to visit with the guests, and that reduces the pleasure of entertaining.

The best way to find a caterer that you will enjoy working with is by word of mouth. Make a list of the most successful parties that you have attended and ask the hosts for their recommendations.

You should be able to depend on the experience and expertise of a good caterer. He or she should have a staff, including bartenders, trained to work together, and is the one to decide how many service people will be needed and what their duties will be. He also has access to rental equipment and can offer advice about the items that they will provide and the ones that need to be rented.

Invite the caterer to your home prior to the party to view the kitchen and service areas. This is the time to determine what time to expect the staff on the day of the party. The more preparation, the less frustration!

From preparation to final clean up, plan on an average of four hours for a cocktail party. The caterer and staff will leave your kitchen as clean as, or cleaner than, they found it. Everything should be washed, dried, and put away before they leave, with no emptying the dishwasher for you.

The method of payment for the caterer and the service people should be understood before the party. Have the payment ready after the party for both the caterer and the service people, who may need to be paid separately. If you feel it is appropriate, a tip to the service people for their hard work is always appreciated.

Sit back, relax, and enjoy your party!

THE CATERING BUDGET

The first issue to discuss with your caterer is the budget, and you should be candid about the amount of money you wish to spend. This will enable the caterer to make the appropriate suggestions concerning menu, rentals, service people, etc. He or she will base it on the date and time of the party; the number of guests, including the number of men and/or women attending; and your service preference, for example, seated, buffet, or family-style. The rule of thumb for entertaining at home is that you should plan to spend the same amount that you would spend if you took your guests to a restaurant with a comparable menu. Keep in mind that entertaining 50 people for brunch is less expensive than entertaining the same 50 people for dinner. The wording on the invitation can also help stretch the budget. An invitation to "drop by for cocktails" will be less expensive than a "cocktail buffet."

Sweetheart Brunch

Celebrate a special occasion by inviting close friends to a brunch with you and your sweetheart. Occasions can range from a Valentine's Day party, complete with cupids, chocolate hearts, and pink and red decorations, to a wedding anniversary celebration, replete with wedding memorabilia. Guests should come for the festivities between eleven o'clock in the morning and one o'clock in the afternoon.

This is a wonderful time to laugh and reminisce with cherished friends. Set the mood by the invitation sent, then carry the theme throughout the party with the same motif in decor and table setting. Don't forget the possibility of party favors, such as a beautifully wrapped and sinfully rich chocolate truffle for each guest as he leaves the party.

MENU

CLASSIC BRUNCH CASSEROLE *(page 208)*
SWEET BACON *(page 215)*
HOT FRUIT COMPOTE *(page 214)*
ANGEL BISCUITS *(page 163)*
ASSORTED JAMS AND JELLIES
APRICOT LEMON CAKE *(page 180)*
FRESH RASPBERRIES
MIMOSAS *(page 245)*
MOOD-ENHANCING MILK PUNCH *(page 30)*
COFFEE

FOOD PREPARATION TIMELINE

One week before:	Prepare and freeze the Angel Biscuits. Prepare and freeze the Apricot Lemon Cake. Prepare and freeze the Classic Brunch Casserole.
Two or Three Days before:	Prepare and freeze the Mood-Enhancing Milk Punch.
Day before:	Prepare and chill the Hot Fruit Compote. Thaw the biscuits, cake and casserole in the refrigerator.
Morning of:	Prepare the Sweet Bacon.
One hour before:	Bake the brunch casserole. Remove the milk punch from the freezer.
Thirty minutes before:	Bake the fruit compote. Heat the biscuits. Prepare the Mimosas. Prepare the coffee.

Shortly after we were married, my husband and I bought and renovated a home. During the planning stages of our first Open House, my husband's mother reminded me that, when entertaining, "you can't have it all." Several years and parties later, her words have remained true. According to her, the three "E's" of entertaining are: ease, elegance, and economy. She said that you can have two, but never all three, at once.

Mary Varga Daugherty

229

Holiday Shopping Drop-In

During the busy holiday season, give your friends a warm and friendly respite from last-minute shopping and treat them to lunch. Invite them to drop in between eleven o'clock and two o'clock for good food with good friends. Give guests a chance to chat and serve themselves in a casual setting.

Your own seasonal decorations will set the scene for a relaxed gathering of old and new friends during this harried time of the year.

MENU

MINESTRONE *(page 48)*
FOCACCIA *(page 173)*
SYMPHONY COOKIES *(page 192)*
TEA COOKIES *(page 189)*
HOT SPICED TEA *(page 26)*
SPARKLING WATER

FOOD PREPARATION TIMELINE

One week before: Prepare and freeze the Minestrone.

Day before: Prepare the Symphony Cookies.
Prepare the Tea Cookies.
Prepare the Hot Spiced Tea.
Prepare the Focaccia.
Thaw the minestrone in
the refrigerator.

Thirty minutes before: Heat the focaccia.
Warm the spiced tea.
Warm the minestrone.

FUN ON THE RUN

After a run, walk, or early-morning tennis game, invite your guests for a casual breakfast on the patio. Set up a central buffet of "light and healthy" fare, with the time chosen to fit the time of the activity. Decorations, limited only by your imagination, can include athletic paraphernalia such as balls, water bottles, or clean tennis shoes filled with fresh flowers. Offer Low-Fat Orange Bread (page 220), chilled nonfat yogurt cups, fresh seasonal fruits, Cranberry Spritzers (page 27), and bottled water.

Box Lunch

A box lunch is a fabulous way to serve a "make ahead" luncheon. Before your guests arrive, pack attractive boxes with all the lunch goodies. Be imaginative with the containers. Use a clear corsage container lined with fabric and wrapped with a rose and a tulle bow, or a box filled with brightly-colored tissue paper and tied with curling ribbon. Colorful Chinese take-out cartons are wonderful for individual servings.

The attractive boxes will do double duty on the dining-room sideboard as decorations. Don't forget disposable napkins and eating utensils in each box. Pass appetizers and bread in order to keep them warm. Place dessert in the box or serve it later. Seat guests at a table or provide lap trays for convenience in unwrapping all the edible treasures.

MENU

HOT SPINACH DIP *(page 23)*
ITALIAN PITA WEDGES *(page 21)*
OR
BAKED TORTILLA CHIPS *(page 19)*
TORTELLINI CHICKEN SALAD *(page 126)*
FRESH SEASONAL FRUIT
CELERY SEED DRESSING *(page 67)*
BREADSTICKS *(page 174)*
FUDGE BROWNIES *(page 186)*
ALMOND TEA *(page 26)*
ICE WATER

FOOD PREPARATION TIMELINE

One week before: Prepare and freeze the Hot Spinach Dip.
Prepare and freeze the Breadsticks.

Day before: Prepare and chill the Tortellini
 Chicken Salad.
Prepare and chill the Almond Tea.
Prepare the Fudge Brownies.
Prepare and chill the Celery
 Seed Dressing.
Prepare the Italian Pita Wedges or Baked
 Tortilla Chips.
Thaw the breadsticks in the refrigerator.
Thaw the spinach dip in the refrigerator.

Day of: Prepare and chill the seasonal fruit.
Prepare the individual servings and pack
 the box lunches.

Immediately before: Warm the breadsticks.
Warm the spinach dip.
Warm the almond tea.

Fourth of July Neighborhood Supper

Gather your neighbors, friends, and families for a festive outdoor Fourth of July supper. Think about providing some activities to entertain the children before the food is served. Some excellent possibilities are "Pin the Tail on the Democratic Donkey"—or "Republican Elephant"; sparklers; or red, white, and blue sidewalk chalk on the driveway or patio.

Rouse the patriotic spirit with a children's parade and let the children decorate bikes and tricycles with brightly-colored crepe paper and balloons. Little ones can ride in red wagons or strollers ablaze in patriotic colors. After the buffet supper, the timing should be right for everyone to enjoy a fireworks display!

MENU

SPICY CHICKEN WINGS *(page 12)*
BARBECUED BRISKET *(page 75)*
GRILLED CORN ON THE COB
FIRECRACKER BUTTER *(page 171)*
BEEFY BAKED BEANS *(page 78)*
COLESLAW *(page 62)*
STARS AND STRIPES CAKE
COLD WATERMELON WEDGES
LEMONADE
BEER
HOLIDAY SANGRIA *(page 30)*

FOOD PREPARATION TIMELINE

One week before: Freeze the ice cube trays for the Holiday Sangria, using blueberries instead of green grapes.

Day before: Prepare and chill the Firecracker Butter.
Assemble and chill the Beefy Baked Beans.
Prepare and chill the Coleslaw.
Make a sheet cake from your favorite packaged mix.
Chill the watermelon.
Prepare the lemonade.

Night before: Marinate the Spicy Chicken Wings.

Day of: Bake the chicken wings; cover with foil and chill.
Cook the Barbecued Brisket.
Decorate the sheet cake as a flag by spreading it with white frosting and adding blueberry stars and sliced strawberry stripes.
Mix and chill the sangria.
Slice the watermelon, cover, and chill.

Thirty minutes before: Reheat the chicken wings.
Reheat the barbecued brisket, if necessary.
Bake the beans.
Grill or boil the corn.
Add the ice cubes to the sangria at the last minute.

FUN FOR KIDS

Face Paint is an easy treat for kids. Mix 1 teaspoon cornstarch with 1/2 teaspoon cold cream, 1/2 teaspoon water, and 2 drops of any food coloring. Repeat the process for other colors.
Ice Cream in a Bag is also fun for little hands. Combine 1/2 cup milk, 1 tablespoon sugar, 1 teaspoon salt, and 1 1/2 teaspoons vanilla in a sandwich-size zip-top bag. Place in a large zip-top bag filled with ice and 6 tablespoons salt. Work the small bag around in the bag of ice for about 5 minutes for one individual serving of ice cream.

New Year's Day Supper

What better way to begin the new year than with a very casual afternoon party to enjoy good food and watch the bowl games with friends. Every guest should feel comfortable to relax before the television with his plate and enjoy the games. This menu was selected for its suitability to remain at room temperature during the party.

Arrange the room so that guests will be able to see the game, even if that includes pillows on the floor—or open up the house with several television sets to ensure that everyone can catch a glimpse of his favorite football team. This also encourages circulation and conversation among friends.

MENU

FRIED WALNUTS *(page 25)*
JALAPEÑO CHEESE SPREAD *(page 18)*
SALSA *(page 158)*
ASSORTED CRACKERS AND TORTILLA CHIPS
PORK TENDERLOIN TERIYAKI *(page 84)*
GARLIC CHEESE GRITS *(page 215)*
POOR MAN'S CAVIAR *(page 17)*
BOSTON BIBB AND RED LEAF LETTUCE SALAD
HONEY MUSTARD VINAIGRETTE *(page 69)*
BROCCOLI CORN BREAD *(page 164)*
CHOCOLATE BUTTER GOOEY *(page 194)*
BEER & WINE
CHILLED SOFT DRINKS

FOOD PREPARATION TIMELINE

Two or three days before: Prepare the Chocolate Butter Gooey.
Prepare the Fried Walnuts.
Prepare and chill the Salsa.

Day before: Prepare and chill the Poor Man's
   Caviar.
Prepare and chill the Jalapeño
   Cheese Spread.
Marinate the Pork Tenderloin Teriyaki
   in the refrigerator.

Day of: Prepare and chill the Garlic
   Cheese Grits.
Wash, tear, and chill the salad greens.
Prepare and chill the Honey Mustard
   Vinaigrette.

One hour before: Ice the beverages.
Bake the pork tenderloin.
Bake the grits.
Prepare and bake the Broccoli
   Corn Bread.

Immediately before: Toss the salad greens with the
   Honey Mustard Vinaigrette.

The best party I have ever attended was a surprise 65th-birthday party my brothers and I had for our father. We invited guests to a one-time showing of "Harry's Museum"—the perfect theme for a man who never gets rid of anything! The museum was an empty warehouse in which we displayed memorabilia from my father's life. For over six months, we gathered old photographs and, in many cases, the actual items that were in the photographs. Items on display included a childhood go-cart and a picture of Dad as a young boy riding in the cart, and my parents' wedding clothes displayed on mannequins, along with their wedding picture. Food was served on an old flat-bed trailer that Dad had once used in the family business. A continuous video of photographs of Dad and his life were shown on one wall of the warehouse throughout the evening. Not only was this a wonderful party which was truly representative of Dad, but the video also gave each of us a pictorial history of the Hastings family, which will be cherished for many generations to come.

Cathy Hastings Owen

A Southern Tea

The South has always evoked thoughts of hospitality and graciousness. A tea, the epitome of Southern hospitality, conjures up visions of white-gloved ladies sipping tea and eating dainty sandwiches. Though the tradition has evolved through the years, it is still a Southern favorite for feting brides and celebrating other special occasions. Business suits may have replaced the white gloves, but Southerners still enjoy the warmth and camaraderie enjoyed with tea.

The traditional British High Tea is held between the hours of five and six o'clock in the afternoon and is the equivalent of the Southern supper. Our tea, a version of the American cream tea, would begin between three and four o'clock and end by half-past five. It includes the customary sandwiches, scones, sweets, and tea. We have also chosen to serve coffee from a silver service at the end of the table opposite the tea.

MENU

CHICKEN SALAD SANDWICHES *(page 58)*
ROASTED RED PEPPER SPREAD SANDWICHES *(page 50)*
CUCUMBER SANDWICHES *(page 51)*
SCONES *(page 167)*
PRESERVES & CLOTTED CREAM *(page 167)*
MINTS *(page 185)*
SUGARED PECANS *(page 24)*
MOLASSES COOKIES *(page 190)*
SUGAR COOKIES *(page 188)*
LEMON WAFERS *(page 190)*
SOUR CREAM POUND CAKE *(page 182)*
FIVE-FLAVOR POUND CAKE *(page 181)*
COCOA BONBONS *(page 185)*
TEA & COFFEE
CREAM   SUGAR CUBES   LEMON

Plan to serve two to three cups of tea per person. Each guest should have a cup, saucer, and spoon. If serving tea brewed from loose leaves, the tea should be poured through an attractive tea strainer. If using tea bags, each guest should have a fresh tea bag for each cup of tea. Tea or dessert plates may be stacked at each end of the table with tea napkins placed between or beside the plates. Each food selection should be served on both sides of the table. Tea sandwiches are made of thinly-sliced fresh bread. Each piece of bread should be spread with a very thin layer of butter to prevent the bread from becoming soggy. The cucumber sandwiches traditionally provide a refreshing foil to the richness of the other foods. The scones, a sweet cousin of the Southern biscuit, may be served with butter, jam, clotted cream, or the truly Southern choice of whipped cream. Mints and nuts are always served, and cookies, cakes, and a taste of chocolate finish the menu.

FOOD PREPARATION TIMELINE

One week before:
Bake and freeze the pound cakes.
Select the serving pieces, polish the silver, and prepare the linens.

Two or three days before:
Bake the Molasses Cookies and Sugar Cookies.
Prepare and chill the Roasted Pepper Cheese Spread.
Prepare the Mints.
Prepare the Sugared Pecans.
Prepare the Cocoa Bonbons.
Set the table and protect it with a dust cover.

Day before:
Prepare the Chicken Salad.
Prepare the Cucumber Spread.
Prepare the Lemon Wafers.
Thaw the pound cakes in the refrigerator.

Day of:
Prepare and bake the Scones.
Prepare all sandwiches; cover and chill.
Organize the coffee- and tea-brewing equipment and supplies.
Prepare and chill the Clotted Cream.
Slice the lemon.

Immediately before:
Place the food in the serving dishes.
Brew the coffee and tea and place in pots warmed with hot water.

239

A Southern Tea

*Plan ahead, and then plan some
more! When you are prepared,
you will be relaxed, and your
guests will be, too.*

*Keep a party diary in a notebook
and include the names of guests,
dates, times, themes, and menus,
along with a drawing of table
seatings. This will avoid confusion
for future planning. Keep the wine
labels as well and store the diary
with your cookbooks.*

*Review your recipes several days
before preparing a meal for guests.
In addition to your shopping list,
make a list of items that need to
be chopped, shredded, or blanched.*

*Mark the items that can be
prepared several days in
advance. Items such as onions,
celery, green peppers, carrots, and
cheese can be prepared ahead and
stored in zip-top bags.*

*For large parties, remember the
rule that two-thirds of the invited
guests can be expected to attend.*

*Although the tea party is a very old chapter in the book of entertaining,
it still manages to retain a contemporary freshness. A table laden with pretty
china, flowers, and lace provides the backdrop for a hostess to set out an array of
delectable dainties. A Southern tea offers a cozy and gracious respite
from the hurried demands of modern living.*

240

A Formal Dinner

Set the table(s) and serving area, including serving trays, bowls, and serving utensils, several days prior to the event.

Place the name of each item in the intended serving dish to ensure that you have the proper dishes for the party. It will also make it easier for someone to help you on the day of the party.

Plan lighted candles, fresh flowers and soft music for a special atmosphere. Louder music may be tolerated during the cocktail and mingling hour, but it may cause audio-indigestion during dinner.

To clean fine linens after the party, wash them in a mild detergent the same night they are used. Remove them from the washer wet, fold them and place in a zip-top bag. Store linens in the freezer or refrigerator until you are ready to iron them.

To celebrate a special occasion, nothing is more in order than a formal, seated dinner. This party needs careful planning because the presentation and serving of food follow definite patterns. To be sure, a formal dinner does require extra work, but the obvious appreciation and pleasure of the guests is more than adequate reward for the time and effort.

A Formal Dinner

Consider hosting the most formal of parties—a seated dinner. There is no better way to celebrate a momentous occasion or to honor special guests. This is a wonderful time to use the finest china, crystal, and silver. Fresh flowers and candles enhance the atmosphere. Crisp linens, whether a tablecloth or placemats with napkins, add to the elegance of the setting. The setting of the table should allow approximately one foot between each guest, because a crowded table is difficult to serve. Silver is placed in order of service from the outside toward the plate. The dessert fork and spoon are placed at the top of the plate. At a formal dinner, a butter plate is optional. A salad plate may be placed on the dinner plate and removed after it is used. While formal glassware need not match, all the glasses for a particular service need to match. Place wine glasses in the order of use, with the closest being the first to be used. Wine should be served with the appropriate course and the glass removed after the course. The water goblet is placed above the knife closest to the dinner plate.

MENU

CHEESY PESTO CROSTINI *(page 11)*
SMOKED TOMATO SOUP *(page 47)*
DINNER CRACKERS *(page 173)*
SMOKED TROUT *(page 118)*
DILL SAUCE *(page 119)*
ORANGE-BASIL SORBET *(page 198)*
BEEF TENDERLOIN *(page 79)*
BURGUNDY MUSHROOMS *(page 11)*
ASPARAGUS WITH CAPER
MAYONNAISE *(page 145)*
GRUYÈRE POTATOES *(page 147)*
OLD-FASHIONED YEAST ROLLS *(page 172)*
MIXED FIELD GREENS WITH RASPBERRY
VINAIGRETTE *(page 68)*
CHOCOLATE CREME BRÛLÉE *(page 196)*
STILTON CHEESE AND PEARS WITH PORT
COFFEE   MINTS *(page 185)*

FOOD PREPARATION TIMELINE

One week before:

Prepare, bake, and freeze the Rolls.

Two or three days before:

Prepare and chill the Burgundy Mushrooms and Raspberry Vinaigrette.
Prepare and freeze the Mints.

Day before:

Smoke and chill the Smoked Trout.
Prepare and chill the Smoked Tomato Soup.
Prepare the Dinner Crackers.
Prepare and chill the Dill Sauce.
Prepare and freeze Orange-Basil Sorbet.
Prepare and chill the Gruyère Potatoes.
Marinate the Beef Tenderloin.

Day of:

Prepare the mixed field greens.
Prepare the Chocolate Crème Brûlée.
Thaw frozen items except sorbet.
Prepare the Caper Mayonnaise.
Prepare the Cheesy Pesto Crostini.

One hour before:

Cook the tenderloin, asparagus, and potatoes.
Warm the soup and mushrooms.
Remove cheese from the refrigerator.

Just before:

Broil the brûlée and crostini.
Assemble the salad.
Warm the rolls.

I have always enjoyed entertaining, no matter what the occasion. Over the years, I have tried to simplify things so that I can enjoy my guests, too. Whether I'm having ten friends for dinner or 100 for a wedding brunch, I always have to "visualize" ahead of time by thinking through the party from start to finish; I remembered the candles for my daughter's birthday cake that way! I love trying new recipes, but if I don't have time to test them, I always have some tried and true favorites that never fail. I also try to have more of fewer dishes, for it's when I try to do too many things that there is trouble. I also never hesitate to pick up a wonderful bread or dessert at the bakery if I'm short of time. It's nice to know that someone will be up baking at 4:00 in the morning— and that it won't be me! Perhaps the thing I enjoy best about entertaining is setting the table. I try to think of unusual ways to combine various collections of depression glass, red Bohemian glass, and crystal. The mismatched look was in style at my house long before it was in vogue!

Sharon Deckleman Mosley

A Cocktail Buffet for Fifty

A cocktail buffet with a hearty menu and a full bar is an appealing alternative to a seated dinner and is an elegant way to entertain a large gathering. It can include both old and new friends— a mix of people who are already acquainted and those who are not.

The menu should be designed to simplify serving by requiring only a salad plate, fork, and napkin. Wrapping the fork in the napkin and tying it with a decorative ribbon makes handling the silverware easier. Candlelight and flowers will enhance the cordial atmosphere.

Set up several bars, appetizer stations, and dessert trays in different locations to avoid crowding and to encourage circulation.

MENU

TRI-COLOR TORTELLINI ON WOODEN SKEWERS

FRESH PESTO *(page 19)*

SUMMER BRUSCHETTA *(page 14)*

ROSY SHRIMP DIP *(page 23)*

PORK TENDERLOIN WITH MUSTARD SAUCE *(page 84)*

SLICED SMOKED TURKEY BREAST

ASPARAGUS VINAIGRETTE *(page 58)*

HERBED GARDEN MUSHROOMS *(page 14)*

TRADITIONAL YEAST ROLLS *(page 172)*

MINIATURE BROWNIE FUDGE TARTS *(page 202)*

MINIATURE LEMON CURD TARTS

FOOD PREPARATION TIMELINE

One week before: Prepare, bake and freeze the
                        Traditional Yeast Rolls.

Day before: Marinate the Pork Tenderloin.
                        Prepare and chill the Mustard Sauce,
                        Pesto, and Asparagus Vinaigrette.

Day of: Prepare and chill the Rosy Shrimp Dip.
                        Prepare the Tri-Color Tortellini and
                        place on wooden skewers.
                        Prepare the French bread for the
                        Summer Bruschetta and place in an
                        airtight container.
                        Prepare and chill the tomato topping.
                        Prepare and chill the Herbed
                        Garden Mushrooms.
                        Prepare the Brownie Fudge Tarts using
                        the filling from Fudge Pie.
                        Prepare the Lemon Curd Tarts using
                        a filling of prepared lemon curd.
                        Use baked frozen tart shells.
                        Thaw the rolls.

One hour before: Bake the pork tenderloin.
                        Bake the mushrooms.
                        Assemble the remaining menu items.

Thirty minutes before: Warm the rolls and bruschetta.

MIXING IT UP

*For a **Manhattan**, combine 2 ounces of bourbon with 1 dash of sweet or dry vermouth. Serve over ice in a highball glass or chilled up (by stirring or shaking with ice and draining) in a martini glass; garnish with a cherry.*

*For a **Martini**, combine 2 ounces of gin or vodka with a dash of dry vermouth. Serve over ice in a highball glass or chilled in a martini glass; garnish with olives or a lemon twist.*

*For a **Mimosa**, combine 1 part champagne and 2 parts fresh orange juice. Serve in a champagne flute and garnish with a mint sprig or orange slice.*

*For a **Champagne Cocktail**, combine 2 teaspoons of sugar, a cherry, and 2 dashes of bitters in a champagne flute. Fill the flute with champagne.*

*For a **Gimlet**, combine 2 ounces of gin or vodka with a dash of lime juice. Serve over ice or chilled up in a martini or cordial glass; garnish with a lime wedge or lime wheel.*

*For an **Old-Fashioned**, combine a slice of orange, a cherry, a teaspoon of sugar, and 2 dashes of bitters in a snifter and mix. Fill with ice, add 2 ounces of bourbon, and fill with soda.*

COCKTAIL PARTY FOR FIFTY

The following suggested bar guide is appropriate for a cocktail party that begins at 7:00 p.m. and ends at 9:00 p.m. Two or three drinks per person is a fair allowance for the evening.

––––––

TOOLS/EQUIPMENT

Ice Bucket	Bottle Cap Remover
Ice Tongs	Lemon Peeler
Sharp Knife (cutting fruit)	Cocktail Shaker
Corkscrew	Cocktail Napkins
Jigger	Lemons, Limes
Bar Towel	Green Olives
Martini Pitcher	Cocktail Onions
Bar Spoon	Ice (¾ to 1 pound per
Strainer	person)

MIXERS

Sparkling Water	Diet Cola
Bottled Water	Lemon/Lime Carbonated
Club Soda	Beverage
Tonic	Tomato Juice
Ginger Ale	Orange Juice
Cola	Sweet/Sour Mix

LIQUOR AMOUNTS

Beer	3 cases	Vodka	1.75 liters
Bourbon	1 liter	Wine: 750 milliliters each	
Gin	1.75 liters	White	10 bottles
Rum	750 milliliter	Red	6 bottles
Scotch	1 liter	Zinfandel	2 bottles
Vermouth	750 milliliters		
(if serving martinis)			

1 liter (33.8 ounces) serves 22 drinks (liquor)
750 milliliters (25.4 ounces) serves 16 drinks (liquor)
750 milliliters serves 5 (5-ounce) servings (wine)

EASY HORS D'OEUVRE IDEAS

All of your social occasions can benefit from some easy suggestions for an hors d'oeuvre that is a little more innovative and sophisticated than chips and dip in presentation, but still requires very little time in the kitchen. Remember that presentation is part of the secret, and a garnish is in everyone's garden, refrigerator or pantry. Try magnolia leaves to line the platter, and decorate with ivy, edible flower blossoms, sliced oranges, grapes, cucumber slices, lemon slices or wedges, celery leaves, or fresh herbs. For some quick ideas, try:

––––––

- Goat cheese served with roasted red peppers and crackers
- Boursin cheese topped with sun-dried tomato tapenade
- Cheddar spread topped with spicy apricot-pepper spread
- Brie topped with pesto sauce and pine nuts
- Paté with grainy raspberry or mango mustard and cornichons
- Smoked salmon with capers and dill dip
- Vegetable caponata with pita chips
- Cheese fondue served with crunchy breadsticks
- Small pastry shells filled with chocolate nutella or lemon curd
- Small liqueur cups filled with mascarpone cheese and topped with Melba sauce

RENTAL EQUIPMENT GUIDE

The following may be utilized at any function
and is intended as a checklist:

China:
Dinner or luncheon plates
Salad/dessert plates
Bread and butter plates
Soup bowls (rimmed or cream soup
    with service plates)
Coffee/tea cups and saucers
Finger bowls

Beverage glasses:
Wine
Water
Iced beverage
Champagne
Barware

Linens:
Tablecloths and overlays
Chair covers
Coat racks with hangers
Luncheon/dinner/cocktail napkins with rings

Coffee and tea service:
Coffee urn or teapot
Cream pitcher, sugar bowl, waste bowl

Additional items:
Water and/or iced beverage pitchers
Ice containers for service and in service area
Punch bowl/ladle and cups
Coffee pot (50 cups or more)
Place card holders
Candelabra or candlesticks
Trays and other service pieces
Chafing dishes
Cutlery and serving pieces
Tables and chairs
Tenting and passage covering
Ashtrays, if needed
Large trash containers
Recycling bins
Flooring (for outdoor event)

PARTY TIME GUIDE

These times serve as a general rule and may vary according to the host's preference or geographic traditions.

Breakfast *is between 7:30 or 8:00 and 10:00 A.M.*
Coffee *is between 9:30 and 11:30 A.M.*
Brunch *is between 10:30 or 11:00 A.M. and 1:00 P.M.*
Luncheon *is between noon or 1:00 and 2:00 P.M.*
Tea *can begin as early as 3:00 P.M. and ends at 5:30.*
Informal cocktails *are between 5:30 or 6:00 and end promptly at 7:30 P.M. If an invitation gives a range of time, it invites the guests to drop in during that period of time.*
Dinner *begins between 8:00 and 9:00 P.M. and may be preceded by cocktails beginning at 7:00 or 7:30 P.M.*

PARTY PLANNING FORM

Type of party: _____

Host(s): _____

Theme: _____

_____

Time: _____

Gift: _____

Guest(s) of honor: _____

Number of guests _____

Invitations: _____

Invitation mail date: _____

RSVP date: _____

Caterer: _____

Service people: _____

Bar: ❏ yes ❏ no

Bar Type: ❏ liquor ❏ wine ❏ Champagne
❏ beer ❏ Non-alcoholic drink(s)

Bar Needs: (Liquor, mixers, ice, cocktail napkins)

_____

_____

Bar Service: ❏ bartender ❏ self-serve

Bar time open: _____

Bar time closed: _____

Appetizer(s): _____

_____

Dining: ❏ buffet ❏ family-style ❏ seated

Dining time: _____

Beverage(s) served with dinner: _____

_____

Wine(s) served with dinner: _____

Menu: _____

_____

_____

_____

_____

_____

Dessert: _____

Apéritif: _____

Coffee: _____

Guest tables:
  Size: _____ Number: _____
  Location(s): _____

Food service tables:
  Size: _____ Number: _____
  Location(s): _____

Bar service tables:
  Size: _____ Number: _____
  Location(s): _____

Chairs: _____
  Type: _____
  Number: (per table) _____
  Number: (total needed) _____

China:
  Type: _____ Number needed: _____
  Type: _____ Number needed: _____
  Type: _____ Number needed: _____
  Type: _____ Number needed: _____
  Type: _____ Number needed: _____
  Type: _____ Number needed: _____

Beverage/Barware:
  Type: _____ Number needed: _____
  Type: _____ Number needed: _____
  Type: _____ Number needed: _____
  Type: _____ Number needed: _____
  Type: _____ Number needed: _____
  Type: _____ Number needed: _____

Linens:
  Type: _____ Color: _____
  Size: _____ Number: _____
  Type: _____ Color: _____
  Size: _____ Number: _____
  Type: _____ Color: _____
  Size: _____ Number: _____

Rentals:

Contact: _____

Telephone: _____ Method of payment: _____

Delivery time: _____ Pick-up time: _____

_____

_____

_____

Decorations:

_____

_____

_____

Entertainment:

_____

_____

_____

Comments:

_____

_____

_____

Room Layout

Table Layout

The party planning form on these pages can furnish the nucleus for your party diary. Make multiple photocopies of both pages and punch them to fit in a loose-leaf notebook. Use plastic photograph sleeves to display photographs of table settings, decorations, and centerpieces.

NUTRITIONAL PROFILE

Nutritional information for these recipes is computed from information derived from many sources, including materials supplied by the United States Department of Agriculture, computer databanks, and journals in which the information is assumed to be in the public domain. However, many specialty items, new products, and processed foods may not be available from these sources or may vary from the average values used in these profiles. More information on new and/or specific products may be obtained by reading the nutrient labels. Unless otherwise specified, the nutritional profile of these recipes is based on all measurements being level.

- **Artificial sweeteners** vary in use and strength so should be used "to taste," using the recipe ingredients as a guideline. Sweeteners using aspartame (NutraSweet and Equal) should not be used as a sweetener in recipes involving prolonged heating, which reduces the sweet taste. For further information on the use of these sweeteners, refer to the package.
- **Alcoholic ingredients** have been analyzed for the basic ingredients, although cooking causes the evaporation of alcohol, thus decreasing caloric content.
- **Buttermilk**, **sour cream**, and **yogurt** are the types available commercially.
- **Cake mixes** which are prepared using package directions include 3 eggs and 1/2 cup oil.
- **Chicken**, cooked for boning and chopping, has been roasted; this method yields the lowest caloric values.
- **Cottage cheese** is cream-style with 4.2% creaming mixture. Dry curd cottage cheese has no creaming mixture.
- **Eggs** are all large. To avoid raw eggs that may carry salmonella, as in eggnog or 6-week muffin batter, use an equivalent amount of commercial egg substitute.
- **Flour** is unsifted all-purpose flour.
- **Garnishes**, serving suggestions, and other optional additions and variations are not included in the profile.
- **Margarine** and **butter** are regular, not whipped or presoftened.
- **Milk** is whole milk, 3.5% butterfat. Low-fat milk is 1% butterfat. Evaporated milk is whole milk with 60% of the water removed.
- **Oil** is any type of vegetable cooking oil. **Shortening** is hydrogenated vegetable shortening.
- **Salt** and other ingredients to taste as noted in the ingredients have not been included in the nutritional profile.
- If a choice of ingredients has been given, the nutritional profile reflects the first option. If a choice of amounts has been given, the nutritional profile reflects the greater amount.

Pg #	Recipe Title (Approx Per Serving)	Servings	Cal	Prot (g)	Carbo (g)	T Fat (g)	% Cal from Fat	Chol (mg)	Fiber (g)	Sod (mg)
17	Poor Man's Caviar	10	45	3	9	<1	7	0	2	391
20	Smoked Catfish Paté	16	147	7	1	12	73	45	0	329
21	Caponata	12	46	1	7	2	34	0	2	201
23	Hot Spinach Dip	16	123	6	4	10	71	30	1	259
27	Cranberry Spritzers	6	93	<1	23	<1	2	0	<1	3
30	Holiday Sangria	10	56	<1	6	<1	2	0	<1	18
44	Gazpacho	6	100	2	14	5	39	0	2	727
48	Minestrone	10	200	8	34	5	21	3	8	756
50	Veggie Sandwiches	6	342	7	34	20	53	8	5	765
58	Asparagus Vinaigrette	8	150	2	6	14	80	0	1	57
59	Black Bean Salsa Salad	20	81	5	16	1	8	0	5	359
66	Indian Spinach Salad	8	148	2	12	11	63	0	1	176
68	Tomato Basil Salad	6	189	1	6	19	84	0	2	400
78	Mexican Casserole	8	332	19	32	14	39	53	2	841
80	Santa Fe Stew	10	596	41	56	25	37	97	11	1774
82	Pork Loin Roast-Blueberry Sauce	8	442	36	27	19	39	105	1	1118
84	Pork Tenderloin Teriyaki	6	192	25	3	9	42	67	<1	658
94	Chicken Fiesta	6	867	78	14	53	56	243	1	925
96	Chicken Stroganoff	4	288	28	20	10	32	69	1	363
97	Oven-Crispy Chicken	8	315	31	38	3	10	73	2	1653
99	Chicken-Black Bean Enchiladas	6	580	33	72	19	29	60	6	1561
101	Grilled Game Hens Merlot	4	693	59	30	35	46	203	1	746
114	Venison Manicotti	8	485	25	38	26	49	64	4	926
116	Grilled Fish with Shrimp	2	555	41	3	42	69	269	<1	753
117	Pompano en Papillote	4	423	35	15	25	54	98	3	6231
118	Salmon with Rosemary	6	420	71	2	12	27	185	<1	1402
120	Shrimp Kabobs	6	245	9	9	20	71	55	2	609
126	Tortellini Chicken Salad	8	330	22	24	17	46	59	3	363
127	Fiesta Pasta	4	348	12	54	10	25	5	4	569
128	Low-Fat Tomato Basil Pasta	4	291	8	49	8	24	0	4	337
128	Spinach and Tomato Pasta	4	594	24	95	14	21	19	6	892
130	Gourmet Chicken with Pasta	6	574	59	38	16	26	146	2	471
132	Italian Chicken Pasta	6	394	24	47	13	28	42	3	338
133	Chicken Pasta Raphael	6	385	26	43	13	30	45	4	1029
147	Special Potato Casserole	8	402	9	44	21	47	84	3	251
152	Oven-Roasted Winter Vegetables	8	250	4	37	11	37	0	8	60
152	Zucchini Casserole	6	127	6	14	7	43	3	3	184
154	Lemon Rice	6	178	7	26	5	26	11	1	595
156	Lime Peanut Rice	4	561	15	54	35	53	0	5	20
166	Bran Muffins	16	132	3	24	4	23	22	2	228
168	Almond Lemon Yogurt Bread	24	271	5	34	13	44	29	1	182
199	Island Fruit Trifle	10	677	11	76	36	47	162	3	148
210	Canadian Bacon Quiche	12	339	14	20	23	60	109	1	525
211	Mexican Green Chile Quiche	6	211	18	18	8	32	108	2	516
216	Baked French Toast	4	223	10	36	4	17	107	2	381
219	Layered Apple Coffee Cake	10	585	7	88	24	37	85	3	405
220	Low-Fat Orange Bread	12	168	3	28	5	25	0	1	149
221	Good-for-You Cinnamon Rolls	20	157	4	29	2	14	11	1	91
222	Orange Muffins	30	120	2	21	4	26	23	1	95
223	Banana Whirl	2	255	8	44	7	22	25	2	91

HERB CHART

*There are no strict rules governing
the use of herbs with food. The
best rules are those you devise
through experimenting.
The guidelines in the herb
complement chart can help you
become more confident. However,
there are a few general tips. Don't
overpower the main dish with
herbs. Be subtle. The herbs
should enhance, not dominate,
the main flavor. Dried herbs
are stronger than fresh
cut herbs. In general, 1/4 teaspoon
dried herbs equals 2 teaspoons fresh
herbs. Scissors are the best tool for
cutting fresh cut herbs onto your
dish. When cooking, add the herbs
during the last five minutes.
If you are unfamiliar with the
flavor of an herb, try adding it to
a small amount of butter,
margarine, or cottage cheese. Let
the mixture sit for about an hour
to absorb the flavors, then try it
on a plain cracker. Store your herbs
in glass jars or pottery. Keep away
from light and heat. With careful
storage, the flavor should last
about one year.*

Beverly S. Fennell
Herbarist

Dill

Chives

Lavender

Rosemary

- **Beef:** bay, chives, cumin, garlic, hot pepper, marjoram, oregano, rosemary, savory, thyme (gingerroot in oriental dishes).
- **Breads:** anise, caraway, coriander, dill, marjoram, oregano, rosemary, thyme.
- **Cheese:** basil, chives, curry, dill, fennel, garlic, marjoram, oregano, sage, thyme.
- **Eggs:** basil, dillweed, garlic, oregano, parsley.
- **Fish:** chervil, dill, fennel, French tarragon, garlic, parsley, rosemary, thyme.
- **Fruit:** candied angelica, anise, cinnamon, candied ginger, ground coriander, lemon verbena, nutmeg, rose geranium.
- **Lamb:** garlic, marjoram, mint, oregano, rosemary, thyme.
- **Pork:** coriander, cumin, garlic, ginger, hot pepper, sage, thyme.
- **Poultry:** chives, oregano, rosemary, sage, savory.
- **Salads:** basil, borage, burnet, chives, cilantro, dill, French tarragon, garlic chives, sweet marjoram, parsley.
- **Soups:** bay leaves, French tarragon, lovage, marjoram, parsley, rosemary, savory, thyme.
- **Vegetables:** basil, chervil, chives, dill, French tarragon, marjoram, mint, oregano, parsley, thyme.

About the Junior League of Little Rock

These are exciting times for the Junior League of Little Rock. In 1997, we celebrated our 75th year of doing together what we cannot do alone—celebrating projects that over the years have resulted in well-known community institutions for Little Rock and our state, like The Arkansas Arts Center, The Parent Center, and Riverfest, a family festival held on the Arkansas River banks in downtown Little Rock. Over the decades there have been projects and programs that addressed specific needs in our community at that time, such as the Visiting Nurse Association in the 1930s, the Pulaski County Council on Aging in the 1960s, the Child Abuse Seminar in the 1970s, which resulted in SCAN, and Safety Town in the 1980s. In the 1990s, we have tackled issues like prejudice reduction with the *Green Circle* project, and AIDS with the *RAINbows and Ribbons* project.

Today, we are actively engaged in projects that affect children's issues, such as hunger reduction with *Potluck*, youth voluntarism through *Cornerstone*, the family structure with *Growing Through Divorce*, and options for critically ill children through *Arkansas Children's Hospital KIDS' TV*. To give flexibility in meeting membership and community needs, we developed *Community Bank* to match community agencies and volunteer hours on a short-term basis. We have recently begun a project with the Museum of Discovery called *Education and Outreach through the Museum*. Also, we have made a pledge toward the Imagination Station at the museum's new site in the River Market District.

As we prepare for a new century, the Junior League of Little Rock remains committed to being a force and voice for positive change in our community. By training volunteers, providing community programs, and developing the potential of women, we are dedicated to community service and making our community a better place for all. Our approach to community service is to identify a need, develop a project to meet that need, ensure the success of the project, and, at the appropriate time, turn it over to the community. This formula has served both Little Rock and our Junior League well. We intend to continue it into the twenty-first century, making a difference in the future as we have in the past.

Mission Statement

The Junior League of Little Rock, Incorporated, is an organization of women committed to promoting voluntarism, developing the potential of women, and improving the community through the effective action and leadership of trained volunteers. Its purpose is exclusively educational and charitable.

ACKNOWLEDGMENTS

The Junior League of Little Rock greatly appreciates the tireless effort of countless individuals who have helped make this book a reality. We hope this listing is complete, but if we inadvertently made an omission, please forgive us!

Arkansas Cattlemen's Association
Arkansas Cooperative Extension Service
Arkansas Game & Fish Commission
Arkansas Poultry Federation
Arkansas Soybean Foundation
Pam Blank
Catfish Farmers of Arkansas
Chester Storthz Advertising
The Country Club of Little Rock, Scott Irwin
Diane's Gourmet Luxuries, Diane Knight
Dillard Department Stores, Inc.
Ellon and Rogers Cockrill
Et Cetera
Beverly S. Fennell, Herbarist
Fifth Season
The Full Moon
Heights Fine Wines & Spirits
Mrs. Jay Hill
Mike Ibsen
Leslie and Mark Lee
Brenda Majors
National Broiler Council
National Live Stock & Meat Board
Pulaski County Cooperative Extension Service, Beth Phelps
Pulaski County Cooperative Extension Service, Nancy J. Winterbauer
Mary Rice
Anne Speed
Tipton & Hurst
The University of Arkansas, Fayetteville
U.S. Department of Agriculture
USA Rice Council

To the active and sustaining membership of the Junior League of Little Rock for their help in recipe testing, our sincere gratitude for your time, money, suggestions, and hosting of testing parties.

To the 1996–97 and 1997–98 Junior League Boards of Directors, our gratitude for their support and ethusiasm.

To our family members, friends, and loved ones, our thanks for their wonderful attitudes, endless sacrifices, and enduring support for this labor of love called a cookbook.

To Little Rock chef, Peter Brave of Brave New Restaurant, special thanks for sharing his Smoked Tomato Soup recipe. Also, special thanks to Chef John Currence of the City Grocery in Oxford, Mississippi, for sharing his Shrimp and Grits Recipe.

COMMITTEES

COOKBOOK COMMITTEES

CHAIRMAN
Beth Ann Waldrup

EDITOR
Lisa Rice Baxter

CO-EDITOR
Carolyn Brabston Gunn

RECIPE DEVELOPMENT
Tanya Phillips Barnes

RECIPE TESTING
Julie Grundfest Shindler

CREATIVE DESIGN
Stacy Johnson Hurst

MARKETING
Angela Newsom Hopkins

SUSTAINER ADVISORS
Cindy Coates Miller
Belinda Housely Shults

Subcommittees

RECIPE DEVELOPMENT
Marilyn Luke Barlow
Martha Shackleford Chisenhall
Becca Rasco Cope
Catherine Cothran Fox
Rebecca Meggs Harris
Beth Hathaway
Kathy Bennett Perkins
Myra Murrah Pope
Terri Schriber Simpson
Lynn Isgrig Topp

RECIPE TESTING
Dana Beaird
Sandy Beck Charlton
Amy Connell
Caroline Ward Fox
Cindy Blyth Howard
Ginger Beeson McCaleb
Paula Klimovich Montanez
Beth Wade Page
Lee Sharp

CREATIVE DESIGN
Martha Camferdam Baldwin
Alice Hudgens Cooner
Andrea Warzecha Cordell
Mary Ellzey
Carolyn Landfair Harrison
Ellen Powell Yeary
Sustainer Advisors:
Katherine Ann Hahn
Sharon Deckleman Mosley

MARKETING
Samantha Cross Adamson
Andrea Dillingham Cain
Kristi Kellam Clark
Catherine Cothran Fox
Jennifer Schueck McCarty
Elizabeth McGee

NON-RECIPE CONTENT
Andrea Makris Gary
Martha McKenzie Hill
Nancy Allenbaugh Puddephatt
Janet King van der Werff
Leslie Welch
Sustainer Advisor:
Victoria van Zandt Saviers
Provisionals:
Gina Scerbo Bilger
Kelly Kinard Ford
Jeanne Yarbrough Joyner

EXECUTIVE COMMITTEES

1996-97
PRESIDENT
Mimi Myer Hurst

PRESIDENT-ELECT
Jan Nelson Cooper

COMMUNITY VICE-PRESIDENT
Cindy Adams Hedges

MARKETING VICE-PRESIDENT
Cathy Hastings Owen

RECORDING SECRETARY
Nancy Allenbaugh Puddephatt

CORRESPONDING SECRETARY
Leighton Maestri Weeks

TREASURER
Sue Overholt Tull

1997-98
PRESIDENT
Jan Nelson Cooper

PRESIDENT-ELECT
Cindy Adams Hedges

COMMUNITY VICE-PRESIDENT
Donna Kordsmeier Sell

MARKETING VICE-PRESIDENT
Martha McKenzie Hill

RECORDING SECRETARY
Lisa Abercrombie Beach

CORRESPONDING SECRETARY
Melissa McIlroy Hawkins

TREASURER
Sarah Pruitt Campbell

CONTRIBUTORS

Kem Embrey Aburrow
Samantha Cross Adamson
Cathy Cahan Alexander
Cathy Gessler Allen
Jan Phillips Alman
Deanna Smith Alguire
Allison Anthony
Shannon Benafield Aston
Kathleen Wright Atkins
Joyce Bradley Babin
Christine Siebert Bailey
Jennifer Rice Bailey
Kimberly Frazier Baker
Melissa Ragan Baker
Dana Yeatman Baldwin
Martha Camferdam Baldwin
Mina Goffin Baledge
Marilyn Luke Barlow
Tanya Phillips Barnes
Anne Coleman Barnwell
Linda Isenman Barry
Dana Winter Bauer
Lisa Rice Baxter
Sam Baxter
Mary Jane Stuckey Baxter
Dana Beaird
Andria Nowlin Beckham
Denny Richardson Bellingrath
Maggie Hornor Bently
Leanne Crenshaw Bernhard
Gina Scerbo Bilger
Susan Jones Boe
Sharon Foster Bowman
Virginia Lynn Boyd
Kathryn DeRoeck Boykin
Billy Ragan Brabston
Catherine Anne Ragan Brabston
Mary Frances Brackett
Connie Blasingame Bracy
Susannne Lawrence Brandon
Wendy Warmouth Brandon
Peter Brave
Trish Brierley
Mary Jane Goodson Briggs
Robin Shively Brown
Brent Bumpers
Jan Getty Burks
Emily Lewing Burrow
Brianne Faulkner Bush
Deanna Kelley Bushman
Renata Jenkins Byler
Sarah Pruitt Campbell
Martha Carle
Rhonda Wells Carter
Sidney Buckley Carter
Susan Barnes Carter
Cindy Camp Cathey
Mary Bryant Cavin
Patricia Frost Chaffin
Shana Hollaway Chaplin
Lori Beardsley Chapman
Joye Trimble Christian
Kristi Kellam Clark
Dorothy Clement

Kay Parette Clevenger
Bill Clinton
Hillary Clinton
Stuart Chapman Cobb
Carmen Comer
Juliet Lyons Compton
Robyn Taylor Compton
Lisa Taylor Cooley
Marilyn Cooley
Alice Hudgens Cooner
Jan Nelson Cooper
Becca Rasco Cope
Beth Hatfield Cousins
Leigh Ann Crain
Maurine Walker Crank
Mary Varga Daugherty
Irene C. Davis
Pat Davis
Rhonda Rowell Davis
Renay Dowling Dean
Polly Montgomery Deems
Brian Deloney
Linda Lusk Deloney
Phil Deloney
Tracey M. Dennis
Laura Doramus
Lisa Garner Douglass
Marjorie Tedford Dudley
Sheffield Christian Duke
Rosemary J. Dyke
Mary Ellzey
Kelley Holt England
Elisabeth Gornatti Estes
Alice Eudora Lincoln Eubanks
Kimberly Henderson Evans
Louise Boggs Feron
Karen Heard Fetzer
Kathy Gray Findley
Linda Leigh Flanagin
Monica Lowery Fletcher
Kelly Kinard Ford
Caroline Ward Fox
Kate Erwin Frazier
Charlotte Hudspeth Gadberry
Pam Pangle Gadberry
Victoria Clement Garrett
Ferris Cook Garrison
Jan Gardner Gattis
Lisa Gearhart
Brooks Gibson
Stacy Reynard Gibson
Bernadette Barry Gifford
Sara Gillison
Vanya Webb Gilmore
Julie Nester Golla
Julianne Honey Gonzalez
Ruthmary Heyd Goodhart
Anne Goodman-Massey
Anna Kay Frueauff Grace
M'Lissa Meyer Gravelle
Pamela Horton Greer
Allie Mae Whitmore Giffin
Bonnie Sokora Griffin
Kathryn Lawson Griffin

Maxine Hughes Griffin
Julianne Dante Grundfest
Lisa Lewis Guerra
Carolyn Brabston Gunn
Julie Price Gunnell
Katherine Ann Kumpuris Hahn
Mary Hall
Priscilla McEntee Hamilton
Betty Lou Hamlin
Ruby Hampton
Debra Wright Harris
Rebecca Meggs Harris
Sheila McCown Hartzell
Laura Camacho Hathaway
Melissa McIlroy Hawkins
Blair Biggers Hederman
Cindy Adams Hedges
Pam Flemister Herget
Anne Hickman
Martha McKenzie Hill
Barbara Hodnett
Cathy Hooker
Wanda Gammons Hoover
Barbara Hope
Lisa Bocquet Hope
Abigail Howe
Mary Katharyn Howell Hope
Angela Newsom Hopkins
Sherrill Barrett Hosto
Cindy Blyth Howard
Michelle Howard
Lois Hughes
Linda Humphries
Mim May Hundley
Mimi Myer Hurst
Stacy Johnson Hurst
Barbie Hawkins James
Deanna McCain James
Leslie Jewell
Jill Thompson Johnson
Katherine Karlovic Johnson
Lisa Dickerson Johnson
Gail McNeal Jones
Kim Cook Jones
Marcella McMillon Jones
Ravonda Wilson Jones
Jeanne Yarbrough Joyner
Valerie Ford Kellam
Elicia Sinor Kennedy
Susan Rhea Kennedy
Anne Plastiras Kerr
Cindy Skinner Kolb
Kim Marble Kullander
Mikel Kullander
Dena Ladd
Lisa Ellis Lagrone
Ashley Yandell Lamb
Leah Lasley
Sandy Ledbetter
Tina Hoffman Ledbetter
Ann Curry Leek
Adele Lloyd
Janie Turner Lowe
Patti Turner Lueck

Suzanne Ownbey Mackey
Cynthia Jernigan Maddox
Brenda Johnson Majors
Kimberly Jack Marchant
Gina Marchese
Janet Kernodle Marshall
Doug Martin
Patti Freemyer Martin
Janell Lundine Mason
Holly Whiteman Mathisen
Catherine Remmell Matthews
Beth McCain
Ginger Beeson McCaleb
Jennifer Schueck McCarty
Heather Davenport McCastlain
Pat VanPellen McClellan
Carolyn Pharis McCone
Elizabeth McGee
Missy Baker McKee
Becky McKinney
Georgea B. McKinley
Melinda A. Meier
Sonya Ray Mendelsohn
Courtney Hawkins Menz
Vickey Hum Metrailer
Marcella Meyer
Robin Westbrook Mickel
Carolyn Miller
Cindy Coates Miller
Kelli Nicholson Miller
Michelle Bass Miller
Mimi Miller
Toni Rowley Miller
Marie Keesee Milwee
Lindy Eubanks Mitchell
Peggy Watkins Mitchell
Cathy Ydarraga Moffett
Lynn McCleary Monk
Paula Klimovich Montanez
Mary Ann Giller Moore
Debbie Joyner Morgan
Kathy T. Moss
Elizabeth Crow Mowery
Susie Douglas Munson
Tia DeVito Murchison
Teresa Carter Murphy
Michael Nestrud
Sue Gibbons Nestrud
Linda Baird Newbern
Margaret M. Newton
Kelley Riggs Nichols
Linda Murphy Norton
Mary Elizabeth Norton
Lynn Alphson O'Connor
Martha O'Farrell
Christi Brown Oliver
Melanie Orintas
Sallie Carter Overbey
Heather Horner Overton
Cathy Hastings Owen
Beth Wade Page

Elizabeth Cooley Paris
Kelly Parisi
Kelly Wortsmith Parker
Jan Pine Paulus
Susan Payne
Bonnie Bailey Peek
Ann Penick
Kathy Bennett Perkins
Rebecca Pfauser
Allison Dyke Pickell
Debbie Williams Plyler
Carolyn Lindsey Polk
Marcia Ellis Pollock
Myra Murrah Pope
Virginia Hamman Porta
Jane Felton Proffitt
Nancy Allenbaugh Puddephatt
Cindy Thomas Pugh
Patricia Shelton Pyle
Ginger Garrett Quinn
Elaine Kordsmeier Raby
Claudia Hopkins Ragon
Linda Seymour Ramey
Evelyn Jennings Rand
Marge Anna Mosley Ray
Tracy Reynard
Susan Stover Reynolds
Beth Stuckey Rice
Mary Adcox Rice
Deborah Truby Riordan
Mary Carol Roach
Cathey Campbell Robbins
Sarajane Phillips Robertson
Beth Lee Robinson
Cecile Stuckey Rose
Susan Boyer Rosenthal
Mallory Lemon Rottman
Kellie Reed Rush
Barbi Rushing
Paige Lester Rystrom
Cherise Champeaux Sale
Kirsten Joyce Sanders
Judi Scerbo
Jennifer McGhee Schmidt
Erin Fergusson Schoen
Carol Schmidt Scholtens
Lisa Miller Schuster
Suzette Ellisor Schutze
Donna Kordmeier Sell
Lee Sharp
Libby Brandon Sheard
Julie Grundfest Shindler
Laura Shiver
Sherrie Barnett Shollmier
Joyce Siebert
Beth Sigler
William B. Sigler
Terri Schriber Simpson
Tawnya Neal Skokos
Heather Ellis Slay
Cindy Smith

Cydney Elslander Smith
Lucy Stephenson Smith
Susie Smith
Judy Glisson Snowden
Holly Cravens Speed
Kay Gaines Stebbins
Martha Sawrie Stephenson
Catherine Ann Stewart
Linda Llewellyn Stickley
Lynn Godfrey Strickland
Karen Hannahs Suen
Tracy Hight Sykes
Deandra Tate
Jane Cockrill Taylor
Gayle Swann Teague
Gina Turner Terry
Stephanie Fess Tharp
Elizabeth Thomas
Mary White Thomas
Mona Flowers Thompson
Susan Nix Tinker
Lynn Isgrig Topp
Michelle Midyett Townsend
Shannon Phelps Treece
Julie Wood Truemper
Luraette Tucker
Shelly Herzfeld Tucker
Janet King van der Werff
Donna Gay Rutledge Van Hemert
Linda Burrow Van Hook
Ginger Creed Wade
Stephanie Haught Wade
Beth Ann Waldrup
Beth Adams Walker
Betty Walt
Kristina Weaver
Jamai Wallis Weber
Doug Weeks
Leighton Maestri Weeks
Jennifer Jeffries Welborn
Leslie Welch
Bonnie Wellborn
Suzan Hayden Wellborn
Susie Whitacre
Sharon Brocato White
Kathy Wilkins
Susan Wilkinson
Joyce Williams
June Williams
Shonna Green Williams
Terry Williams
Christie Young
   Williamson
Mark S. Williamson
Ann Willis
Rebecca Hodges Winburn
Sherry Wilkins Wortsmith
Genny Wrape
Ellen Powell Yeary

INDEX OF RECIPES

258

INDEX OF PHOTOGRAPH RECIPES

MY FAVORITE RECIPES

My Favorite Recipes

NOTES

NOTES

NOTES